THE MODERN SCOTTISH DIASPORA

To Scott, Donna & Graham,
all part of the least heralded diaspora
MSL

To the late Andrew Sim,
a reluctant member of the diaspora
DS

THE MODERN SCOTTISH DIASPORA

CONTEMPORARY DEBATES AND PERSPECTIVES

EDITED BY
MURRAY STEWART LEITH AND DUNCAN SIM

EDINBURGH
University Press

© editorial matter and organisation Murray Stewart Leith and
Duncan Sim, 2014
© the chapters their several authors, 2014

Edinburgh University Press Ltd
The Tun – Holyrood Road
12 (2f) Jackson's Entry
Edinburgh EH8 8PJ
www.euppublishing.com

Typeset in 11/13 Adobe Sabon by
IDSUK (DataConnection) Ltd, and
printed and bound in Great Britain by
CPI Group (UK) Ltd, Croydon CR0 4YY

A CIP record for this book is available from the British Library

ISBN 978 0 7486 8140 2 (hardback)
ISBN 978 0 7486 8141 9 (paperback)
ISBN 978 0 7486 8142 6 (webready PDF)
ISBN 978 0 7486 8143 3 (epub)

Contents

Acknowledgements

As editors, there are a number of people we wish to thank. We would firstly like to thank the various contributors who have helped to produce what is an impressive collection of papers. We would also express our thanks to the many individuals and organisations among the Scottish diaspora, as this collection owes a great deal to them, their ongoing connection with Scotland and their willingness to talk with the academics whose work is contained within this volume. Thank you for taking the time and the effort to speak to researchers such as us.

We are grateful to our university, the University of the West of Scotland, for their support, and to the Carnegie Trust for the Universities of Scotland, who funded some of the research we have reported on here. Simply put, without them, we would not be able to do what we do.

Thanks also to staff at Edinburgh University Press for their help and advice. In a long-held academic tradition, we were slightly late in delivering our manuscript to them but it seems altogether very fitting that it was completed on St Andrew's Day.

MSL
DS
30 November 2013

Contributors

Alan Bairner is Professor of Sport and Social Theory in the School of Sport, Exercise and Health Sciences at the University of Loughborough, England.

Jenny Blain is an independent researcher, recently retired from being Senior Lecturer in Sociology in the Department of Psychology, Sociology and Politics at Sheffield Hallam University, England.

Edward J. Cowan is Emeritus Professor of Scottish History at the University of Glasgow, Scotland.

Ewan Crawford is Lecturer in Journalism in the School of Creative and Cultural Industries at the University of the West of Scotland in Hamilton, Scotland.

Mike Danson is Professor of Enterprise Policy in the School of Management and Languages at Heriot-Watt University, Edinburgh, Scotland.

Michael Fry is a historian and freelance writer.

Euan Hague is Professor and Chair of the Department of Geography at DePaul University, Chicago, USA.

Murray Stewart Leith is Senior Lecturer in Politics in the School of Social Sciences at the University of the West of Scotland in Paisley, Scotland.

Jim Mather is a former Scottish Government Minister and is now Visiting Professor at the University of Strathclyde, Glasgow, Scotland.

Andrew Mycock is Reader in Politics in the School of Human and Health Sciences at the University of Huddersfield, England.

Michael Newton is Technical Lead for the Carolina Digital Humanities Initiative at the University of North Carolina, Chapel Hill, USA.

Duncan Sim is Reader in Sociology in the School of Social Sciences at the University of the West of Scotland in Paisley, Scotland.

Kim Sullivan is an independent researcher and writer. She gained her doctorate from the University of Otago in Dunedin, New Zealand.

Stuart Whigham is Lecturer in Physical and Sport Education in the School of Education, Theology and Leadership at St Mary's University College, Twickenham, London.

Introduction: The Scottish Diaspora

Murray Stewart Leith and Duncan Sim

INTRODUCTION

There has been a significant and developing interest in diasporas during the last thirty years or so. Brubaker (2005), for example, highlights the ways in which the word 'diaspora' now occurs frequently as a keyword in research and the million or so Google hits which it yields. From 1991 to 2007, the journal *Diaspora* provided an important outlet for work in this area. And, hand in hand with this growing academic interest in the subject, the focus of diaspora studies has become both broader and more complex (Cohen 2008).

For those of us working in Scotland, this expansion of interest is particularly exciting. Scotland has long been a country of emigration, with migrant Scots and their descendants scattered across the globe. But it has been the advent of devolution and the establishment of a Scottish Government in Edinburgh in 1999, which has allowed Scottish politicians and organisations to engage with the diaspora in events such as Tartan Day, in a way in which London-based organisations were never likely to do. Tourist developments such as the Years of Homecoming in 2009 and 2014 are significant expressions of this engagement.

In this introductory chapter, therefore, we explore the nature of diasporas and how the terminology has changed over the years. We then discuss the increase in hyphenated identities, whereby members of diasporas adopt a hybrid identity which acknowledges both their host society and their homeland, and the ongoing relationship which they have with their homeland. We explore aspects of the Scottish diaspora more specifically before going on to describe our approach to this edited volume and the plan of the book.

Defining 'Diaspora'

The term 'diaspora' is of Greek origin and refers to a sowing or scattering of seed. The Greeks themselves used it to refer simply to migration, although later it came to be associated with forced resettlement, particularly the dispersal of the Jews from Palestine (Adamson 2008). Later, the term was also applied to other groups who had been forced into exile, such as the Armenians, and Africans taken into slavery; key to understanding the nature of these diasporas were firstly the forcible banishment of these groups from their homelands and, secondly, the continuing importance which those homelands held for them (Brubaker 2005). But in recent years, the term 'diaspora' has been used ever more loosely to cover a range of emigrant groups, many of which have been largely assimilated into their host societies. Thus

> groups that are classified as immigrant groups, ethnic groups or minorities in their state of residence can redefine themselves as belonging to a larger transnational community that exists beyond the state by taking up the label of 'diaspora' (Adamson 2008: 7).

The term itself has therefore become a social construct in which a diaspora reality is based on a range of factors, including a sense of national or group identity, feelings of belonging, mythology, history, memory and dreams (Shuval 2000).

Albeit that 'diaspora' is therefore a slippery concept, various writers have done their best to identify and define different forms of diaspora. Safran (1991) was one of the first to identify what he believed to be the key characteristics of a diaspora. These included (1) dispersal of a group from an original homeland to two or more foreign locations; (2) the retention of a collective memory of their homeland; (3) a belief that they are not – and perhaps cannot be – fully accepted by their host society; (4) an idealisation of the homeland as a place for possible future return; (5) a commitment to the maintenance or, possibly, restoration of that homeland; and (6) a continuing relationship to the homeland.

Safran's list has led to considerable academic debate. Cohen (1996) suggested that there was possibly an over-emphasis on relations with the homeland and that there should be more recognition of the positive virtues of retaining a diasporic identity *per se*. Thus members of a diaspora group may have an identity which binds them to each other as well as to a homeland, particularly important in the case of a homeland which may no longer exist or to which return may not be possible. Cohen also pointed out that migration may not be forced but that many people move for colonial or voluntarist reasons and this led him to seek to identify different types of diaspora.

Five types were identified (see Cohen 2008). The first was the *victim* diaspora which would include forced migration from early times to more recent refugee groups. The Jews and Armenians would be the classic examples but so too would be the Irish. A second group was the *labour* diaspora, which would include indentured workers, guest workers and the like. Examples would include Indians, Turks, and Chinese labourers. A third was the *imperial* diaspora, of which the British (within which many would include the Scots) are possibly the best example, with numerous individuals moving across the globe to defend and administer the Empire. Fourth was the *trade* diaspora, whereby individuals have moved to work in trade, business and the professions. There are examples ranging from the Venetians through to more recent groups such as the Indians or Chinese. A fifth and final group was the *hybrid* or *de-territorialised* diaspora, where there may not be a specific homeland with which to connect. Examples include diasporas which are defined by their religion rather than by a territory, or cross-national groups like the Roma.

In seeking to summarise the thinking on diasporas, Butler (2001) pointed out that most scholars agreed on three basic features. The first was that, after dispersal, there should be a minimum of two destinations; this reflected the original meaning of the term as a 'scattering'. A second feature was that there must be some form of relationship to a homeland, be it real or imagined. Thirdly, there must be a self-awareness of the group's identity as a diaspora community, with links to each other as well as the homeland. This can act as a form of boundary maintenance vis-à-vis the host society or other diaspora groups (Brubaker 2005). Butler then goes on to add a fourth distinguishing feature, namely the existence of a diaspora over at least two generations. She argues that a single-generation diaspora may only be in temporary exile and that true diasporas should be multi-generational.

There is therefore a time dimension to diasporas, and they will change significantly from one generation to the next, often reflecting the position of the group within the host society, and shifts in the relationship with the homeland. A decreasing likelihood of a return to the homeland for many diasporas, for example, will have important effects on how their diasporic identities develop.

DIASPORAS OVER TIME

Just as there are different types of diaspora, so too will they receive different types of reception within their new host society, ranging from the welcoming to the hostile. Some countries have sought to exclude migrant groups from playing their full part in society (Turkish guest workers in Germany are a recent example), while in countries such as the United States, immigrants were generally welcomed, so long as they assimilated and ultimately became 'American'. This approach was known as the 'melting pot' (Schlesinger 1991), whereby migrants of many different nationalities and origins were 'melted' or 'smelted' into American citizens.

In fact, however, it became clear over time that many immigrant identities refused to melt (Novak 1971), and research by Glazer and Moynihan (1963) showed how many individuals continued to have an awareness of their historical identity and to be members of a recognisable ethnic or national group. This self-awareness grew in subsequent decades, aided by the introduction in 1980 of a question on ancestry in the American Census which assisted those interested in exploring their ethnic roots, and also by the enormous success of Alex Haley's novel *Roots*. Published in 1976, it focused on the black experience in America, but its appearance coincided with the American bicentennial and a nationwide interest in the country's history and origins; thus it appealed to white Americans as well.

Radhakrishnan (2003) identified three stages in the narrative of ethnicity for migrants. First, in an initial phase, immigrants were likely to suppress their ethnicity in the name of pragmatism and opportunism. This would represent a phase of assimilation. Second, immigrants might reassert their ethnicity, partly perhaps to keep memories of the homeland 'alive'. Thirdly, individuals may adopt a more hybrid or 'hyphenated' identity combining both a national (host society) identity and an ethnic (homeland) identity.

Certainly, there is now widespread recognition of a hyphenated identity being adopted by many groups within societies such as America, Canada and Australasia, and Glazer and Moynihan's (1963) landmark study showed that, despite assimilation, individuals continued to have an awareness of their historical identity and to be members of a recognisable ethnic or national group. The continuing strength of such groups led social scientists to rethink models of ethnicity which are rooted in assumptions about the inevitability of assimilation. New ideas about ethnicity have therefore stressed the fluid and dynamic nature of ethnic identification, resulting in a model

> that emphasises the socially 'constructed' aspects of ethnicity, that is, the ways in which ethnic boundaries, identities and cultures are negotiated, defined and produced through social interaction inside and outside ethnic communities. (Nagel, 1994: 1001)

Nagel (1994) showed that, increasingly, hyphenated Americans were *choosing* to retain their ethnicity, rather than being assimilated into an undifferentiated American society. Individuals might not necessarily join defined ethnic organisations, participate in events or socialise with others from the same background but they might still *feel* a sense of belonging to a particular ethnic group and declare themselves to be a member. It echoes Waters' (1990: 150) comment about a 'particular American need to be "from somewhere"'.

But while there is undoubtedly a growth in an ethnic consciousness, can we regard groups such as the Italian-Americans, the Polish-Americans or the Irish-Americans as diasporas? Safran (1999) thinks not, and argues that such hyphenated groups cannot be diasporas because they no longer speak the language of their homeland, no longer attend a homeland-orientated church and have no clear idea of their homeland's past. Transplanted minority groups, he states, do not necessarily remain diasporas. Yet he acknowledges that positions do shift and asks the question as to when an ethnic minority actually becomes a diaspora.

In some respects, Safran's stance is at odds with the work of other academics who have highlighted the widespread and growing interest in ethnicity, albeit that such an ethnicity is essentially symbolic (Gans 1979). But there is ample evidence that, in order to be 'from somewhere' (Waters 1990), many people are relearning their homeland languages, rediscovering their roots and taking a renewed interest in their homeland, often returning for visits. So perhaps these hyphenated groups are indeed becoming diasporas? To take a simple example, we can see the establishment of Tartan Day in the United States in 1998 as an example of the Scottish groups there renewing their interest in their heritage, displaying a collective diaspora consciousness and developing a particularly diasporic celebration.

Safran is particularly focused on the links with homeland and the feasibility of a return there, a particular issue for victim diasporas. He asks:

If an expatriate community (1) removed itself voluntarily from its homeland, (2) has a homeland to which it can return but chooses not to do so, and (3) has remained abroad for so long that it has only an indistinct memory of its place of origin, no longer has cultural links with the homeland, and is no longer capable of effectively perpetuating its culture, is it still a diaspora? (Safran 1999: 265)

We would argue that Safran's third point has lost some of its validity, given the changing nature of many diasporas. As expatriate communities increasingly renew their interest in their culture, their history and their homelands, it is precisely the 'indistinct memory' of the homeland that is attractive. This allows diasporas to mythologise and romanticise the homeland, so that their knowledge of it becomes more imagined than real. In relation to the Scottish diaspora, for example, Roberts (1999) writes about the characteristics of Highland Games in America:

This isn't Scotland, of course: Scotland isn't so self-consciously *Scottish* ... This is, in fact, Jefferson County, Florida. The food is more barbeque than haggis and half the guys in kilts also wear Florida State T-shirts. But they've come to celebrate a place – or at least the idea of a place – most of them have never seen. (Roberts 1999: 24)

This relationship between diasporas and their homelands will clearly vary depending on the nature of the diaspora and if it is, to use Cohen's classification, a 'victim', 'trade' or 'imperial' diaspora, for example. It will also change over time and across the generations. It is important therefore to reflect further on this relationship.

DIASPORAS AND THE HOMELAND

Much of the literature on diasporas focuses on relationships with the homeland and this relationship is demonstrated in a variety of ways. For example, diasporas may remit funds to relatives 'back home', they may support political movements and, indeed, may in some circumstances retain a vote in their homeland. Members of diasporas may travel home if they can, although the connections may weaken over time. The remittance of funds is particularly significant: on a global scale, annual remittances from diasporas to home countries exceeded $251 billion in 2007 (Esman 2009).

In terms of politics, diasporas are recognised as important lobbies for change in homelands, sometimes campaigning for regime change. They are 'increasingly able to promote transnational ties, to act as bridges or as mediators between their home and host societies, and to transmit the values of pluralism and democracy' (Shain and Barth 2003). Yet diasporic activities may lead to violence and instability in the homeland; we may be familiar, for example, with the activities of the Irish Northern Aid Committee (Noraid) in America, which raised financial support for the nationalist movement in Northern Ireland and which was accused by government of being a front for the IRA (Wilson 1995).

In fact, as Shuval (2000) points out, diaspora relationships are essentially triangular ones, involving the diaspora group itself, the host society, and the homeland which may be real or virtual. The relative strengths of these different relationships depend on a range of factors, including the attitude of the host society to the homeland, the degree to which the diaspora has been made welcome within the host society, and the attitude towards the diaspora by the homeland itself. These relationships change over time, with later generations possibly less concerned about the maintenance of a homeland connection. Thus, 'when they have a choice, many people do not choose to return to their homeland because it is often too disruptive or traumatic to leave the diaspora' (Shuval 2000: 47).

Certainly there is a recognition that, for many members of diasporas, views of the homeland change over the generations. Thus for Butler (2001: 5), 'diasporan representations of the homeland are part of the project of constructing diasporan identity, rather than homeland actuality'. This echoes Handlin (1973), who suggests that the upheavals and hardships involved in migration cause many migrants to look back fondly to their previous life, even though they may know that it is a past which is already changing and to which they can no longer belong. Hall notes how diasporas are affected over time by the larger society in which they are located. So cultural identities may be historical but nevertheless undergo constant transformation, being subject to the continuous play of history, culture and power. Diaspora identities therefore are those that are 'constantly producing themselves anew through transformation and difference' (Hall 1990: 237).

Within homelands themselves, attitudes to diasporas have also undergone significant change. Victim diasporas will always have perhaps a difficult and tortured relationship with their homelands, particularly if they are unable ever to return. But elsewhere, expatriates claiming a homeland identity have sometimes been viewed with suspicion and regarded at best as outsiders by the indigenous population (Conner 1986). Partly this arises because the homeland sought by the diaspora bears little relationship to reality. Dezell (2002: 206), for example, writes of the Irish Americans heading 'home' to Ireland, crossing the country in tour buses, 'longing for an illusory place'. But, in fact, there has been a noticeable shift in attitudes towards diasporas from many homelands.

For example, Pires-Hester (1999) refers to the changing relationship between the government and inhabitants of the Cape Verde islands and their descendants in the United States. There was an apparent shift from simply ignoring the Cape Verdean diaspora to seeing it as an important resource for levering investment and influence. Closer to home, the then president of Ireland, Mary Robinson, in an address to the Houses of the Oireachtas in 1995 argued strongly that Ireland should cherish its diaspora. She referred to the huge numbers of Irish people living across the world, and suggested that Ireland needed to respond to desires for dialogue, interaction and practical links involving trade and business. The diaspora therefore can be seen as a significant potential resource.

Brinkerhoff (2009) highlights the various ways in which homeland governments can provide an 'enabling' environment with which diasporas can engage. She notes that diasporas can contribute to homeland economies (through remittances, investment or skills transfer), they can contribute politically, and they can contribute in moral and informational ways. One of the most significant developments in the last twenty or so years has been diaspora tourism, assisted by the growth of the internet and developments in cheaper air travel. Timothy (2011) and Basu (2007) refer to the large numbers of tourists revisiting homelands to undertake genealogical research or to visit sites of personal meaning. Some homelands operate 'homecoming' events such as the Scottish Year of Homecoming in 2009 (Sim and Leith 2013), the 2013 Gathering in Ireland, and the Birthright Israel and Israel Experience programmes for Jewish youth from across the globe (Timothy 2011).

The development of diaspora tourism is a significant shift in the relationship between diasporas and homelands. It reflects the fact that, over the generations, many diasporas may still wish to visit the home of their ancestors, without having a desire to move back themselves. Thus a 'homing desire' may be seen as something quite separate from a desire for a homeland (Brah 1996). Indeed, some diasporas may become relatively deterritorialised and cease to have a meaningful relationship with the homeland at all. Recent work by Adamson (2008) suggests a 'constructivist' approach to diasporas which treats them as 'imagined communities' (Anderson 1983) that transcend national boundaries. So a diaspora becomes a global community beyond any single state in which they may be a minority. It may be a means of asserting a national or religious identity on a transnational basis; thus one may speak of a 'Muslim diaspora' which is not linked to any particular territory. Brubaker (2005: 13) similarly refers to 'identity' as crossing state boundaries, such that diasporas should not be thought of necessarily as bounded entities but rather, 'it may be more fruitful, and certainly more precise, to speak of diasporic stances, projects, claims, idioms, practices and so on'. In this way, membership of a diaspora may be seen as highly flexible.

So the relationship between diaspora and homeland is complex and changing. For members of the diaspora,

> the concept of home emerges as a highly contextual and ambivalent notion, referring to multiple places and spaces in past, present and future in various ways. Home can be remembered, lived, longed for. Notions of home are fluid and bound to change as one moves in time and space. (Stock 2010: 27)

We move on now to consider the Scottish diaspora, in particular, and to try to judge the extent to which it may be thought to fit within the various theoretical frameworks which we have described above.

THE SCOTTISH DIASPORA

Estimates of the size of the Scottish diaspora vary tremendously and nobody really knows how many people across the world claim Scottish ancestry. Politicians Kenny MacAskill and Henry McLeish (2006) suggested that estimates range from forty to eighty million, in comparison to a 'home' population actually residing in Scotland of just over five million. On the other hand, the Scottish Diaspora Forum, part of the country's 2009 Year of Homecoming, referred in its online publicity to a diaspora of 'more than thirty million'. Either way, the numbers are huge, relative to the Scottish homeland population.

Although the diaspora may be found in all parts of the world, the largest groupings are generally acknowledged to be in North America and Australasia. Data from the 2010 United States Census, for example, show that 5.5 million people in the US claimed Scottish ancestry, making the Scots the eighth-largest ancestral grouping. In Australia, in 2006, 1.5 million people claimed Scottish ancestry, over 7 per cent of the total (Prentis 2008).

The members of the diaspora are, of course, very varied. There are substantial numbers of individuals who were born and brought up in Scotland and who have migrated as adults, often for employment reasons. While clearly a part of the diaspora, such individuals are first generation migrants, whose migration may not be permanent and who may return or retire to the homeland. Chapter 8 of this volume, for example, explores the experiences of the Scots in Europe, many of whom are Scots-born and who have moved as adults. But in countries like America and Australia, those who claim Scottish ancestry may be the second, third and fourth generation diaspora, often claiming a hyphenated and 'symbolic' identity.

If we examine the Scottish diaspora using Cohen's (2008) classification, then the Scots would fall into at least three categories. Some Scots emigrants could be classified as a 'victim' diaspora, forced from the homeland for economic or political reasons. Perhaps the most significant series of events relate to the Highland Clearances, where thousands of Highlanders were forcibly removed from their crofts and smallholdings by landowners in the eighteenth and nineteenth centuries. Additionally, some left of their own accord, either because they feared forced clearance or because it was becoming increasingly difficult to farm relatively poor land (Devine 1994; Richards 1999, 2000). Other examples of forced exile relate to political events such as the conflicts involving the Covenanters in the seventeenth century, or the Jacobite risings of 1715, 1719 and 1745 (Pittock 1998), after which defeated Jacobites fled or were expelled to the colonies.

A second category of migrants would be a 'trade' diaspora, and there are numerous Scots who moved overseas to work. Within the United States, for example, there were farmers in Carolina, miners in Appalachia, and weavers and textile workers in New England (Calder 2006). Some Scots established significant business enterprises in the countries to which they migrated. American examples include Andrew Carnegie from Dunfermline, who made his fortune in the steel industry before becoming a leading benefactor; Alexander Graham Bell from Edinburgh, the inventor of the telephone and founder of the Bell Telephone Company; and David Dunbar Buick from Arbroath, who established the Buick Motor Company. Elsewhere, the rise of Hong Kong as a centre of trade and wealth owes much to the activities of William Jardine and James Matheson from Sutherland, who established the Jardine Matheson company there.

Thirdly, some Scots emigrants would be classified as part of an 'imperial' diaspora, helping to administer the British Empire, and forming a disproportionately large part of the British army over the years (Fry 2002).

Because of the range of these diaspora experiences – and the obvious successes of some Scots emigrants – Vance (2005) suggests that Scots might not legitimately be considered as a diaspora, as the term has connotations of victimhood and hence forced migration. However, we have already seen that this is really too narrow an interpretation of the term and at odds with the work of other academics in this field.

It is clear that the Scottish diaspora is large and geographically dispersed, while being composed of both recent migrants and the descendants of earlier ones. The relationship between the Scottish diaspora and the homeland will vary between these different groups, reflecting the likelihood or not of a return 'home'. So some diaspora members may have a current – and realistic – relationship with Scotland, while others, whom we may call 'ancestral' Scots, have perhaps a more sentimental attachment. MacGregor (1980 v), writing as an American Scot himself, suggests that there are in fact three Scotlands, which he distinguishes as:

(1) the never-never land of *Brigadoon*, where kilted Rockettes dance in the moonlight on heather hills, and men, having greeted the dawn with a quaich of Scotch, sally forth to shoot a deer or two for breakfast; (2) the Scottish Homeland, an area of just over thirty thousand square miles inhabited by five or six million people on the northern part of the island we call Britain; and (3) the Scottish Diaspora, consisting of the vast millions of people of Scottish birth or ancestry dispersed throughout the world (in the United States alone an estimated five times as many as in the Homeland) who look to the Homeland with that deep affection and occasional exasperation that people never bestow on anyone but their mother.

Although the *Brigadoon* version of Scotland may still have currency, it is becoming harder to take it seriously, even in the diasporic context. As is discussed in later chapters in this book, the Scottish diaspora is increasingly better informed about modern Scotland, thanks to the internet and to improvements in the availability of air travel. The key relationship for us in this volume is therefore between the second and third of MacGregor's categories.

PLAN OF THE BOOK

There is a growing interest in the Scottish diaspora. In part, this reflects an increased focus by academics on aspects of international migration and diasporas, as discussed above; Scotland, with a substantial diaspora in most parts of the world, has therefore been a subject for study by a number of historians and sociologists. But there has also been a political interest in the diaspora, with the Scottish Government developing a diaspora strategy, not least in order to encourage 'roots tourism', as those individuals of Scots descent come back to visit their 'homeland'. The 2009 Year of Homecoming was an important manifestation of this strategy.

But although there is now an important body of academic work on the Scottish diaspora, we would argue that it is nevertheless rather limited; by field if not by focus. There have been a significant number of historical studies of the Scottish diaspora (for example, Hunter 1994, 2005; Fry 2001; Harper 2003; McCarthy 2006; Devine 2011). There has also been a major body of work within the social sciences, particularly in sociology and anthropology (for example, Ray 2001, 2005; Basu 2007). And there have also been studies of individual diasporas, such as Sim's (2011) work on America and Prentis' (2008) on Australia.

There are, however, significant gaps. The diaspora is also of interest to politicians, to public policy makers and to Scottish business; it is of interest to those working in the media, in sport, in literature and in music. But material on the connectedness of the diaspora to the homeland in these areas is very hard to find. We believe therefore that only some aspects of diaspora research are adequately covered in existing work and that there are a number of other perspectives which are much less visible. The aim of this edited work is to explore a fuller range of perspectives on the Scottish diaspora and make it available for a wider audience.

Following this introduction, the chapters in the book may perhaps be grouped into four main areas. Chapters 2, 3 and 4 are broadly historical, explaining the nature of emigration from Scotland, the creation of the Scottish diaspora and the Scottish organisations within it. Edward Cowan's chapter traces the various stages of Scottish emigration, from the pre–1700 period when Scots were essentially concerned with establishing trading opportunities usually in Europe, to the later period when Scots began to look towards the New World. Scottish traders, he notes, were often sympathetic to native peoples because they were pragmatists, needing native support for their trading enterprises. He notes the differences between the approach of the Scots (and the French) in Canada with that taken by immigrants to the United States who sought to eradicate native peoples to make way for white farmers.

That is not to say, of course, that the Scots were a uniquely enlightened people, and Scotland played its part in the British imperial adventures. Chapter 3 by Michael Fry describes the Scottish presence in various parts of the globe and the impact which this had at home – from the sugar refiners of Greenock to the tobacco merchants of Glasgow. Like Cowan, Fry stresses that the Scots were essentially more interested in using the Empire for trade rather than conquest, instancing the fur trade in Canada, sheep-farming in Australia and trade in the Far East which led to the establishment of Singapore and Hong Kong. But as he correctly states, the Scots often merged into the societies in which they settled and did not require the mutual support which would have led them into 'communal coherence'.

This might suggest that the Scottish diaspora was rather weakly defined. But, although Scots may not have clustered in specific settlements, they did establish a range of social organisations, Presbyterian churches and the like, which helped to preserve a sense of 'Scottishness'. Kim Sullivan is therefore able in Chapter 4 to describe the associational culture which has long existed within Scottish diasporas in many parts of the world. The earliest associations were established in the early years of the nineteenth century and many are still flourishing today. Focusing in particular on clubs and societies in Australasia, Sullivan brings the story of these associations up to date, demonstrating that, despite their sometimes romanticised view of the homeland, they 'nevertheless continue to provide an outlet for the expression of their identity for thousands of diaspora Scots'.

For many in the Scottish homeland, such diaspora Scots were sometimes seen as an embarrassment because of their fondness for tartan, clans and the historical trappings of Scottishness – things which many homeland Scots saw as largely irrelevant to modern Scotland. But attitudes within Scotland have changed significantly in recent years, not least because devolution and the establishment of a Scottish Parliament has allowed Scots to engage more directly with their diaspora, perhaps following in Ireland's footsteps. So successive Scottish governments have developed diaspora strategies and held Years of Homecoming to attract back diaspora Scots, and the diaspora is increasingly seen as a resource – for business, for investment and for tourism.

Danson and Mather's chapter (Chapter 5) focuses on the business connection between Scotland and its diaspora, suggesting that the diaspora could have an important role to play in the economic and social revitalisation of the country. They note the historical wariness displayed by some homeland Scots towards the diaspora and emphasise the importance of encouraging indigenous Scots to realise the potential of diaspora engagement – a process, they argue, which will require a 'reappraisal of core–periphery relations'.

Such relationship changes are a focus of Leith's chapter (Chapter 6), which describes the shifts in Scottish politics, identity and belonging which have taken place particularly in the years since devolution. He explains the growing desire of the Scottish Government for diaspora engagement and the development of a Diaspora Strategy. He also begins to explain the different Scottish diasporas which exist – ranging from the 'far' diasporas in North America to the much nearer diaspora elsewhere within the UK. The relationship between Scotland and this 'near' diaspora is particularly complex, not least in the context of the Independence Referendum, where Scots within the UK but not within Scotland will be unable to vote. He also touches upon the reverse diaspora or 'new Scots', without whom the numbers in the Homeland would be decreasing. Albeit not members of the Scottish diaspora, they are a diaspora with which Scotland has to engage.

This chapter allows us to move on to consider some of the different Scottish diasporas which exist. Mycock in Chapter 7, for example, notes how the Scottish diaspora in England is a very distinctive entity – an intra-state diaspora, in which Scots living in England may retain their own sense of identity but within an overarching construction of Britishness. He also points to the possible implications of a changing Scotland, whereby the internal diaspora that is the Scots in England may become the nearest diaspora abroad, should the current minority of those favouring an independent Scotland become a majority prior to September 2014. The implications of this action will impact upon the diaspora as greatly as they will upon the homeland.

In Chapter 8, Leith and Sim describe a much-neglected diaspora, that of the Scots in Europe. In contrast to the more ancestral diasporas of North America, many of the Scots living in Europe are first generation and have moved for work, often since the UK became a member of the European Union. So their links to the homeland are usually current ones and many people expect to return or retire back to Scotland at some point. The chapter debates if such a group can be considered a true diaspora, in that it has not existed over more than one generation, but concludes that it is increasingly acting like one, with the establishment of a range of Scottish diaspora organisations over recent years.

In Chapter 9, by contrast, Michael Newton's focus is very much on an ancestral diaspora. There has been a substantial amount of previous research on the Scots in North America and so Newton focuses on a specific group, namely Scottish Gaels. He describes the Gaelic traditions which were exported from Scotland to North America, in language, music, dance and song, and how they are being revitalised by a present generation which has a growing interest in Gaelic culture. He notes how this revitalisation reflects a growing investment in Gaelic in Scotland itself, although he points out that developments in Scotland and North America may differ, and may not necessarily offer the same vision of Gaelic culture. This provides a useful reminder to us of the differences between homeland and diaspora versions of a Scottish identity.

This leads us on to the following four chapters which are essentially concerned with representations of Scotland within the diaspora, and which sometimes illustrate some interesting disconnects between the two. Heritage tourism, for example, is of growing importance to the Scottish economy and, with the expansion of transatlantic flights, many ancestral Scots from North America are finding their way 'home'. Travel from other parts of the globe may be less easy but the growth of the internet and the opportunities which it provides for online genealogical research are hugely significant. Jenny Blain's chapter describes this growing phenomenon.

Those who travel back to Scotland and who undertake research into their ancestry may end up with a reasonably realistic view of what modern Scotland is like – unlike those who remain in the diaspora and simply read about it. Euan Hague explores in Chapter 11 the relatively recent expansion of romantic fiction which uses Scotland as its focus. He describes the growth in the numbers of novels about periods of Scottish history, many of which use time travel as a device to enable romance to flourish. Such fiction is already having an impact in Scotland itself, with some hotels now catering for American tourists seeking to experience for themselves the 'romance' which they have read about in these novels.

In Chapter 12, the focus shifts to the ways in which the media have portrayed Scotland, often depicting images of tartanry and 'kailyard' to the exclusion of more modern pictures of Scottish life. As Ewan Crawford shows, such images are often enjoyed by those within the diaspora, but there is sometimes irritation at home at the seeming inability of the media to produce output which reflects the diversity of Scotland. At a time of constitutional debate, when Scotland may (or may not) become an independent country, he argues that we need to ensure that we really 'do have the capability to hold a mirror up to the country'.

This group of chapters concludes with a contribution by Alan Bairner and Stuart Whigham which explores the importance of sport for the Scottish diaspora. Supporting Scotland in a team sport – or supporting a Scottish athlete like Andy Murray – allows diaspora members to distinguish themselves from other migrant groups. In addition, diaspora Scots may be eligible to represent Scotland through a Scots-born parent or grandparent. Sport then, can help to create in diaspora Scots a sense of belonging to the homeland, to Anderson's (1983) imagined community of Scots.

The final chapter is the conclusion, in which we as editors reflect on the contributions made in the book. We begin with a reflection on the nature of diaspora, and then shift to a consideration of the themes evident within, and among, the chapters. As we sought to bring the discussion of the diaspora beyond the current limited discussion, we consider not history, legacy or the diaspora of yesterday, but rather, we firmly move our analysis into the contemporary diaspora and the Scotland and Scottishness that exist in the wider world. We seek, in short, to move the debate to today, and for it to continue tomorrow.

2

Scottish Emigration and the Creation of the Diaspora

Edward J. Cowan

It could be said that migration commenced when the first specimen of *Homo Sapiens Sapiens* took her or his first step some 200,000 years ago. Migration has been part of the human condition ever since. Immigration and emigration are, of course, refinements of the core element, which essentially encapsulates movement from place to place. Modern migration studies have been concerned to broaden the subject beyond the familiar transatlantic examples to regard the subject as a worldwide phenomenon. It is pointed out that while 60 million people participated in the Atlantic migration during the period 1850–1940, around 50 million were involved simultaneously in north Asian migrations and a similar number in south-east Asian population movements (Lucassen, Lucassen and Manning 2011). Given such figures, Scottish migration may seem a drop in the ocean but emigrants are not misunderstood lemmings jumping from a hypothetical cliff; they are individuals with their own unique experiences. Types of migration have been defined as local (short distance), circular, which might involve employment some distance away but which always implies return, chain migration through family or work, and career migration through which people anticipate betterment or achievement of ambition by removing considerable distances. These categories, however, do not adequately accommodate such matters as military service, slavery, the transportation of criminals, or the forced migration of millions of people as dictated by the likes of Hitler, Stalin and Mao Tse-tung, on a scale unimaginable in a Scottish context.

Though there are exceptions, most Scottish emigration can be regarded as aspirational. John Herries McCulloch from New Abbey, Galloway wrote, with pardonable exaggeration, that during his boyhood in the earlier twentieth century hundreds of thousands emigrated to the Dominions annually; 'the life-blood of Scotland was being drained away at a fearful rate, but nobody cared' (McCulloch 1954: 22). Pundits tend to overstate the number of emigrants, most of whom were voluntarily contributing to the haemorrhaging. The artist and novelist Alasdair Gray is recently reported as saying that when he was at school it was expected that the cleverest boys would emigrate. John Logan Campbell, founder of the city of Auckland, lamented his failure to achieve a different kind of aspiration when he reflected that 'we can fly away from man and places and things, but we cannot fly away from ourselves' (Stone 1982: 236).

I write as an academic who had no notion of emigration but who was invited to leave Scotland (fortunately by Canadians rather than Scots!), who emigrated in 1979, who now enjoys dual citizenship and who returned to Scotland in 1993. If Canada is not really the extension of Scotland that John Buchan discerned, it is certainly a country which Scots find congenial. Too many historians, in my view, write about emigration without having very much idea about, or sympathy for, the actual process (Cowan 2012). For years Scots had little interest in their compatriots abroad. Much of the propaganda surrounding the supposed pain of emigration appears to be designed for the comfort of those who stayed at home. At embarkation the emigrant may experience a combination of anticipation, adventurous exhilaration, guilt at leaving family behind (especially parents), sadness at abandoning the familiar, and above all doubt. Often both voluntary and coercive elements are involved. Many studies examine push/pull factors but economic recessions and the battle of Culloden do not explain everything. In Dumfries and Galloway, for example, many people seem to have emigrated quite casually to England or the New World, often returning as planned. England offered chapmen or peddlers the opportunity to acquire a stake with which to found a more settled business, while significant numbers of young men were sent out to the American plantations to serve apprenticeships as managers and overseers.

Many others at different times wished to escape the suffocating restrictions of Scottish society, notably the feudal practices of farmers and landlords, who initially opposed emigration until self-interest and new agricultural opportunities, in both Highlands and Lowlands, made them think again. The much-vaunted Scottish pursuit of freedom was more achievable abroad than it was at home. While numerous Scots lost their identity without regret in pursuit of prosperity and independence, some of their prosperous descendants now visit

Scotland for genealogical research. In all my years in Canada, from sea to shining sea, I never met a Canadian Scot who had the remotest interest in returning permanently to the Auld Country. Such people may be enthusiastic about kilts, whisky, dinners and bagpipes, but for them the culture is vastly more attractive than the country. For some abroad, Scotland is truly an imagined community spoiled by acquaintance with the real thing. Others have rediscovered their Scottish origins while some have reinvented themselves as Scots.

Scotland, like most European countries, is a somewhat recent phenomenon. It is only in the last millennium or so that 'Scotland' has emerged as the nomenclature for a place on the map or in the heart. For the first thousand years of the Christian era, since Scotia is part of an island, the inhabitants were probably much more familiar with immigration than they were with emigration, though the latter cannot be ruled out.

Older studies tended to be obsessed with migrations in the proto-historical and early historical periods but then fashions shifted and theories were advanced about migrations of cultures rather than people, reflected in language changes, as static populations came to terms with new economies and technologies. It was long held that the *Scoti* migrated from Ireland to Scotland in the fourth or fifth centuries but archaeological evidence suggests that Dalriada (roughly modern Argyll) belonged to the same cultural zone as Ireland (Fraser 2009). This entire controversy arises in part from an imperfect understanding of migration, the notion that, for example, the 12 miles from Antrim to Kintyre is too short to justify the word. Migrationists would no longer accept that premise. Recently the entire debate about early historical European migration has been fruitfully and positively reopened (Heather 2009).

It is said that the first two questions that any human being asks are 'Who am I?' and 'Where do I come from?' The early peoples of Britain, in common with those of Europe and virtually every known culture on the planet, concocted origin legends to explain their existence. Thus the Picts supposedly originated in Scythia, the Angles and the Vikings claimed Odin, or Woden, as their ancestor, and the Britons traced descent from Brutus of Troy. All of these fabrications were totally bogus but they seem to have conferred some sort of antique respectability in the minds of scribes and bards (Cowan 1984).

The Scots, according to legend, claimed descent (unusually) from a female, Scota daughter of Pharaoh, who supposedly quit Egypt shortly after the Israelites crossed the Red Sea. Travelling through the

Mediterranean, they settled in their land of choice, having driven out the Britons and destroyed the Picts. Resisting attacks by Norwegians, Danes and English, they lived free until the outbreak of the Wars of Independence (Cowan 2008). Traditionally then, the Scots, the people who gave their name to the country, were themselves immigrants.

From the time of the Angles and the Saxons who appear in the late Roman period, England has been a constant source of population replenishment, as well as something of a magnet for Scots travelling in the opposite direction. They were a Germanic tribal people forced to migrate to a declining Roman Britain because, due to global warming, rising sea-water was inundating their settlements. One incursion which has been intensively studied is that of the Vikings, the dazzling sea-raiders, mostly Norwegian in Scotland's case, who were driven out through pressure of population in the homeland where the people outstripped the resources necessary to maintain them. They settled in Shetland, Orkney, Sutherland, Caithness and the Western Isles, maintaining a presence in Scottish waters for half a millennium. Their heroic and shameful exploits alike were preserved in poetry and saga, arguably the greatest literary achievements of medieval Europe. These stories and verses are greatly concerned with ancestor worship and with the rebirth of certain personal characteristics from generation to generation.

They also contain much information about Viking emigration to the British Isles, Ireland, Iceland, Greenland and North America, all made possible by their highly developed ship technology. One of the earliest studies of the Norse in Scotland was by a prominent Norwegian historian who explicitly drew parallels with the emigration of 800,000 Norwegians who departed for America in the nineteenth and early twentieth centuries (Brøgger 1929).

In the eleventh century, English asylum seekers fled William the Conqueror's brutal conquest and, in particular, his devastation of the north of England. A chronicler related that farmhouses and cottages throughout the south of Scotland were overrun with English refugees, 'both men and maidens', including Princess Margaret, who would become the queen of Malcolm III. Their sons would supervise a kind of Anglo-Norman cultural conquest of Scotland in the twelfth and thirteenth centuries, which would bring north, not only many Normans, but also adventurers from all over Western Europe, as well as their ideas of warfare and government. They continued to come in successive reigns, Anglo-French warriors encased in steel, frontier adventurers accustomed to living by their wits and their weapons, who could be exploited in the expansion of the Scottish kingdom to the north and west but who were also valued for their expertise in land management, justice and administration. Many of these incomers must have married native women for we must never forget in considering genealogy that the name is only half of the story, and with the passing of time, an ever-reducing fraction of it – the male version. Although incomers always show a touching desire to belong, we may think it was often the mothers who turned their sons and daughters into Scots.

Robert Louis Stevenson once observed that it is the mark of the Scot of all classes 'that he remembers and cherishes the memory of his forebears, good or bad, and there burns alive in him a sense of identity with the dead even to the twentieth generation' (Stevenson 1896: chap. 5). Certain names, unmistakably Scottish, can be solemnly intoned in the nation's proud roll-call of heroes and achievers – Bruce, Wallace, Stewart, Lindsay, Hay, Sinclair, Ramsay, Grant, Fraser, Gourlay, Menzies, Boswell, Barclay, MacLeod, Gunn, Lamont, MacLachlan, to name but a few. Yet every single name on this list indicates that the original founder of the family originated somewhere else, that the revered ancestors were not Scottish at all, but rather incomers. In strictly genealogical terms a surprisingly high proportion of us have come from away. Indeed, although historians have perhaps expended a disproportionate amount of ink upon clans and families, one of the main dynamos driving Scottish history since medieval times has been the fortunes of 'New Scots'.

Foreign merchants and craftsmen from the Low Countries and the Baltic left their architectural mark on east coast burghs. Refugees from civil war and religious persecution in England found shelter in Scotland. Also there were sizeable groups of overseas traders throughout the entire period in the east coast ports. The rich fisheries around the waters of Shetland were controlled by the Dutch in the sixteenth and seventeenth centuries. From medieval times Gaels moved freely between the Gàidhealtachd and Ireland.

Between 1057 and 1625 Scotland was ruled by twenty-three monarchs. Of those, eleven married English women, three sought brides in Scandinavia and one in Gueldres, a Netherlands duchy. Surprisingly only two monarchs found spouses in France – James V and his daughter, Mary; the former had two consecutively. The three Roberts married Scots, but all before becoming king. Only one monarch was dumb enough to marry *two* of her own subjects during her personal reign – Mary, Queen of Scots. It was thus well understood, by most, that exogamous marriage was good for the bloodline. It seems to have been similarly recognised that external infusion, in the shape of immigrants, was good for the kingdom.

It is impossible to know when the first Scottish emigration took place. Some unfortunates were carried off into slavery by Romans. St Patrick wrote to a king of Strathclyde asking him to desist from slave raids on Ireland. Vikings transported *fir gorma,* 'blue' or 'black' men from North Africa, to the slave markets of Dublin. When the Norwegians colonised Iceland they took Celtic slaves and concubines from the Hebrides with them. Some of the earliest emigrants are likely to have been in religious orders. Travelling monks are almost universally depicted as solitary celibates but they were probably often accompanied by females. Medieval churchmen ventured furth of Scotland for study and advancement; many did not return. There was much interaction between Hebrideans and the Norwegian court in the High Middle Ages. By the fourteenth century *Der Schotte,* Slavic *szkot,* was becoming synonymous with peddler or chapman in Germany and Russia, as in other parts of Europe attracting the same reputation they had at home as roguish conmen (Worthington 2012). From solitary packmen to wealthy merchants, trade was the lure offered by Europe, closely followed by military service. It is estimated that 10,000 Scots fought in the Hundred Years' War and they continued to bleed for foreign countries and causes in the continental wars of the sixteenth century, the Thirty Years' War and later. Soldiers always intended to return but many found a grave in the 'High Germanie' of the ballads. Others forsook their native land for love or lucre or both.

An important article published in 1994 demonstrated a remarkable expansion in Scottish emigrant activity in the seventeenth century (Smout, Landsman and Devine 1994). The authors made claims which seemed extravagant at the time, now largely accepted, that around 100,000 Scots, including an estimated 20 per cent of the male population under thirty, emigrated in the course of the century, thus outnumbering, it is thought, those who departed in the eighteenth century. Their main destinations were Ireland, Poland (Devine and Hesse 2011) and Scandinavia. Recent estimates suggest even larger numbers throughout the century: over 100,000 to Ireland, half in the 1690s, 30,000 to 50,000 to Poland-Lithuania (Fitzgerald 2005; Kowalski 2009). There were also significant Scottish presences in the Netherlands, Norway, Denmark, Sweden and Russia. The seventeenth century was a fraught period of intense discomfort at home as the population experienced a serious decrease in average temperatures, leading to famine, disease and the abandonment of upland farms. There were vast upheavals in church and state as civil war – the Wars of the Covenant – raged from 1639 to 1651. Many soldiers returned to fight on one side or the other and thousands died in battle. The Stewart Restoration in 1660 brought little relief in economic conditions, in which famine and plague remained regular occurrences, and a prolongation, by different and less obvious methods, of earlier strife as the state attempted to crush dissidence of all kinds. There must have been significant population loss due to internal circumstances as well as through emigration, though the data does not exist for accurate measurement of trends for either. This was the century in which the words 'migration', 'emigration' and 'immigration' entered the English language for the first time. It was also the era which undoubtedly brought about the creation of the Scottish diaspora, a term which, despite having infiltrated migration literature, remains somewhat contentious.

The Greek word, which means 'dispersion', first appears in Deuteronomy 28 but does not appear in English until 1876. Had it been in use in the Covenanting period it would have been recognised, fearfully, as a symptom of the wrath of God, because it appears in the context of a lengthy sustained curse upon the Jewish people by the petulant and vengeful deity. The Scottish emigrant experience was never comparable to the Jewish diaspora, the God-ordained punishment of an entire nation. It is in the prophecy of the Dispersal that the texts so often associated with emigration are quoted:

And the Lord shall scatter thee among all people, from the one end of the earth even unto the other; ... And among these nations shalt thou find no ease, neither shall the sole of thy foot have rest; but the Lord shall give thee a trembling heart and failing of eyes, and sorrow of mind. (Deuteronomy 28: 64, 65)

Diaspora, and hence emigration, were for losers who had earned God's awesome anger. This was victimhood *par excellence*, which served, once again, to bolster those who remained, rather than the departed. However misleading and inaccurate though the word is, it has now been adopted by the Academy. Recent discussions of the term by Devine (2011) and Sim (2011b) do not really convince since neither of them dwells on its negative connotations.

Movements pre–1700 were concerned with Scots establishing communities for trading opportunities in nations that were often multilingual, some of them establishing families and businesses that were long-lived. Yet another seventeenth-century innovation was that Scots began to look, somewhat tentatively, westwards towards the New World. Thomas Henderson from Fife joined the Jamestown experiment to become the first known Scottish settler in America (Smout, Landsman and Devine 1994), if the Scots couple of the Vinland sagas, Haki and Hekja, are discounted (*Vinland Sagas* 1965). Jim Hewitson's candidate, Tam Blake, who was a member of the Coronado expedition in 1540, was an explorer rather than a settler (Hewitson 1993). David Dobson has counted some 7,000 transatlantic Scots who followed before 1700 (Dobson 2005). However, Atlantic migration was quantitatively and qualitatively different from the European experience. Distance was such that emigrants really did not expect to return. Some were involved in colonial enterprises where monarchical authority, French, Spanish or English, was thin on the ground, if it was present at all. Colonists could expect to settle beside people who spoke their own language or a variety of English. The seventeenth century marked the beginning of the English, and thus the British, empire (Canny 1998). Unlike earlier migrations, the participants might travel vast distances to settle abroad yet still be subject to British rule and law, albeit somewhat diluted. However strange the environment, there would still be much that was reminiscent, reassuringly or otherwise, of the homeland.

Most intriguingly of all there was a native population to consider, the like of which few settlers had hitherto encountered. Exceptions were those Scots who served on the frontiers of the Danish-Norwegian empire, such as John Cunningham who, as a district governor in Finnmark, had extensive dealings with the Sami people (Hagen 2003; Murdoch 2003). The First Nations of North America were literally exotic – alien, outlandish, barbarous, savage and heathen. The Greeks and the Romans had developed their own vocabularies for describing such peoples, applied by classically trained Scottish historians in the sixteenth century to their own *indigines*, the Gaels, and thus handily available to be recycled with reference to the native peoples of the Americas and elsewhere (Cowan 1998). Furthermore, it was believed that study of First Nations might shed light on the hidden past of the Scottish nation. William Fyffe, a plantation owner in Charlestown, perfectly encapsulated the view of the Enlightenment conjecturalist when he wrote to his brother in Dundee in 1761, 'I look upon these Savages to be [in] much the same state as our Forefathers were in Alex the Great's time or, if Scotland was not inhabited then (tho' it must have been) in Julius Caesar's time' (Woodward 1963: 56).

John Mair, the sixteenth-century philosopher, theologian and historian who enjoyed an international reputation, once opined, 'our native soil attracts us with a secret and inexpressible sweetness and does not permit us to forget it', an early articulation of the *maladie du pays* from which most exiles supposedly suffered. He also infamously remarked in 1519 that the native peoples of the Americas were, by nature, slaves and hence deserved to be conquered. This passage, as Anthony Pagden and Arthur Williamson have pointed out, was eagerly seized upon by Spanish commentators to justify their depredations in the New World. Later, James VI wrote in his *Counterblaste to Tobacco* that 'the pockie Indian slaves' were a people who were barbarous, beastly, wild, godless and slavish (Williamson 1996). In 1610 a royal official, doubtless reflecting James' own view, opined that the troublesome Neil Macleod of Lewis, who was resisting the king's colonial scheme for Lewis and Harris, should be deported to Virginia, where his barbarous language – Gaelic – would facilitate communication between him and the savages of America (*Collectanea* 1847: 49). Yet when Scots prepared to establish colonies in, or when they actually encountered the native peoples of, America the ideas of Mair and James appear to have been largely forgotten.

Much is to be learned about attitudes to emigration, as well as native peoples, in the earliest extant Scottish literature relating to colonial activity, *An Encouragement to Colonies* (1624) (Laing 1867: 1–47) by Sir William Alexander, later Earl of Stirling and Viscount Canada, and dedicated to Prince Charles, who would succeed James the following year. He commended Charles's support for colonisation:

> This is the way (making the Gospell of Iesus Christ knowne in unknown parts) by supplying the necessities of many, with a lawfull increase of necessary commerce, to procure glorie unto God, honour to your selfe, and benefit to the World; By this meanes, you that are borne to rule Nations, may be the beginner of Nations, enlarging this Monarchie without bloud, and making a Conquest without wronging of others.

While all exploiters of the New World paid lip service to the conversion of the heathen, Alexander devoutly wished to bring it about, advocating the importance of trade in securing that end. He believed that the Scots who taught the natives cultivation and agrarian skills (not that they required such instruction) would be regarded by the natives like the gods of the ancients. The stressing of bloodlessness and peaceful conquest is truly noteworthy. Alexander had read such material as was available and he had interviewed people with transatlantic experience.

He begins his tract with a history of plantation or colonisation drawing upon the Old Testament and classical sources which, he thinks, provided models for the recent plantation of Ireland – in his view, a great success. He is critical of colonial schemes undertaken by the Spanish, the French and even the English, while emphasising the potential riches of all colonies (Laing 1867: 1–28). Virginia, for example, one of the richest, suffered from native attacks as well as divisions among absentee owners. A further problem he notes, anticipating Andrew Fletcher of Saltoun and the revolutionary Americans of the following century, is that the colonists must labour like family servants, purchasing their food and clothing from England in exchange for tobacco, 'as they are directed by their Masters, many whereof are Strangers ... intending to settle none of their Race there', and having no care except exploitation for profit (Laing 1867: 29–30).

He proceeds to recount the frustrating tale of Scotland's first colonial adventure. He had granted the island of Cape Breton to a Galloway laird, Robert Gordon of Lochinvar, who promptly renamed it New Galloway. Alexander sent a ship to Kirkcudbright at the end of May 1622, in order 'that the businesse might beginne from that Kingdome, which it doth concern'. Gordon was nowhere to be seen; local merchants tripled the price of supplies. Locals were reluctant to embark. Eventually the ship sailed but was forced to over-winter in Newfoundland. The expedition's minister and blacksmith both died. Others drifted away but a few went on to gain a very favourable impression of the natural resources of Nova Scotia. Returning to Newfoundland, the group finally dissipated, most finding berths home on English ships (Laing 1867; Cowan 1999).

Alexander believes that the American plantations resemble in purity those,

> that in the infancie of the first age did extend the multiplying generations of Mankind, to people the then Desert Earth, for here they may possesse themselves without dispossessing of others, the land either wanting Inhabitants, or having none that doe appropriate to themselves any peculiar ground. (Laing 1867: 37)

In Europe previous invasions had toppled nations that were already civilised, for reasons of avarice and glory. Alexander intends that his colonists should civilise rather than subdue the natives, whose ruin would bring neither glory nor benefit, resulting in infamy and the loss of a population, which would gain by conversion and the introduction of trade and industry. He is delighted that God has chosen to keep America 'locked up so long amidst the depths', concealing it from the ancients to be discovered by posterity. He speculates that America was at one time connected to Europe and Asia by a land-bridge but is content to leave such matters to 'the unlimited libertie of the imagination of man' (Laing 1867: 40–1).

He argues that the possibilities inherent in colonisation are endless. Instead of living in poverty at home, men can become rich beyond imagining. Those with money may encourage others to accompany them and so perhaps create a town named after themselves. Once settled, individuals can enjoy a solitary existence when it suits them, or they can be sociable. Opportunities for hunting and fishing are virtually limitless. There is the challenge of new geographical discoveries, of building churches in the wilderness and of converting thousands of natives. For some, new beginnings may be possible, 'serving God more sincerely than before, to whom we may draw more neere, by retyring our selves further from hence'. In other words one might become a better person and a better Christian by emigrating. He warns would-be colonists, however, at some length, that much labour is required to succeed. He wants confident, optimistic settlers rather than nay-sayers or shirkers. He was among the first, however, to be convinced that Scots, where emigration was concerned, were peculiarly 'fit for purpose', 'having dareing minds', contempt for danger, strong bodies and a keen desire to work their own land.

On his map of New England and New Scotland, Alexander named four rivers Tweed, Solway, Clyde and Forth, the first of many conferred Scottish place-names designed to appeal to would-be emigrants back home. It is often stated that Scots migrated to Canada because it reminded them of Scotland, and while this is true in some parts it represents pure propaganda in others. Many Scots would have found the former lakebeds of southern Ontario as alien as the prairies, the endless stretches of forest and the snow-blasted flat-lands of the north. Nevertheless, place-names represent the footprints of predecessors and in Alexander's case they were emphatically lowland inventions.

The future Viscount Canada was a poet and a visionary who foresaw a Canada that was not torn and split by religious strife, where Protestant and Catholic could live side by side, as the lion lay down with the lamb, a manifestation which Canada, surely one of the most tolerant countries on the planet, has largely achieved.

Sir Robert Gordon of Lochinvar was up to his ears in skullduggery, a hell-raiser and reiver, drowning in debt, who was accused, among other crimes, of theft, slaughter, adultery, murder and arson, and of oppressively seizing ships. He can be seen as one of the last of the Border reivers, yet one of the first Scots to set their sights on the New World. Remarkably his pamphlet, *Encouragements For such as shall have intention to bee Under-takers in the new plantation of Cape Briton, now New Galloway in America, by Mee Lochinvar* (1625) (Laing 1867) is, like Alexander's, an underrated classic in the literature of colonisation. He regarded Adam and Eve as the first colonists. He too noted conversion of the heathen as a major motive for plantation, but he proceeded to list the main justifications for emigration, anticipating the many who wrote on the subject in future years. These were: enlargement of the dominions, in this case specifically Scottish; national and personal enrichment; the checking of sedition at home; and to 'settle security against enemies abroad'. Other motives included glory, adventure and the conferment of great benefit upon one's fellow human beings. He favourably reviewed the activities of explorers and settlers in America during the previous sixty years, finding them inspirational for himself and others. He was particularly concerned to persuade his fellow Scots of the benefits of emigration:

> We are not born to our selves: but to help others, and our abilities and means are not so much unlike at the first hour of our birth, and the last minute of our death: and it is our deeds good or bad that all of us have to carry to Heaven or Hell after this life. (Laing 1867: B2v)

To persuade his countrymen to acquire a kingdom overseas he provided a detailed account of the economic potential of New Galloway, the physical closeness of which might require a passage of only eighteen days (Laing 1867: D), the earliest-known attempt to advertise the supposedly short distance between Old and New Scotland in order to lure potential migrants. He highlighted the classless nature of emigration by indicating that in Ireland gentlemen had become peers, and artisans gentlemen. He urged members of his own class, crushed by debt like himself, to become involved. They should follow the example of the Italians who were not afraid to dirty their hands on trade (Laing 1867: Ev).

As might be expected of a man with his reputation, he was less well disposed towards the *indigenes* than Alexander. It was the duty of Christians to preach God's message to all the world, closely followed by the gospel of commerce. It was lawful to possess part of the native lands and defend them against the Indians. The best way to convert them was 'by daylie conversation, where we may see the Life, and learne the Languages each of others'; for good measure he included some native words in his tract. Commendable though Gordon's latter intention may have been, he was emphatic that there was plenty of land for native and newcomer alike. He cited numerous precedents to demonstrate that acquisition of further land was legitimate (Laing 1867: B3–B4v). He concluded with a description of the native people, 'so fewe, so poore, so base, so incivile, and so savage, as wanting both multitude, power or airte (art) to harme us'. If war with them transpired, their only defence would be retreat (Laing 1867: Dv). He thus, in displaying the ugly side of Scottish racial attitudes, perfectly complemented Alexander's more benign view.

Encouragements ends with 'The Offers' which Gordon made to potential colonists, the first such surviving examples of Scottish contracts. Ministers and their families were to travel free of charge with support for their first three years in the colony, in which time it was hoped parishes would be established. All colonists must conform in religion, obedience to the king and the laws of Scotland. Gentlemen, their families, their household staff, and supplies for a year's sustenance were promised free passage. Their lands would be granted in fee and heritage to them and their heirs forever, to be held of Gordon and his successors, according to Scots law. Compensation would be paid for possessions destroyed or stolen. Tenants and farmers would be granted three life-rents followed by nineteen-year leases. Craftsmen of all kinds would enjoy free transport and free rents for life (Laing 1867: D3–E). Thus between them Alexander and Gordon anticipate most of the issues which would persist throughout the Scottish emigrant experience irrespective of destination.

That his scheme was a failure was no disgrace since many early colonial ventures were no more successful but his enterprise, only two years after the *Mayflower* left English shores, should be better known. In 1626 he was created Vice-Admiral of the Southwest Coast of Scotland and Lieutenant-General of Charles Island in America. Though it was a far cry from Loch Ken, he was given permission by Charles I to send two ships south of the Equator in order to claim his American lands but death intervened to foil the ambitions of this Galloway imperialist.

In the event, Cape Breton was to be visited briefly by Alexander's son, also Sir William Alexander, in 1629 before he moved on to Port Royal. On board a ship returning to England that autumn was an Indian chief, Sagamore Segipt, and his family. The purpose of his voyage was to perform homage to Charles I and to seek his assistance against the French (Insh 1922). In this there was the germ of an idea that the Scots were to develop at century's end.

According to the pioneering study of George Pratt Insh, the earliest settlers seemed inclined to follow the example of Alexander rather than Gordon in their benign views of native peoples (Insh 1922). A recent study has significantly illuminated Scottish colonial activity in the seventeenth century but it rather ignores the question of race relations (Macinnes 2007). In July 1698 the directors of the Company Trading to Africa and the Indies ordered the colonists who were about to embark for America to plant a colony to be named Caledonia, 'in some place or other not inhabited ... or in any other place, by consent of the natives and inhabitants thereof'. When the homely Scots reached the West Indies one isle was described as 'like the Bass'; another was not so broad as Inchkeith while a third appeared to them at night-time 'just as the Castle of Edinburgh does to any going up from Leith'. Travellers always look for the familiar in the exotic, establishing a lasting trope in the literature of emigration; everywhere looks like somewhere else.

In two separate treaties of friendship, union and perpetual confederation were agreed between the Council of the Colony of New Caledonia and Chief Diego Tucuapantos 'Supreme Leader of the Indian inhabitants of the lands and possessions in and about the River Darien'. The conditions involved mutual defence of persons, lands, territories, dependencies and properties by land and sea; liberty of movement, of commerce and of the possession of and cultivation of land (Hart 1930, Watt 2007). When the news reached Edinburgh it was gleefully received. 'The Indians are now in league with the Scots and have joyfully received them into their country.' The Scots had peacefully entered upon their new colony 'without force or fraud; they can now liberate the natives from their hideous conditions under the Spanish' (*Defence* 5–6, 14). What becomes clear in a number of contemporary commentaries about Darien is that native and newcomer shared a reciprocal belief that each was exploiting or manipulating the other.

Complementing these sentiments were the careful observations of the natives by almost all expedition memorialists who provided sympathetic anthropologies which are striking for their neutrality and objectivity. Devine (2011) has provided a totally inadequate discussion of race relations which seriously underestimates the complexity of the subject. He is slightly more temperate in his brief discussion of Australia which is badly skewed because he highlights the atrocities of Angus MacMillan while omitting any mention of John Dunmore Lang who was well-disposed towards the aborigines. Scots felt a certain empathy for First Nations people not because of some romantic notions about shared clans and kindreds but because they were pragmatists. The fur trade could not operate without native support. Sometimes both sides treated one another harshly, but the issue was one of mutual respect. As it happens, Scots and French had similar approaches which became the Canadian way in relating to native peoples, whereas in the United States the authorities were hell-bent on ridding the land of native occupants in order to make way for European farmers. It has been forcefully argued that the differing foreign policies of Canada and the US are rooted in their respective attitudes towards the First Nations (Hall 2003). There is, however, good evidence that the Scottish attitude sometimes prevailed even in the US. When in 1823 the American government sent Chief William Macintosh of the Creeks to bribe John Ross Chief of the Cherokee nation into surrendering lands for white settlement, he was unsuccessful (Woodward 1963). This is not to deny that Scots ever committed atrocities for they did, especially the Scotch-Irish, but Scottish ideas of enlightened enquiry, social union, equality and respect for humankind greatly informed emigrant assumptions and aspirations. Such values would be transmitted by Scottish diasporans, if such they were, as their main contribution to their chosen host countries, wherever in the global emporium they settled.

3

The Scottish Diaspora and the Empire

Michael Fry

Scotland has in historic times probably always exported its own people but the age of European imperialism, dawning in the sixteenth century, allowed the diaspora to take new forms and to follow new channels (see Devine 2011).

In the Middle Ages mercenary warfare had led Scots to Ireland and to France, some to settle permanently. Or else peaceful trade sent them across the North Sea to the Netherlands and through the Sound to the Baltic region, where again a certain amount of permanent settlement followed. Still, most of those Scots who left returned at some point, and those who stayed away seldom kept up any connection with the mother country beyond the first generation; their descendants simply became assimilated to the host communities. Such families ceased to be Scots in all but their names and their memories, and no Scottish population formed in any neighbour nation. It was therefore not the same sort of medieval migration as, for example, drove the Germans to settle in compact masses on the many linguistic islands of eastern Europe that remained German-speaking till the twentieth century (Higounet 1976, Gründer and Johanek 2006, Piskorski 1999).

This general picture changed with the onset of imperialism, which before long extended the presence of European maritime nations to other continents (Césaire 1955, Osterhammel 2004, Tignor 1998).

The presence was of two kinds. One took the shape of colonisation, with the emigrants conquering, occupying and seizing possession of the territories of indigenous peoples. These, mounting a vain resistance against technological superiority, were dispossessed, subdued, often enslaved or even exterminated, if they did not succumb to the unknown infectious diseases that Europeans brought with them. Such was the normal pattern in the Americas especially. With catastrophic falls in the native populations, and sometimes their entire disappearance, European colonies established themselves overseas as early as the sixteenth and seventeenth centuries. From the eighteenth century, large regions had a population of non-indigenous origin, as they still do today (Bailyn 2005, Hinderaker and Horn 2010). The second sort of presence kept the European incomers and the indigenous peoples at arm's length except for trading contacts. In this case the purpose of the merchants and sailors who undertook the hazardous oceanic voyages was to conduct commerce rather than to take over territory. It was a presence of transients, not of permanent settlers, even where the trading outposts were themselves permanent, or semi-permanent. Trade could often, though not always, be carried on without any military or political control over the exchanges, over the hinterland of the emporiums where they took place or over the people participating in them (Luxemburg 1913, Fry 2001).

In the Far East, trading partners such as China and Japan were anyway ancient empires with governmental structures well able to control commerce on their own terms and, if necessary, to deal firmly with foreign devils (Fairbank and Teng 1979, Lester 2012). In India, on the other hand, the early European contacts came at a time of instability and decline in the Mughal Empire (Ali 1975, Black 2012). Even so, seaborne traders seldom found it straightforward or easy to establish a secure base here or anywhere else. It was in part a matter of the distances needing to be covered. To the Orient, the Europeans had to take the long oceanic route rather than the shorter overland route because of the hostility of the Islamic powers in between. Along that route, the coasts of Africa were too inhospitable to admit of any presence except in precarious outposts (the sole exception being at the Cape of Good Hope). Once arrived at their destination, the Europeans had no choice but to seek a perch amid the flurries of local conflict; if their side lost, they were toppled too.

Where then did the Scots fit into the troubled and uncertain character of these early intercontinental relationships? Before 1707, the independent nation hoped to benefit from them as other European countries were doing. Competition in distant parts of the world waxed ferocious, and wars originating in European politics were often also carried on in a colonial setting.

It might have been thought this gave an advantage to the greater European powers, yet in practice things did not always work out that way. By the end of the seventeenth century, the first European empires, formed by Spain and Portugal, were already stagnating, while the English and French empires had not yet risen to match them. There was a window of opportunity here for small countries to find some foothold in a distant continent. The Dutch offered the prime example, and in this era they ran the most profitable of all the empires with their monopoly of the lucrative traffic to the Spice Islands in modern Indonesia (Boxer 1965). But there were colonial initiatives from a range of other small countries or even from semi-autonomous provinces of the great powers: the Austrian Netherlands (modern Belgium) (Serruys 2005), Denmark (Larsen 1907), Sweden (Frängsmyr 1976), Brandenburg (in the Holy Roman Empire) (van der Heyden 2001) and Courland (modern Latvia) (Archibald 1987). It is into this category that the Scots fit, notably with their attempt to set up the colony at Darien in 1698–1700 (Watt 2007).

A common feature of these initiatives was that they did not establish, or aim to establish, colonies of settlement like the Spaniards in South America or the English along the eastern seaboard of North America. There were simply not the numbers of people available from the small countries to attempt such imitations of their native societies in distant regions of the globe.

Darien offered a typical example. Even if this had been planned as a colony of settlement the appalling death rate from tropical disease would soon have put paid to the idea. But that was never the intention anyway. When William Paterson, the originator of the scheme, who himself took part in it and lost his wife for his pains (indeed, he almost died himself), set out its supposedly glittering prospects to his countrymen, the trading opportunities were what he stressed above all:

Trade will increase trade, and money will beget money, and the trading world shall need no more to want work for their hands, but will rather want hands for their work. Thus, this door of the seas and the key of the universe, with anything of a sort of reasonable management, will of course enable the proprietors to give laws to both oceans and to become arbitrators of the commercial world without being liable to the fatigues, expenses and dangers, or contracting the guilt and blood of Alexander and Caesar. (Bannister 1859: 22)

For Scotland, this small country's pattern of colonialism continued long after it had been admitted to the empire of a big country on the formation of the United Kingdom in 1707. The most profitable part of that empire was the West Indies, where English colonies dated from the previous century. It did not take long for Scots to appear in them

(Karras 1992). Indeed, a few might have ventured there already; a West Indian voyage is listed in the records of the Scottish customs for Leith in 1611 (Carswell 1937). There must certainly have been some sort of Caribbean connection by the middle of the seventeenth century, because by the end of it four companies, three in Glasgow and another in Leith, were refining imported sugar and distilling rum. All survived the Union too, and by 1775 Scotland had ten such refineries. Later the commerce and processing were concentrated in Port Glasgow or Greenock, where sugar long remained a staple of the local economy (Smout 1961).

The British Empire in India was originally a transient traders' empire as well. The easiest way for any subject of the crown to get there and set about making his fortune was to sign up as a servant of the East India Company, in origin an entirely English enterprise granted a monopoly on trade with the Orient by Queen Elizabeth I in 1601. After 1707, Scots penetrated its ranks (McGilvary 2008). Because this offered one easy way for the government in London to satisfy their expectations of the Union, the Prime Minister, Sir Robert Walpole, made sure a fair share of Indian appointments was put their way. In the course of the eighteenth century it grew into something much better than a fair share.

In 1793, Henry Dundas, the political manager of Scotland, became also President of the Board of Control for India (the statutory authority which, in London, supervised the activities of the Company). The English soon complained they were now the ones excluded from a colonial operation dominated by Scots. As in the West Indies, these Scots were transients, who went east because they had some need to, but meant to return home and use their often ill-gotten gains to advance the social status of themselves and their families. They won the hostile nickname of nabobs (Fry 1992).

Even in the thirteen English colonies of settlement in North America, the Scots arriving after 1707 tended to treat them as commercial emporiums. The strongest link between Scotland and these colonies was the trade in tobacco from Virginia to Glasgow. In Virginia, the first part of America to be settled by the English, Scots arrived more than a century later as a small minority of strangers. That did not stop them penetrating up-country and supplying the frontiersmen with cheap goods shipped from Scotland. In return they bought up tobacco to be carried back as cargo in the returning ships. The raw crop was processed in Glasgow and exported all over Britain and Europe. The traffic formed the foundation of the city's later prosperity (Devine 1975).

None of this required Scottish settlement. Anyway, no rush of emigration to America followed the Union. Before the end of the Seven Years' War in 1763, Scots just seemed disinclined to make such a permanent move. Between then and the American Revolution, however, about 40,000 Scots did go, representing one-third of the entire British outflow of the period and perhaps 3 per cent of the total Scottish population at the time (Bailyn 1986). Towards these migrants, Americans seemed often to share hostile English prejudices akin to those being orchestrated in London by John Wilkes. They revealed themselves in the mind of Thomas Jefferson when he wrote the first draft (hastily amended by colleagues) of the Declaration of Independence in 1776, claiming that King George III had sent 'Scotch and foreign mercenaries, to invade and deluge us in blood'.[1] In fact, back in Edinburgh, most of the great names of the Enlightenment did disapprove of the revolting Americans: they favoured social evolution rather than political revolution. Still, after the United States won its independence, Scots continued to go and settle there. According to the new republic's first census in 1790, there were 260,000 of them, 8 per cent of the total population (Dollarhide 2001).

Part of the same movement was the surge of Scottish emigration to Canada after Britain annexed it from France in 1763. Among the first to settle were Highland troops who had taken part in the capture of Quebec in 1759. It was the aim in London to secure this northern half of the continent by introducing a British population. Since the defeated French already occupied the province of Quebec, newcomers pushed further up the St Lawrence River into what is now Ontario. Beyond lay the West, still empty of all but native tribes, yet economically valuable because of the furs it yielded from ceaseless slaughter of its wild animals. This business was largely taken over by Scots, operating in commercial partnerships set up in Montreal and then by penetration of the originally English enterprise, the Hudson's Bay Company chartered in 1670, on the analogy of their earlier penetration of the East India Company. With a mixture of guile and force, and the purchase of favourable legislation, these Scots managed to keep the Canadian West empty of European settlement till Confederation in 1867: a stark contrast to what was happening south of the border in the United States (Fry 2001).

The third major colony of British settlement was Australia. Here again the Scots' involvement tended at first to follow a pattern somewhat at variance with English norms. Since this began as a settlement for criminals condemned to transportation by the courts in England, the population was in the early decades English or Irish for the most part, with only a small proportion of Scots. Scottish interest centred rather on the vast tracts of the outback suitable for sheep-farming, land of no more than moderate quality but distantly comparable with the Scottish Highlands – parts of which were also now, through the Clearances, being emptied of people and filled with sheep. With such experience behind them, Scottish pastoralists could develop the outback in the same way, with the purpose of making it profitable rather than populous (Brown 1941–71).

This was all consistent besides with the part played by Scots in two other colonial outposts, Singapore and Hong Kong. The foundation of Singapore in 1819 is usually attributed to Stamford Raffles, the man then in charge of efforts to extend British influence in south-east Asia. He had at the same time to accommodate the Dutch interests in the region, and his answer was to set up a new settlement on the Strait of Malacca. In fact Raffles stayed only a single night in the colony he founded, leaving it afterwards to the Scots he had brought with him, mostly traders from India. They continued to develop the commercial network already linking Britain with its oriental outposts (Braddell et al. 1991). The foundation of Hong Kong in 1841 by Lord Napier formed part of the same process. Scottish trading houses such as Jardine Matheson were already trafficking with China. But that often led to political complications, culminating in the two Opium Wars of 1839–40 and 1859–60. Provision for these houses of a base in sovereign territory (or at least what the British regarded as sovereign territory) offered the solution to the problem (Napier 1995).

Up to the middle of the nineteenth century, then, there had been a fairly consistent pattern in Scottish imperial involvement, one reflecting the legacy of the independent nation before 1707. The mentality of the Scots remained that of a small nation, not seeking political dominance over distant regions of the globe with a view to emigration, yet all too happy to trade with the natives on equal terms. But from the middle of the nineteenth century Scotland became, through a variety of factors ranging from the industrial revolution to the crises in all its traditional national institutions, an altogether more British kind of country. Its imperial attitudes changed accordingly.

Now there followed the first really large waves of emigration from Scotland. In the Highlands a rapid increase in the indigenous population reached a peak in 1841, according to the census of that year, despite the clearances already carried out by some landlords. The following decade saw repeated failures in the potato crop, now the source of the Highlanders' staple food. A mass exodus followed with the effect of creaming off the entire natural increase till the end of the nineteenth century, when the population entered on steady decline. Yet the movement out of the Lowlands was also high, here with the decision to move abroad being nearly always a matter of economic aspiration. Whatever the reasons, Scotland as a whole lost between a tenth and a half of the natural increase in population in every decade till the First World War, and in the first decade afterwards the population of the country as a whole fell (Flinn et al. 1977).

The phenomenon of mass emigration did for the first time allow the formation of what might be regarded as Scottish colonies, in the sense of reasonably compact masses of population of Scottish origin able to preserve such signifiers of identity as Presbyterian religion and educational aspirations for all.

Canada was from Scotland the nearest destination, by this time a mere week or so away by steamship. The heaviest concentration of Scots formed in Nova Scotia. This had actually been the site of the earliest Scottish colony, or attempt at a colony, to which the first expedition set out in 1621. Still, nothing remained of that project except the name, and the Scots population here was mostly the product of emigration from the Highlands in the Victorian era. It was the only other part of the world where Gaelic language and culture took root, surviving right down to the present, if nowadays somewhat precariously (see Newton's chapter in this volume). Elsewhere in Canada, there was a strong Scottish imprint on the commercial community of Montreal and on the rather gloomy city of Toronto. The building of the Canadian Pacific Railway, essential to the unification of the country by opening the prairies for settlement, was in large part a Scottish enterprise (Bumsted 1981, Campey 2005).

Traces of Scottish emigration during the Victorian era also remain in Australia, New Zealand and South Africa. Today in these countries, as in North America too, those traces are most readily seen in the superficial paraphernalia of Scottishness. There are Highland games, and celebrations of Hogmanay and Burns Night. People wear the kilt, toss cabers, dance Strip the Willow. They may cultivate a sort of worship of the ancestors. All this serves, among other things, to mark them out from newer groups of immigrants unable to boast anything like the same colourful yet distinguished history. In America the invention of the so-called cracker culture in the former Confederacy, for example, adds Scottishness to its dominant strand of nativism. The message is that the primitive virtues of American tradition need to be preserved amid the floods of later immigration and the multi-culturalism they have created (today almost an official ideology of at least the liberal establishment in the United States). Tracing the roots of true American culture still deeper into the Old World underlines the message. And there seems to be nothing so visibly authentic as the component in it of Scottish culture – except, of course, that this is anything but authentic in the form in which it has been received (McWhiney 1988).

The fact is that none of these places, with the exception of Nova Scotia, really manages to preserve elements of the life of the mother country in a colonial setting. The overseas concentrations of Scots and their descendants were simply not big enough to achieve that in any continuous fashion. Rather, in the Victorian era as in the remoter past, the emigrant Scots assimilated within a generation to the society of the host country, which was partly English in origin and partly adapted to the exigencies of a new environment. Again, they retained little of Scotland but their names and their memories. Modern embellishments of that minimal identity are mere fabrications, usually less rather than more historically informed.

There were good socio-economic reasons for all this to have happened. Victorian Scotland equipped its people for success in the outside world by its well-developed system of education, its pioneering of the agricultural and industrial revolutions, its excellence in engineering and medicine. There were few other parts of the world where Scots could not use the skills their own country had taught them. Because they then tended to be successful emigrants, it was all the easier for them to integrate into the host societies. They had no need to cluster in the defensive ghettoes from which immigrant communities such as the Irish and the Italians often struggled in an alien and hostile environment. In the United States especially the succeeding waves of emigrants followed this latter example, with the result that ethnic identity and politics remain strong to this day. But this has not been the Scottish way of coping with the stresses of immigrant life (McCarthy and Hague 2004). It is true Scots sometimes did feel an impulse to compensate themselves for the actual loss of identity by rooting around in their cultural baggage and pulling out a few gaudy scraps. They were never enough to propel expatriate Scots into communal coherence like that of the Jews or the Sicilians in the United States, let alone the French in Canada or the Afrikaners in South Africa. These peoples retained a range of religious, educational, linguistic and where possible political and legal structures meant to preserve their identity against the odds at whatever cost. This was because they needed such mutual support, while Scots did not.

Here, then, is how the Scots have actually acted in their diaspora. But what did they have to say about it? The earliest significant corpus of Scottish writings on imperialism is that of William Paterson, the man behind Darien. While not wholly consistent in their outlook, they do by and large advocate an empire of trade rather than of settlement. That is also the basic message in the imperial thinking of the Enlightenment, set out in the writings of David Hume (Greig 1969), Adam Smith (1976) and Adam Ferguson (McDaniel 2013). On the whole they take a dim view of empires as productive of corruption and tyranny. Smith, who in 1776 called back the proofs of *The Wealth of Nations* so he could add to his text some salty comments on the outbreak of revolution in America, believed Britain would be better off without its thirteen colonies on the opposite side of the Atlantic.

Yet, despite what many feared at the time, the American Revolution was not the end of British imperialism, only of its first phase. The comments of enlightened Scots therefore continued to echo in the nineteenth century. For the United Kingdom, the imperial structure it then re-erected became the main prop of its status as a great power, something quite different in kind from that of great powers still emergent, such as the United States and Russia, which could rely on their indigenous resources.

The earlier enlightened thinking informed most obviously the radical side of Scottish politics. Scotland's dominant Liberal party in the Victorian era was a broad church. It drew support at one end from Whigs of a comfortable landowning or legal background and at the other end from urban activists who after the Reform Act of 1832 mobilised the newly enfranchised voters and called for the vote to be given to the majority not yet enfranchised (Hutchison 1986).

A typical figure was Joseph Hume, MP for the Aberdeen Burghs from 1818 and for the Montrose Burghs from 1842. He had a reputation as the most boring man in the House of Commons for his long speeches on the detail of public expenditure. But he could come alive when he turned to imperial affairs. There was a crisis in Canada in 1834 after an incursion by an irregular American force hoping to provoke revolt against the corrupt Tory clique then running the colonial government. Hume's reaction was something less than true-blue: in fact he supported this effort at separation from Britain. In an open letter to William Lyon Mackenzie, later Prime Minister of Canada and then serving as mayor of Toronto, Hume hoped that the violent incidents were something 'which will terminate in independence and freedom from the baneful influence of the mother country, and the tyrannical conduct of a small and despicable faction in the colony'.[2] It was a deduction from a typical radical line of argument: a diaspora into a colony of settlement leads logically to the independence of the territory.

The radical inheritance was later claimed by William Gladstone, leader of the Liberal party and from 1879 MP for Midlothian, where he reinstated himself as a Scot (which he was in blood, though he had spent his life elsewhere: he was just as good at pretending to be a Welshman at his country house of Hawarden in Flintshire, and an Englishman on all other occasions). This new identity also completed a long journey he had made in politics, from the high Toryism of his youth (and defender of the slave trade, no less) to the populism he now espoused. In his celebrated electoral campaigns for Midlothian he denounced the imperialist policies of Benjamin Disraeli's government in terms designed to pluck at the heartstrings of Presbyterian internationalist idealism: 'Remember the rights of the savage, as we call him. Remember that the happiness of his humble home, remember that the sanctity of life in the hill villages of Afghanistan, among the winter snows, is as inviolable in the eye of Almighty God, as can be your own' (Gladstone 1971).

Yet by this time the Empire was an inescapable reality in British politics and every government had to adopt some sort of policy towards it. The radical Gladstone might have wanted disengagement, followed by freely chosen association among the colonies of settlement. But, as soon as he got back again into Downing Street, he faced one urgent imperial crisis after another. In 1882 he reluctantly agreed to the occupation of Egypt – a step that would ultimately lead to the death of General Gordon at Khartoum, for which Gladstone was widely blamed. Much more serious in the event was how this exercise of British imperial muscle fuelled a wider European competition for colonies, in particular the scrambles for Africa and the Pacific. It was against a rapidly changing global background that Gladstone sought to hold fast to a radical view of the Empire; but he merely came across as a verbose hypocrite. Finally his espousal of Irish Home Rule in 1886 split the Liberal party and put it out of office for the better part of two decades (Matthew 1995).

The day of a primarily commercial imperialism seemed to be done. If the British Empire was to survive, it had to be secured by the exercise of power, by the occupation of territory and by colonial settlement.

For the first time, this point of view was coherently articulated in Scottish politics, through the secession from Gladstone's Liberal party that assumed the name of Unionism. The Unionists went on in the general election of 1886 to win seats in most parts of Scotland but especially in the west, where Clydeside's economy was in large part an imperial economy, dependent on markets in the Empire for its output of steel, ships, locomotives and so on (Cawood 2012).

Now a fierce debate on imperialism raged in Scotland. The radical critique continued to develop. A major contribution came from James Bryce, MP for South Aberdeen from 1885 to 1907, who held various posts in the Cabinet till he went as ambassador to Washington. He was a scholarly man who wrote on imperial and American constitutional history. In one of the most learned of these works he compared the original imperialism of the Romans with the British imperialism of his own day, especially in India:

> The fact that their dominions were acquired by force of arms exerted an enduring effect upon the Roman Empire and continues to exert it upon the British in imprinting upon their rule in India a permanently military character. (Bryce 1914: 12)

This had obliged Britain to make itself mistress of the seas, just as the Romans had needed to build roads everywhere: 'To make forces so small as those on which Rome relied and those which now defend British India adequate for the work they have to do, good means of communication are indispensable.' The rule of law was also necessary to both: 'It has contributed not only to the easier defence of the frontiers, but also to the maintenance of a wonderfully high standard of internal law and order' (Bryce 1914: 20–1).

Other effects were not so much to Bryce's radical taste. The government of India

> is virtually despotic. Whatever may have been done for the people, nothing was or is done by the people. There is in British India no room for popular initiative, or for popular interference with the acts of the rulers, from the viceroy down to a district official. (Bryce 1914: 28)

It did not bode well for the future: 'No more in India than in the Roman Empire has there been any question of establishing free institutions either for the country as a whole, or for any particular province.'

And a further effect is what we would call (the phrase never occurred to Bryce) institutional racism:

> As a rule, Anglo-Indian officials approve the course [of excluding Indians from the Indian Civil Service, usually recruited from the universities of Oxford and Cambridge]. But I know there are some who think that there are natives of ability and force of character such as to fit them for posts both military as well as civil, higher than any to which a native has yet been advanced. (Bryce 1914: 43)

Only a few decades later these people would make India an independent republic free of British control.

A streak of anti-imperialist radicalism also entered into the nascent Labour party. Keir Hardie went on a worldwide tour in 1907–8 that took him to South Africa, India and Australasia, so to a representative sample of imperial territories: one with a native population governed by British officials and secured by British arms; a second where a white minority held down a black majority; and finally two countries peopled by settlers. His support for Indian nationalism and condemnation of the official policy of divide and rule, setting Hindus apart from Muslims, made him unpopular enough in the British and colonial press. It got even worse when he arrived in South Africa and Australia, where white workers were angry and fearful of competition from imported Indian coolies, already present in the one case and threatening to come in the other. The Labour movements in both countries, expressing the views of their members, insisted that jobs should be reserved for white men. Hardie would have no truck with this, so fell out with the very South Africans and Australians who were supposed to share his political outlook. The affair showed, from a novel angle, how hard it was to uphold radical ideals in an Empire of settlement (Hyslop 2006).

Meanwhile in Scotland the imperialist point of view was enjoying much clearer articulation in the speeches and writings of Archibald Primrose, Earl of Rosebery. At the schism of the Liberal party in 1886 he stayed loyal to Gladstone, expecting to succeed him in its leadership. Yet in practice there was little difference in his imperial views from those who went over to Unionism.

In 1884 Rosebery, after resigning a junior ministerial post in charge of Scottish affairs, had gone on a worldwide tour that reshaped his view of the Empire. He decided it might be transformed into a powerful federation if the white colonies were placed, at least in principle, on a par with the mother country. During a speech in Adelaide in Australia, he became the first man to use the term Commonwealth: 'There is no need for any nation, however great, leaving the Empire, because the Empire is a Commonwealth of Nations' (McKinstry 2005: 121).

It seems unlikely, though, that Rosebery used the term quite in its present-day meaning. While he was at this point Gladstone's protégé, he had in fact already arrived at an imperial outlook rather different from his mentor's. Rosebery initially followed in espousing Irish Home Rule, yet this was the first policy he ditched after he succeeded as Prime Minister in 1894. He provoked a huge outcry when he at once announced that Ireland could only get Home Rule if England, as the senior of the three kingdoms in the British Isles, agreed to it. Such an unexpected reversal on the dominant issue of the day, after Gladstone had spent so much political capital in dealing with it, shocked not only Liberals but also the Irish Nationalist party at Westminster on which they relied for their majority. It was a defeat for the radical view of Empire and put off Irish Home Rule till after the First World War – when it turned into Irish independence. And that was the first occasion since the American Revolution that the United Kingdom gave up sovereign territory against its will (McKinstry 2005).

Finally we might take a look at a Scottish Unionist thinker on the Empire, John Buchan. In 1901 he got his first job after leaving university under Alfred, Lord Milner, who had been put in charge of the former Afrikaner republics conquered in the Second Boer War. Milner recruited round him a group of enthusiastic young officials known as the Kindergarten. They were meant to form the nucleus of a new, progressive civil service in the Transvaal and Orange Free State. For two years Buchan contributed to this exercise in comprehensive postwar reconstruction, with the aim of turning truculent and backward provinces into model dominions within the Empire, partly by settling British immigrants in them. His first task was to close the overcrowded death-traps of the concentration camps (at which he was horrified) where many Boer civilians had been interned during the hostilities. The reunited families were settled on land newly made available to them. This was done partly by taking it from the blacks, and Buchan's humanitarianism petered out at that point. Indeed, he himself fantasised about becoming one of a new breed of gentlemen settlers and establishing a colonial squirearchy on the high veld, living in much the same style as he enjoyed among the Border or Highland lairds at home (Smith 1965).

The attitudes towards race and class are utterly different from anything that would be acceptable today. Yet Buchan was not a brute. The colony of settlement became for him an ideal rather than just a policy. He hoped a good number of the settlers would be Scots. South Africa, he assured his fellow countrymen, was 'a sort of celestial Scotland' (Buchan 1906: 213). The core of his small but diverse body of African writing is the problem of colonial white settlement on the dark continent, with the purpose of shaping a new identity based on and rooted in this wild and exotic landscape. That preoccupation is in many respects a typically Scottish one. Buchan reflects on nation-building, on the question of how to master a demanding environment so that, imaginatively and literally, the settler comes to belong to it. It is hard to conceive of an Englishman being so moved by such a question, yet to a Scot, with the ambiguities of his own nationhood, the dilemmas posed themselves naturally.

What brings this range of writers and thinkers together is in essence the backdrop of diaspora, the idea of a Scotland that can be formed in some other place than Scotland itself and of its relation to the mother country. The concept arose not in a vacuum but out of a practical question. Scots were leaving their own shores in large numbers and it was legitimate to ask whether they would in effect be lost to the nation or whether they could in their new and different conditions construct alternative Scotlands to stand in a fruitful relationship to the original one. The radical answer was no, this could not be done, and the emigrant communities must be left to go their own way: the loss was in that sense absolute. The imperialist answer was the opposite, but obviously depended on an untiring Scottish commitment to the Empire that in the event was not sustained, if only because the Empire in the end vanished despite all the efforts that Scots, among others, had put into it.

This whole field is, I think, something that will repay continued study in the future. As things stand, treatment of it has been left in an unsatisfactory state through the invention by Devine and his acolytes of the idea that Scots at home and abroad are united by 'Highlandism' (Devine 1999), precisely the phoney and superficial aspects of Scottishness dealt with earlier in this essay. The fact is that till recently most Lowland Scots felt little affinity with the Highlands and their symbolism. Only with the recent rise of nationalism, and of course the Tartan Army's inexplicable devotion to one of the world's lousiest football teams, has that changed somewhat.

Devine's most recent book, *To the Ends of the Earth* (2011), attempts to substitute the term globalism for the imperialism previously assumed as the rational justification for Scots to move abroad. He makes the valid point that since figures for emigration demonstrate that their opportunities were not confined to territories under British rule, it is little surprise to find that Scottish emigration knew no such limitation either. Even so, we should always look at what the people of the past had to say for themselves, rather than treating them as the fodder for modern statistical analysis. Here I have presented just a few salient examples of contemporary Scots' actual engagement with the Empire, and this only scratched the surface of the literature. By contrast, I have discovered only one author who might properly be said to have tackled the issue of globalism, Sir Halford Mackinder, Unionist MP for Glasgow Camlachie 1910–22, and he is never mentioned by Devine (Mackinder 1907).

Of course, there were no satisfactory answers to these questions of identity that the Scottish diaspora raised. Though it was hard for Scots to maintain their identity thousands of miles from home, so it was hard for the colonial communities they joined to forge some new identity of their own (though this appeared more of a problem at the beginning of the twentieth century than it appears in the twenty-first). And meanwhile identity at home in Scotland was steadily decaying as the country became ever more British. But if other Scotlands could once be imagined overseas, it should not be hard to imagine other Scotlands that may exist here and now, or at least soon.

4

Scots by Association: Clubs and Societies in the Scottish Diaspora

Kim Sullivan

One of the questions at the heart of this volume is whether that vast and diverse array of individuals with a Scottish connection scattered throughout the globe actually possesses a collective awareness as a diaspora community. This proves to be a complex issue, as not all Scots and their descendants living beyond Scotland necessarily identify with that heritage. And while many clearly do, it is often expressed in purely personal terms, and is therefore unconnected to the experiences of others. However, a stratum exists within this wider, largely indefinable 'community' that projects a wholly intentional, shared Scottish diaspora consciousness.

During the British colonial era, Scottish associations such as St Andrew's and Caledonian societies, to name but two of the more popular forms, proliferated throughout the Empire as a medium for the mutual, outward expression of ethnic identity among settler Scots. A remarkable number of these, established principally in North America and Australasia, still thrive today, while others have emerged, and continue to do so, in places that have latterly attracted Scottish migration. Recent additions include, for example, the Caledonian Society of Cyprus and the Moscow Caledonian Club, both formed during the 1990s. Consequently, Scottish clubs and societies overseas have for centuries represented the conscious, deliberate embodiment of diaspora identity for those Scots (and increasingly their descendants) who have chosen to form and join them. The following chapter explores this most visible facet of the broader Scottish diaspora community, tracing the origins and evolution of these enduring organisations, before examining what they represent for their members in the twenty-first century. At a time when a devolved Scottish nation is reassessing its own identity – a process in which the diaspora looms large – Scottish associations provide a valuable window into the nature and outlook of that other, vast external Scottish community.

It is unclear precisely when Scots first began forming clubs and societies as a means of collectively asserting their shared ethnic identity in places other than home. However, British imperial expansion triggered an intensive period of both the invention and propagation of these bodies throughout, and ultimately beyond, the colonial world. And while organisations of this nature manifested in a great variety of forms, they generally fell into one of two overarching categories – those that were generically Scottish in character and those with a specific regional orientation. Among the former were St Andrew's, Caledonian and Scottish societies, Burns and Thistle clubs, each with their own particular purpose, internal identity and ritual culture, but otherwise expressing themselves in undiscriminating Scottish terms. In the latter category were all manner of associations representing regional loyalties, although many of these, such as the Toronto Caithness Society, founded in 1877, were short-lived, presumably owing to insufficient numbers (O'Connor 2008). Others fared better by amalgamating different regional interests, as with the Caithness and Sutherland Association in Dunedin, New Zealand (1873), which, while already representing two Scottish regions at its foundation, quickly expanded to include members from Orkney and Shetland, altering its name accordingly (Harland 2009). However, associations with a broader Highland/Gaelic orientation were perhaps the most successful of this type, with dozens taking root and flourishing throughout the British Empire from its core to its periphery.

The earliest known associations with a specific Highland/Gaelic focus actually emerged within Scotland, although outside of the traditional Gaeltacht, and thus were products of an internal regional diaspora. In Glasgow, migrants from the north established a Highland Society in 1727, and the Gaelic Club of Gentlemen in 1780 (Withers 1985). Four years later, the Highland Society of Scotland came into force in Edinburgh, followed by the Highland Society of Aberdeen in 1816 and the Celtic Society of Edinburgh in 1820.[1] This trend also spread across the border into England in the late eighteenth century, with the establishment of the Gaelic Society of London in 1777, and the Highland Society of London the following year. The latter ultimately spawned several sub-branches overseas, in response to the growing exodus of Highland Scots to the British colonies.[2] Among these was the Highland Society of Canada, founded in Glengarry, Ontario (then Upper Canada) in 1818, which became the umbrella organisation for numerous offshoots across the Canadian territories (Macdonell 1884). Later, in Victoria, Australia, where a substantial cluster of Highland Scots settled during the region's gold rush, two independent and highly successful examples of this type of association also emerged. The Comunn na Feinne (Brotherhood of Fingalians) in Geelong and the Maryborough Highland Society were both established in 1857, and continue to operate, in one form or another, to the present day (Willis 2008).[3] And following a small but significant influx of Highland Scots into Otago in New Zealand, a Gaelic Society formed in Dunedin in 1881, folding only in 2006 after an impressive century-and-a-quarter life span (Entwistle 1981). The first organisation of this kind known to have emerged within the Gaeltacht was the Gaelic Society of Inverness in 1871 (Terry 1909).

Those associations of an all-encompassing Scottish character also originated in the diaspora. The earliest identifiable St Andrew's society was founded in Charleston, South Carolina in 1729,[4] inspiring a flurry of namesakes throughout America's blossoming colonial cities, including Philadelphia (1747), New York (1756)[5] and Washington, DC (1760)[6] (Gardner 1947). St Andrew's societies became prominent across North America, and ultimately spread into Canada where, for instance, early versions sprang up in Hamilton and Toronto during the mid–1830s.[7] By 1914 at least twenty others had formed across Upper Canada alone, alongside roughly twenty sub-branches of another locally popular form of Scottish association known as the Sons of Scotland, and more than a dozen Highland/Gaelic societies of various types, including a Highland Society of Canada sub-branch (Macdonell 1884). The oldest identifiable St Andrew's Society within Scotland appears to have formed in Aberdeen in 1788, several decades after that pioneering North American wave. It was not until 1854 that a St Andrew's Society emerged in Glasgow, with Edinburgh only following suit in 1907 (Terry 1909).[8]

Caledonian societies also first took root beyond Scotland, albeit much later, and much closer to home. The first was founded in London in 1838 (Hepburn and Douglas 1923). From here, this new form of Scottish association quickly spread out to the colonies and beyond, becoming predominant in the emerging Australasian settlements especially, by the end of the century. In Victoria, Australia, for example, the first Caledonian society formed in Melbourne in 1858 at the peak of the gold rush (Chisholm 1950). And with the subsequent intensive spread of settlement throughout Victoria, around thirty more Caledonian societies emerged there during the ensuing half-century. Three of these even managed to coexist independently within Melbourne, despite the city also becoming home to a further dozen Scottish associations of various types by the early 1900s. In fact, so prolific was the spread of Scottish associational culture in Victoria at this time that the president of Melbourne's short-lived St George's Society was compelled to remark to a local journalist that 'Scottish societies were springing up like mushrooms after rain!' (Chisholm 1950: 64). Caledonian societies also dominated the Scottish associational landscape in Otago, New Zealand, where approximately twenty independent versions are known to have been established between the foundation of the region's first, in Dunedin in 1862, and the beginning of the First World War. However, no such body ever appears to have successfully taken root in Scotland. Caledonian societies were therefore not only another expatriate invention, but also one that, unlike St Andrew's, Highland and Gaelic societies, remained an expatriate phenomenon.

Despite their variations, the main impetus behind those Highland and Gaelic forms of association in the colonial diaspora was essentially uniform. This comprised the protection and preservation of Highland culture generally, and the Gaelic language in particular, at a time when both were broadly perceived to be under threat at home. Many, if not most, also restricted membership to Highland Scots and their descendants as a further measure of cultural self-defence (Fraser 1900). As the Gaelic Society of New Zealand's rules made clear: 'Candidates for admission as members ... must be Scottish Highlanders, or the descendants of Highlanders, possessing an acquaintance with and a desire to improve their knowledge of the Gaelic language' (*Otago Daily Times* 1881). However, such strict exclusivity often proved difficult to sustain beyond the first generation of Highland-born settlers. In Dunedin, for example, the children of the Gaelic Society's founding members were often indifferent towards their parents' native tongue, seeing little value in learning Gaelic as they pursued their own futures in an English-speaking colony (Entwistle 1981). Consequently, the Society was compelled to extend membership eligibility to the broader Scottish migrant and descendant community, in the hope that other Scots might at least enjoy learning Gaelic as a pastime – an initiative that helped ensure the Society's survival into the twenty-first century (Entwistle 1981). Ultimately, the Society would remove all ethnic membership restrictions, and even elected an Englishman as its Chief during the 1970s (*Otago Daily Times* 2006).

Two early exceptions to that otherwise prevailing restrictive trend, however, were the Comunn na Feinne and Maryborough Highland

Society in Australia, both of which invited membership from across the multi-ethnic communities in which they operated from the outset (Willis 2008).[9] Additionally, both were careful to counter that inherently insular Gaelic language objective with a more accessible and inclusive expression of Highland culture, namely the staging of an annual Highland Games for the whole community. The success of this strategy is still very much in evidence, as thousands of people of every ethnic background flock to Geelong and Maryborough each summer to be part of these sporting and cultural events whose origins, while firmly rooted in the distant Highlands of Scotland, are also now an ingrained Australian tradition.

The motives behind the formation of those other, broadly Scottish types of association in the diaspora were more varied, and not always necessarily premised on a desire to uphold ethnic identity as a first priority. North America's pioneering St Andrew's societies, for instance, were established principally as a means of generating and distributing charitable aid to what appears to have been a persistent underbelly of desperate souls among the greater mass of migrating Scots. One of the oldest, the St Andrew's Society of Philadelphia, was formed in 1747 by some of that city's established and successful Scottish settlers, in direct response to an influx of less fortunate Scots during the tumultuous post-Culloden era. The Society's historian, Edgar Gardner (1947: 30), vividly described these incomers as 'sufferers from the troubled times: escaped prisoners of war, indentured servants, refugees from Culloden and other victims of misfortune'. Canada's later wave of St Andrew's societies shared this core objective, albeit that the causes of hardship among their prospective beneficiaries were typically of a less turbulent nature. A common problem facing Scots, and other migrants, wishing to settle in Toronto, for example, was simply a miscalculation of both the distance and cost of getting there once landed at far-off Quebec or Montreal (Campey 2005). Besides making direct grants of money to applicants experiencing immediate financial difficulties, these bodies also aspired to provide longer-term solutions for individuals with more complex needs. The St Andrew's Society of Toronto, for instance, sometimes relocated Scots struggling to find work in the city to other towns where suitable job opportunities might be more prevalent.[10] However, underscoring all of these societies' benevolent activities was the principle of self-improvement, and they took great care to select only those candidates likely to use the help given to lift themselves permanently out of hardship. As the Toronto society's annual report for 1879 made clear, 'tramps or vagrants' need not apply.[11]

Although each St Andrew's society was completely independent, they shared another key aspect of their internal culture. The constitution of the Toronto society, founded in 1836, was entirely typical of its kind, stating that both members and the recipients of its charity should be none other than Scots or their descendants.[12] The Toronto body also followed form by making St Andrew's Day the focal point for its fundraising activities, thereby further emphasising its exclusive Scottish orientation. And while no such ethnic discrimination applied over which members of Toronto's high society (and their wallets) to invite to its grand annual St Andrew's Day ball, this pivotal event was no less steeped in Scottish symbolism. Haggis, whisky and oatcakes were regulars at the buffet table, while thick swathes of tartan draped around the hall helped to absorb the noise of the live pipe music accompanying the Highland dancing.[13]

However, despite the huge success of the St Andrew's society model in North America, it made relatively moderate inroads into the later emerging Australasian settlements. Historian David MacMillan (1967: 40) has suggested that in early Australia's case at least, the unfathomable distance from home, along with its as-yet-untested viability as a colony for general settlement, meant that it was rarely the choice of those 'desperate men' so visible within North America's Scottish migrant demographic. Rather, a move to Australia (or New Zealand) more typically represented a calculated risk by those with the requisite means and freedom of choice. One early twentieth-century Australian reference book described these settlers as 'the more energetic, self-reliant, and mentally well-equipped of the uneasy classes in England, Scotland, Ireland, and Wales ...' (*The Cyclopedia of Victoria* 1903: 107). Perhaps, then, there was simply less need for the manner and intensity of charitable services which were the St Andrew's societies' forte. Instead, that newer form of Scottish association, the Caledonian society, flourished in the Antipodes, the overarching impetus for which was a desire among the Scots who formed them to express and celebrate their ethnic origins. Although much as tartan, bagpipe music and Highland dancing came to exemplify a typical St Andrew's society event, so too did Caledonian societies adopt distinctly Highland forms of cultural expression in order to represent their all-encompassing Scottish identity. Yet in both cases, it would appear that early memberships were typically dominated by Scots of Lowland origin (see Sullivan 2010).

In Victoria, for example, the region's first Caledonian society, formed in Melbourne in 1858, made the staging of an annual

Caledonian Games its primary focus. These events typically comprised caber-tossing, hammer-throwing, Highland dancing and bagpiping contests (*The Argus* 1859). As such they differed very little from the more traditionally styled Highland games held by the nearby Comunn na Feinne and Maryborough Highland Society, except that they were packaged and presented to the Melbourne public as a national, rather than a regional, Scottish custom. Yet this alternative version proved no less popular, as the multitude of Caledonian societies that subsequently emerged across the region began staging their own throughout the summer season. In fact, so prolific and well-attended did Caledonian games become in Victoria's outlying towns, that the original Caledonian Society in Melbourne, unable to compete, eventually abandoned the event in favour of regular Scottish music concerts and dances (Sullivan 2010), although again, with a recognisably Highland bearing.

Figure 4.1 A sketch at the Caledonian Ball, Melbourne, 1886. State Library of Victoria, A/S05/05/86/65

A similar story unfolded in colonial New Zealand, where in Otago, for instance, those Caledonian societies initially dominating the Scottish associational landscape became known principally for their annual Caledonian games. The region's first, the Caledonian Society of Otago, founded in Dunedin in 1862, set an impressive benchmark with its games, which regularly attracted crowds in the hundreds, as well as a string of celebrity Scottish sportsmen, including athletics legend Donald Dinnie (*Otago Witness* 1883; Zarnowski 1998). The Dunedin games were even graced by a royal presence on two occasions – the Duke of Edinburgh in 1869 and the Duke and Duchess of Cornwall in 1901.[14] Yet while otherwise following the lead of its forerunners in Australia, and subsequently setting the trend in its own region (and throughout New Zealand), the Caledonian Society of Otago did differ from the vast majority of its namesakes in one important factor. Nowhere in its constitution did it stipulate that members must be Scottish or of Scottish descent. However, this anomaly was likely a reflection of Dunedin's unique origins as an experimental Scottish Free Church settlement, a result of which was a profound overrepresentation of Scots within the population during its formative decades. Historian Tom Brooking (1985: 159) notes that Scots accounted for approximately 80 per cent of all immigrants into Otago up to 1860. As local historian Alison Clarke (2003: 150) argues, therefore, 'a community dominated by Scots took its Scottishness for granted'. That being the case, it may simply have seemed excessive and unnecessary to Dunedin's Scots to exclude ethnic outsiders from their cultural activities, in a city whose character was already so emphatically Scottish. One curious consequence of the Caledonian Society's unusually relaxed membership policy was the gradual swelling of its ranks with Englishmen in particular during the later nineteenth century, many of whom appear to have had no personal Scottish connections. Also present at various times during the Society's first half-century were members from Ireland, Germany, Canada and the United States. And even a local Chinese businessman, Choie Sew Hoy, appeared on the Society's roll in the early 1880s (Sullivan 2010).[15] However, with so many of the city's Scottish business elite among the Society's membership, it is possible that these non-Scots were drawn primarily by the opportunity to engage in professional networking.

Despite the now-distant colonial origins and seemingly outdated impetuses of the various Scottish associations so far described, a remarkable number continue to thrive today, among which are the St Andrew's Society of Toronto, the (now Royal) Caledonian Society of Melbourne and the Caledonian Society of Otago. The remainder of this chapter considers these three long-enduring organisations, and in particular the individuals who keep them going, in the greatly altered contexts of twenty-first-century Canada, Australia and New Zealand.

Now in its 178th year of continuous operation, the St Andrew's Society of Toronto has undergone little change since its establishment, notwithstanding a subtle easing of its original strict Scottish orientation. Its constitution, as it appears on the Society's website,[16] now states that members may be individuals 'of Scottish descent or who support the objectives of the Society', thereby sanctioning potential participation from beyond Toronto's Scottish ethnic community. The Society's core charitable remit has also expanded to include non-Scottish causes, although a particular commitment to helping Scots still remains pivotal. One current member recalls, for instance, an occasion on which the Society purchased replacement tools for a newly arrived Scottish tradesman whose own had been stolen (Sullivan 2010: 284). Today, however, the majority of the Society's benevolent work is channelled through various intermediary agencies dealing with a diverse range of issues from poverty to education, and encompassing the entire community – a reflection, perhaps, of modern-day Toronto's multi-ethnic (and far less Scottish) demographic composition. But the Society still expresses its original Scottish identity via the ever-popular annual St Andrew's Day ball, and has since added a Burns supper to its social calendar. Thus, with membership continuing to run into the hundreds, the St Andrew's Society of Toronto has successfully adapted to the changing social and ethnic landscape within which it operates, without sacrificing the strong Scottish foundations upon which it was built.

The Royal Caledonian Society of Melbourne, which was granted a Royal Charter by King George V in 1921 (Chisholm 1950), has also remained largely true to its original purpose and character, 156 years after its formation. According to its website,[17] the Society's social calendar is still punctuated by Scottish entertainments, in particular an annual St Andrew's Day festival dinner, and 'Hogmanay Australis' – a uniquely Australasian spin on a traditional Scottish event, held in mid-winter each year. However, like the St Andrew's Society of Toronto, the Caledonian Society's rules of membership have undergone a notable degree of relaxation. Its current constitution, available online, notes that prospective members may be 'natives of Scotland or of Scottish descent or association', before noting specifically that 'the spouse or partner of a qualified member may be deemed eligible for membership notwithstanding the absence of a Scottish bloodline'.[18] This clause in fact highlights a fundamental change within all three of the associations under discussion, namely the inclusion of women in what were, at their respective foundations, exclusively male institutions. Consequently, females now constitute a notable presence within each. And while the Society's Secretary notes that membership numbers have dwindled considerably since the nineteenth century,[19] its survival is nonetheless equally remarkable, given the still entirely Scottish nature of its activities.

The Caledonian Society of Otago is now in its 152nd year, and as committed as ever to its popular annual games, although ironically, these have recently been rebranded as Highland rather than Caledonian. Having invited participation from beyond the Scottish ethnic community since its foundation, the Caledonian Society of Otago was always ahead of its time, and consequently its rules of membership have not changed. However, its historic cosmopolitan outlook aside, it remains a distinctly Scottish organisation, playing an active role in Dunedin Scottish Week each November, and collaborating with the region's other Scottish associations, both old and new, in promoting and upholding Otago's unique Scottish heritage.

Facilitating these organisations' continued existence is a generation of members far removed from their nineteenth-century progenitors, and yet who nonetheless presumably find in their respective colonial-era Scottish societies (and their largely unchanged purposes) something to which they can relate. Accordingly, members of all three were invited to take part in a survey in order to establish both a demographic profile of these associations' current incumbents, and an insight into their personal perspectives as some of the more visible upholders of Scottish identity in the contemporary diaspora. A total of fifty-eight individuals ultimately participated.

Naturally, these three societies were founded, and initially dominated by, Scottish settlers. And while a very small contingent of Scots-born remains within the Toronto and Melbourne societies at least, the vast majority of surveyed members in all three were found to be the descendants of Scottish immigrants, by various degrees of removal. Most were the children, grandchildren or great-grandchildren of a Scot, although in Toronto and Melbourne there were members as far as four, and even five, generations removed from their closest Scottish ancestor. Yet despite the broad range of Scottish connections represented among the survey participants, when asked what motivated them to belong to their respective associations, their answers were virtually unanimous. Almost every respondent across the board cited a deep, personal sense of Scottish identity.

Sociologist Herbert Gans (1999) questioned whether this manner of essentially self-ascribed ethnic identification, which he observed as manifest among third-generation descendants of European immigrants in 1970s America, was capable of enduring into subsequent generations, or whether it would decline incrementally with the continued widening of that gap. Regarding the subjects of this survey at least, generational proximity to one's nearest Scottish forebear appeared to have no bearing upon the presence or intensity of that impulse towards Scottish ethnic self-identification. Thus, while continuing to serve as cultural hubs for an albeit profoundly reduced stratum of expatriate Scots, all three associations have largely evolved into sites of what Gans termed symbolic ethnicity (1999: ch. 9) for those Canadians, Australians and New Zealanders of varying degrees of Scottish descent who currently constitute the majority of members.

Given the diversity of Scottish connections within the three associations' memberships, it was anticipated that other ethnicities would also likely be present in many, if not most, of the survey participants' family backgrounds. This broader ethnic picture, and the emphasis placed on those other ethnic connections, where relevant, was considered crucial to fully understanding the Scottish aspect of the members' identities. Consequently, the survey also sought to establish both the presence, and meaningfulness, of any additional ethnic links for those who chose to declare them. The results cast up some unexpected insights. More than half of all the members surveyed cited at least one additional (non-Scottish) ethnic connection. And while this particular finding is commensurate with the multi-cultural nature of contemporary Canadian, Australian and New Zealand society, attitudes towards those other ethnic links proved quite unexpected. None of the St Andrew's Society of Toronto members claiming other ethnicities, for example, chose to engage or identify with them either privately or socially, while only one survey respondent each from Melbourne and Otago claimed to do so. The predominant trend among the respondents at large, therefore, was an open acknowledgement of the presence of other ethnic connections in their backgrounds, yet a relative ambivalence towards them (Sullivan 2010).

The most frequently cited reason for this was a lack of opportunity to express those other ethnic identities, in the sense that there were no equivalents to their respective Scottish associations, or other regular public events, through which to engage with them. One Scottish- and German-descended Caledonian Society of Otago member noted, for example, the absence of any German ethnic associations in or around

Dunedin. Similarly, three Royal Caledonian Society of Melbourne members claiming both Scottish and English ethnic heritage independently noted a lack of local English organisations. One of these members suggested that the absence of a visible English ethnic movement in Melbourne was because 'England is so varied in its different areas that local interest in certain areas (e.g. Somerset in my case) would not attract enough people'. This individual considered the prevalence of regional identities as a counter to the emergence of a broader English ethnic associational culture. However, the persistence of regional loyalties among certain elements of Melbourne's (and wider Victoria's) early Scottish community did not preclude the emergence of a more comprehensive Scottish ethnic movement there. (As noted earlier, both Highland/Gaelic and more general Scottish forms of ethnic association emerged successfully alongside one another in early Victoria.)

Similarly, a dearth of Irish associations was the prevalent explanation among those St Andrew's Society of Toronto members also claiming Irish descent for their lack of involvement in this particular aspect of their heritage. One member noted that the city's St Patrick's Society (which was founded at the same time as the St Andrew's Society) 'died more than fifty years ago from lack of support'. Another member lamented that there was 'nothing for the Irish' in terms of ethnic activity in the city. Yet the greater Toronto area is currently home to numerous Irish associations including the Toronto St Patrick's Parade Society, the Irish Cultural Society of Toronto and at least one Orange Lodge, suggesting that claims to a lack of opportunity were largely unfounded. And in Dunedin, two Caledonian Society of Otago members claiming Irish heritage appeared similarly disinterested in actively exploring this facet of their identities, despite openly acknowledging that there were local outlets through which to do so. As one stated, 'I believe ... St Patrick's Day is always well celebrated in Dunedin. I have never had time to explore this too much.' A fellow Irish-descended member responded by saying, 'There are Irish societies in Dunedin but I have not become involved. I am very busy with other clubs I am involved in plus work and do not have the time.' Another member was less ambiguous on the subject of his lack of engagement with his Irish ethnic heritage, simply stating 'Apathy!' as the reason why, although sadly without further elaboration.

In Melbourne, too, where opportunities to express Irish ethnic identity were duly acknowledged by the Caledonian Society's Irish-descended members, a degree of indifference prevailed. One such member claimed that 'although I have Irish ancestors, I do not feel

Irish at all ... there are plenty of opportunities but I do not wish to avail myself of them'. For another, English-descended member, however, it was not the strength of regional loyalties which precluded her from expressing her English heritage. Rather, it was something more fundamental. 'You could say that the whole of the Australian "establishment" is a manifestation of English-ness ... perhaps this is why there is not really a "society" – it already is ours.' For this member, the very fact of being Australian was in itself a subconscious expression of Englishness, and therefore required no separate articulation. Some interviewees went further, openly conceding a preference for their Scottish heritage over others. One Melbourne Caledonian stated, 'my father's side are all from England so I can identify with them [note 'can', rather than 'do'] but my Scottish side has taken precedence'. Another articulated similar sentiments: '[I] have always identified more closely with [the] Scottish (romantic ideal, father's heritage) but as I get older I realise I am just as, if not more, English than anything else. This creates an obvious conflict!'

Before addressing the matter of why so many respondents claimed disinterest in their non-Scottish ethnic backgrounds, an additional revelation from this particular exercise is worth highlighting. Despite the apparent ease with which the individuals concerned offered up their various immigrant ancestor-derived ethnic connections, only one articulated any sense of ethnic affiliation to their actual country of origin. This exception was a female Caledonian Society of Otago member who, while citing Dutch heritage, stated a preference to regard herself simply as a New Zealander. Those 'ethnic options' (Waters 1990) being exercised by the rest of the interviewees were therefore never inclusive of their actual places of citizenship. Sociologist Mary C. Waters (1990) observed a similar phenomenon when surveying Americans with mixed ethnic backgrounds during the 1980s, noting that they were apt to define their American-ness in nationalistic or patriotic terms, while ascribing their ethnic identities, instead, to the places of origin of their immigrant forebears. This suggests that even now, at a time when so many citizens of post-British colonial countries can trace their ancestral links within them back for numerous generations, a corresponding sense of *ethnic* belonging or rooted-ness to these places has perhaps not yet fully materialised. The Scottish associations under investigation here, therefore, may not so much represent a supplementary ethnic identity for individuals who are, by right of birth, Canadians, Australians and New Zealanders, but rather fill a void where these identities of citizenship have yet to take on a deeper, ethnic meaning of their own.

Returning to the apparent widespread preference among the participants for their Scottish heritage, however, a deeper insight emerged from another part of the survey. The members were also asked why, in their opinion, Scottish identity appeared to have successfully endured in places so far removed from Scotland, a question oriented towards consideration of the particular Scottish associations to which the respondents variously belonged. The most commonly recurring answer was that those activities and events typically employed to express Scottish identity in the diaspora were inherently accessible, attractive and enjoyable. One Caledonian Society of Otago member highlighted the strong entertainment aspect of Scottish ethnic activities overseas, describing them simply as 'fun' and noting that 'when people attend a Scottish gathering or concert they know how well they will be entertained no matter how young or old they are'. A fellow Otago Caledonian, in considering such elements of Scottish identity expression as bagpiping, Highland dancing and marching, suggested that 'many people around the world have an affinity to these activities' by virtue of their broad appeal. Another member concurred, noting 'just the fact that ... the Highland Games events, i.e. Tossing caber/sheaf, etc. is able to be done by anybody and it is a great family environment'.

In a similar vein, two Royal Caledonian Society of Melbourne members alluded to the universal appeal of kilt-wearing and bagpipe music. As one elaborated:

There is a certain attraction to the wearing of Scottish attire ... attending Scottish games and taking part in these, as well as Highland dancing and Scottish country dancing is an enjoyable pastime and people like to be part of a group which offers these to them.

A member of the St Andrew's Society of Toronto went as far as to suggest that relative to some other ethnic groups' outward expressions of identity, their Scottish equivalents generally had more cultural material to draw upon. 'The English don't have a country music tradition ... no one else has tartan. Few others have bagpipes.' Thus, for many respondents, it was the very nature of those symbols and activities commonly associated with Scottish identity in the diaspora, broadly perceived as accessible, entertaining, appealing and fun, which ensured its longevity in these distant places. This may also help explain the apparent preference among those survey respondents with other ethnicities in their backgrounds to most readily identify with the Scottish.

Yet, attached to and underscoring these enduring expressions of Scottish identity is a romanticised and somewhat skewed notion of the homeland they are deemed to represent. Again, in relation to the question of why Scottish identity in the diaspora had proven so durable, a belief that Scots were an historically subjugated people, and therefore more prone to stick together and identify with one another once settled elsewhere, strongly permeated the survey responses. One Caledonian Society of Otago member suggested that, 'having known oppression', Scots overseas were especially inclined to 'celebrate together their past/present/future in an inclusive way'. A similar view prevailed within the Royal Caledonian Society of Melbourne, with one member suggesting that as a people who 'fought for many years to defend their culture', Scots had developed a particular determination to retain their ethnic distinctiveness. Another Melbourne Caledonian cited 'an oppressed history' as a reason for the persistence of Scottish identity in the diaspora, while another referred more specifically to oppression at the hands of the English. Two St Andrew's Society of Toronto members also stated a special impetus among Scottish colonial settlers to protect and uphold their ethnic identity as a consequence of English subjugation.

In addition to the idea of Scots as historical underdogs was that of Scottish society as inherently primitive, a characteristic which numerous respondents also believed to be causal to the longevity of Scottish identity overseas. As one Caledonian Society of Otago member suggested:

I think Scottish heritage thrives as they [Scots] are thought of as previously being a type of barbarian. No respect for law and order or other cultures. I think maybe it is ingrained in us to carry that attitude on. Hence the Highland games, etc.

Among the many responses of this nature was one from a member of the Royal Caledonian Society of Melbourne, albeit his comments regarding Scottish primitiveness were clearly tethered to the present:

Outside large towns and cities in Scotland the communities are small and generally very close due to weather, location, and until recently communications with others was limited. Perhaps this is reflected in that when in the Scottish diaspora Scots stuck together in communities.

This particular respondent was among the Melbourne association's small Scottish-born contingent, making his views appear particularly incongruous. Sadly, however, the individual concerned did not disclose when or at what age he emigrated to Australia, or indeed from where in Scotland he originated. It is not known, therefore, how these factors may have shaped his outlook. Suffice to say that an idea of Scotland as a somewhat archaic culture informed the perceptions of a significant number of survey respondents, right across the immigrant/descendant spectrum.

Cutting across and fleshing out these images of oppression and primitiveness, however, was an equally pervasive tendency to frame Scotland and Scottishness in entirely Highland-historical terms. One Otago Caledonian, for example, concisely described the persistence of Scottish identity in the diaspora as 'a positive outcome from the clan structure', while a fellow member alluded to 'clan allegiances' as a catalyst for the same. Another Otago Caledonian offered a more elaborate explanation:

> The forming of clans or 'septs' where in feuding days a weaker group could survive by joining a clan helped the strong sense of togetherness of the Scottish people ... people years ago would have died for their tartan but as people hopefully become more 'civilised' the clans and septs have over time formed a very strong unity that Irish/English & Welsh have never been able to match!

Three Melbourne Caledonians made similar references to clan structure as a direct influence on the persistence of Scottish identity in Australia, as did two St Andrew's Society of Toronto members in regard to the endurance of Scottish identity in Canada. With so much of what these associations have relied upon to represent Scottishness from their respective foundations having been drawn from the unique culture of the Highlands, it is perhaps only natural that a conflation between the two has persisted. After all, very little has changed in how these associations have chosen to express themselves since the nineteenth century. However, there are hints of a growing awareness among these bodies that their particular representations of Scottishness are out of step with contemporary homeland realities. As the St Andrew's Society of Toronto's President recently articulated to MSPs Kenny MacAskill and Henry McLeish (2007: 65):

The thing we [the Society] do least well is interpreting present-day Scotland to the membership. We are aware of what is happening in and around Scotland, but the depth of our knowledge is not much more than watching TV news or *Braveheart* ... Scotland's high-tech industries are virtually a closed book to most Canadians.

A survey participant from the Royal Caledonian Society of Melbourne reiterated this view, suggesting that 'in recent years we [Scottish associations] have not done enough to off-set the bag-pipes, haggis and och-aye the noo'. Whether this is an issue these bodies will ultimately address in some measure remains to be seen. What is clear is that however outmoded their ideas of Scotland and Scottishness may be, these associations nevertheless continue to provide a successful outlet for the expression of that identity for thousands of diaspora Scots which is evidently meaningful and authentic for them.

Prolific, long-standing and with their popularity undiminished, Scottish associations remain a highly significant beacon of ethnic consciousness within the wider Scottish diaspora community. These bodies have survived profound change within the societies that they operate, as well as a major collective internal demographic shift, from immigrant- to descendant-dominated memberships. Neverthe-less, their modes of expressing Scottish identity, and consequently their outlooks upon the homeland, remain emphatically rooted in the Highland-romantic imaginations of their colonial-era founders. Yet it is precisely the nature of those particular forms of Scottish identity expression, being both widely accessible and enduringly entertaining, which helps ensure the perpetuation of Scottish ethnic consciousness beyond Scotland itself. As modern-day Scotland seeks ways to include its vast, self-identifying overseas community in its own future, there-fore, the influential presence of these associations must surely be taken into account.

5

Doing Business with the Scottish Diaspora

Mike Danson and Jim Mather

INTRODUCTION

When Winnie Ewing MSP 'reconvened' the Scottish Parliament in May 1999, after a gap of 292 years, she arguably was also reconvening the Scottish diaspora, albeit that latter exercise remains work in progress as more effort from more people of goodwill and sound motives is still needed.

This chapter explores the business rationale for embracing the concept and the opportunities which are presented by the existence of a truly purposeful Scottish diaspora, and offers some pointers as to how they might be pursued. Specifically, how the diaspora might come to play a deeper role in the modernisation and innovative development of the Scottish economy is considered. As well as being able to call upon experiences with overseas trading by indigenous enterprises based here (Danson et al. 2005), emigrants to Scotland from the Commonwealth, and more recently from the new member states of the EU (Brown and Danson 2008), have demonstrated the benefits of internationalisation of businesses through their linkages back home. With millions around the world claiming ancestral connections with Scotland (Ancien et al. 2009; Boyle and Motherwell 2005; Devine 2011), there is the potential to grow the business base and so the economy through greater involvement in established supply chains, better business and management practices, and improved access to finance capital. Comparative analyses of the structures and performances of other small independent nations in northern Europe suggest that building enterprises and linkages can successfully overcome many disadvantages of peripherality and apparent lack of internal economies of scale (ESPON 2010; Danson and de Souza 2012).

We begin with a review of Scotland's relative economic position before identifying the key drivers which might lead to improvement. The potential role of the diaspora in contributing to a strategy for change is introduced as a lead-in to the consideration of who they are and how they might fit into national policies. This is followed by an exploration of existing and possible ways to engage with the diaspora to promote economic development, covering both current initiatives and evolving forms of networking and connection. The prospects of this dispersed Scottish community contributing to a new Scottish Enlightenment are then discussed as recognition that their engagement should have wider implications than for narrow business interests alone. The conclusion speculates on the likely future development of a Scottish economy which has better incorporation of its substantial diaspora.

Present Realities and the Potential of the Diaspora

Driven by the long and sustained relative decline of the UK economy (Elliott and Atkinson 2012) and deindustrialisation since the 1970s, Scotland's economic performance has been mediocre compared with our nearest comparators and, without a transformational change, this is projected to continue into the future (Elliott and Atkinson 2012; MacKay 2011). Since the Scottish Parliament was re-established in 1999, successive Scottish Governments have introduced measures to address this, albeit constrained within the confines of devolution (Maxwell 2012) and after-effects of the 2007 Financial Crisis. In summary, measures of the lagging performances include (Danson 2012):

- sustained lower levels of economic growth in the post-war years
- flat-lining population numbers
- low levels of entrepreneurship
- a widening gap between rich and poor
- high levels of emigration of qualified, talented young people

Despite these indicators of a long-term underperformance relative to our nearest neighbours, Scotland does have strengths and opportunities as well as the weaknesses and threats exposed by these statistics. In recent times, there has been much attention paid to the importance of agglomeration economies in explaining why some localities appear to attract economic activities disproportionately, and then continue to benefit from these flows and lower costs. Captured in such theoretical constructs as 'clusters' (Porter 2000), proximity (Moulaert and Sekia 2003) and agglomeration economies of scale and scope (Parr et al. 2002) with derivative strategies and policies of smart specialisation (CEC 2011; Lundvall and Lorenz 2012), they have led to arguments in favour of the Single Market and unfettered competition policy on the one hand (Cecchini 1988) and progressive concentration of industry, finance and commerce in the core of Europe (Farole et al. 2011). Other things being equal, these centripetal forces have worked against the interests of the peripheral regions of Europe; yet, it has been suggested (ESPON 2010) that there are:

> economically successful regions with below average accessibility. Often ... sparsely populated and remote. They can be found in the Nordic Countries, north-east of Spain, Scotland, Ireland and in and around northern Italy. Apparently, accessibility is not a decisive factor for the economic development of these regions. Regions in the Nordic Countries, for example, have overcome their peripheral location by capitalising on current strengths in relation to ICT, research, educational and environmental opportunities and less on improving their accessibility.

So, although not co-located with the other key players in an industrial cluster (as in the economic heartlands of the EU and US), networking and judicial use of indigenous human factors and resources have allowed the businesses of these smaller nations to compete successfully in global markets. Overcoming apparent obstacles to participating in supply chains and acting globally has been possible, therefore, and by energising and activating its latent networks in the diaspora, there should be crucial advantages for Scottish enterprises.

The other approach to addressing the need for diversification of the economy following deindustrialisation has been through the attraction of mobile capital – in other words, through foreign direct investment. Although inward investment by multi-national enterprises has been pursued for several decades and Scotland has a good track record in terms of establishing their branch plants here (Ernst & Young 2012), globalisation and the international division of labour have increased the competition for such footloose investment. As a result, moves to embed these plants in the regional economy and to fill the gaps in the supply chain locally have come to represent a maturing of this particular strategy. Recent economic and financial crises have exacerbated the negative forces and both undermined local economies dependent on branch plants and highlighted the vulnerability of small nations (Skilling 2012; Price with Levinger 2011). However, these peripheral locations have demonstrated such a degree of resilience of late that it suggests that their cohesion and flexibility has much to offer as a model for resistance and success (Martin 2010).

The conclusions of this brief review of the development drivers for small open economies are that a capacity to participate in international markets is crucial. This is dependent on participation in global sectors and supply chains from a position of strength based on optimising the application of high levels of human capital and skills in knowledge-based industries. Theoretical perspectives and practical experiences of what works in this competition stress endogenous growth and the pursuit of smart specialisation (CEC 2011). The Nordic countries are recorded as the most innovative in the European Union, which enables them to overcome many disadvantages from the lack of agglomeration economies and proximity (CEC 2012; EPSON 2010).

STRATEGY AND THE DIASPORA

Scotland, with its history of underperformance, legacy of deindustrialisation, and low rates of enterprise (Danson and Lloyd 2012), nevertheless has designed an economic strategy that is well informed, reflects maturely on good practice elsewhere and often promotes model approaches (Danson and Lloyd 2012). Scotland emphasises those terms which are stressed in the 'new industrial policy' – sustainability, creativity, resilience and economic potential – seeking 'to drive sustainable economic growth and develop a more resilient and adaptable economy', through actions on six strategic priorities: 'Supportive Business Environment; Transition to a Low Carbon Economy; Learning, Skills and Well-being; Infrastructure Development and Place; Effective Government; and Equity' (Scottish Government 2011a). Key sectors, with their inherent needs for international flows of talent and knowledge and for competitiveness based on world-leading staff and connectivities, are prioritised in this strategy, as well as more generic support for new and small enterprises.

Such approaches fit well with the objectives of addressing perceived failures to match competitors' levels of enterprise and entrepreneurship (Brown and Mason 2012) and aspiration, risk aversion and information deficiencies (MacRae and Wight 2011), believed to explain Scotland's weak economic performance. Resolving to restructure and revitalise the Scottish economy and build networks and global companies to pursue those aims, specific measures were introduced from the early 2000s to address this strategic agenda, with the Scottish diaspora seen as a critical component.

Recognition of the role and potential of a nation's diaspora has evolved over the decades to a level of maturity that allows different characteristics to be identified and so typologies to be constructed (Kuznetsov 2011). Within this wider context, the Scottish international network 'Globalscot' was established to engage with and mobilise our diaspora. As a typical 'ideal case' where there is vibrant brain circulation, this was designed to promote synergies and virtuous cycles between the growing confidence of the country and the involvement and return of the diaspora (MacRae and Wight 2011). The remit of this network of 'influential individuals who have an affinity with Scotland and who can contribute and share in Scotland's economic success' (Scottish Executive 2001) was:

- to build an international network that can contribute to Scotland's economic success;
- to mobilise Members to undertake roles that can benefit Scottish Enterprise [the RDA for Scotland] and the economy;
- to maximise opportunities produced by network relationships, knowledge and expertise. (MacRae and Wight 2011: 5)

As a measure of its success, Globalscot has been described by the World Bank as 'a model program for leveraging ... highly skilled professionals' (Kuznetsov 2011: 236). While there are other networks and means for the Scottish diaspora to continue to trade, support and engage with the Scottish economy, this initiative exemplifies the main and more successful means of nurturing and taking forward productive relationships between businesses, customers and suppliers.

WHO ARE THE DIASPORA AND WHERE DO THEY FIT INTO SCOTLAND'S BUSINESS FUTURE?

Engaging the diaspora is unfinished business, because Scotland has yet to develop a collective sense of purpose and hence the means to make a really compelling case for its diaspora to be involved in Scotland and Scottish affairs in a purposeful way. In saying that, there is no doubt that there have been some very worthwhile attempts to activate the diaspora: especially on the part of those who have sought to reconcile the country's practical aspirations to be part of modernity and the evocative perceptions of the largely ancestral and affinity diaspora that is more linked to Scotland's past (see Ancien et al. 2009, *inter alia*, for review of this literature).

Consequently, given that those two sub-sets of the diaspora are so material, numbering many millions of people (Eirich and McLaren 2008), this is a blend, a reconciliation that must be achieved, especially as many of the diaspora come into these categories:

- *Ancestral Scots* – those with a parent, grandparent or an earlier ancestor who came from Scotland;
- *Affinity Scots* – citizens of other countries, who through work or education have lived in Scotland, regular or one-time visitors, people who plan to visit or people who simply love Scotland, its landscape, culture, evocativeness, amenity or people.

The situation is complicated because there are not just *Ancestral* and *Affinity* Scots. As identified by Kingsley Aikins, of the consultancy firm Diaspora Matters, and formerly chief executive and president of The Worldwide Ireland Funds, there are additional categories, all of which apply to Scotland:

- *Lived diaspora* – individuals born in the home country who now live permanently or temporally in a host country.
- Next generation diaspora – younger members of the diaspora, typically under the age of thirty-five, who are fundamental to engage in order to ensure the sustainability of current diaspora strategies.
- Returning diaspora – diaspora members who have lived in a host country and who have come back to the home country. (Aikins 2011)

These five categories and their different histories, perceptions and needs give us a better basis for engagement and understanding and the potential of better, richer conversations. Arguably, in the Scottish context they all have something to offer and for most of them the realities and perceptions of Scotland are very important, because its history, culture, image and national wellbeing combine to be the tap root of who they are.

Indeed, that connection, that joint and several shared ownership of what Scotland is and can be, is the key starting point of the dialogue that Scotland must have between its diaspora and the current people of Scotland: especially in the formulation of a worthy, altruistic and unifying sense of national purpose.

Therefore, as argued above, there is a challenging national agenda for regeneration and revitalisation. In particular, the high levels of emigration on the part of qualified talented young people is especially poignant and personal to many people in Scotland in that, while it increases the numbers within the Scottish diaspora, it sees many move away beyond easy reach. There are other obvious losses to Scotland from this emigration of human capital (Ancien et al. 2009), including the possible reduction of the size of the 'creative class' (Houston et al. 2008; Boyle and Motherwell 2005), as has been studied over several decades (MacKay 1969).

To put this in clear focus, *Scotland's Diaspora and Overseas-Born Population* records that this population 'equates to about 20 per cent of Scotland's current population (over 1 million people). Of these, over 835,000 live in the rest of the UK' (Carr and Kavanagh 2009: 2). This goes some way to explaining why the population has stagnated over the past century – along with the very disproportionate loss of life suffered by Scotland in the First World War with the population growing at a fraction of the rate achieved in Norway and other small countries:

Table 5:1 Comparative population change Scotland and Norway, 1913–2013

	1913	2013	Growth 1913–2013	Source
Scotland	4,728,932	5,250,000	9.93%	http://www.gro-scotland.gov.uk/files1/stats/1855–2006-population.pdf
Norway	2,447,000	5,038,000	51.43%	http://en.wikipedia.org/wiki/Demographics_of_Norway

These realities and the potential for the diaspora to be more fulfilled in its connection with Scotland are all coming into focus at a time when there is 'an elephant in the room', and that is the 2014 Referendum on Scotland's constitutional future: an issue that is as likely to divide the diaspora as it has divided opinion in Scotland (see Chapter 6 in this volume). For it is clear that some successful members of the diaspora, whose forebears fought the British Establishment in their own country's quest for Independence or were transported by that establishment, are keen to see Scotland reject independence (Devine 2011).

Equally, there are divisions in the ranks of the Scots, who have migrated to other parts of the UK to advance up the career escalator in London and the South-east (Fielding 1992), with many more of them having a bias towards the Union than would have been the case had they had the better opportunities to invest lives, capital and life-chances in Scotland. So it could be argued that, if the most is to be made of the economic potential offered by the diaspora, there is a need to find a set of common goals that would unite those in favour of Independence with those in favour of the Union. That would need a unifying definition of national purpose that was aligned with helping Scotland, its people and its diaspora being all that they can be.

ENGAGING THE DIASPORA

Improved internationalisation of indigenous Scottish companies is one major objective of involving the diaspora more effectively. Research on the efforts of both enterprises and development agencies to promote such developments have emphasised the importance of social capital, effective relationships and networking (Lundvall and Lorenz 2012; Kuznetsov 2011). Recent studies confirm this approach with the 'connection with the customer, tacit knowledge and vision and product-service complexity ... the strongest influences on the decision to internationalize, which is moderated by the strength of the business case and resource-based risk tolerance' (Perks and Hughes 2008: 310). Similarly, evaluations of Globalscot have demonstrated the importance of international gatherings and networking events to support outward trade and development activity (MacRae and Wight 2011; Ancien et al. 2009), along with traditional trade missions and facilitated contacts (Danson et al. 2005). This confluence of strategic approaches suggests that the endorsement by the World Bank of Globalscot and associated initiatives is well-founded (Kuznetsov 2011). As well as linking up those in North America and elsewhere – though, as with the equivalents for China, India and Taiwan, the US tends to dominate such networks – who have an affinity with Scotland, these processes are also relevant for new Scottish communities including those from the 'Commonwealth', China and Poland.

There have been several distinct stages in the development of the Globalscot network: first, engaging members and managing expectations, leading to the need to stimulate demand from businesses in Scotland for their services and maintaining a supply of members from the diaspora; second, establishing an infrastructure and servicing relationships between targeted participants; and third, mobilisation and matching through facilitated engagement and brokered connections. Reaching maturity is a key phase of such a networking activity with the need for 'disintermediation' (with the agency catalysts withdrawing so that staff working directly with companies could be the facilitators of bilateral connections). The capabilities of both these government agencies and private sector stakeholders are recognised as key in the success of engaging the diaspora and of sustaining such reciprocal relationships (Kuznetsov 2011; Ancien et al. 2009); ownership of the connections is also an essential element in raising the awareness and access of the network and of the benefits of networking in this context (MacRae and Wight 2011: 14).

The experiences recorded in the evaluations of Globalscot, which have captured a number of analogous initiatives and other means of connecting the diaspora with businesses in Scotland, have been consistent with the expectations of those in academia and in practice. So a range of 'soft' outcomes (e.g. networking events and meetings) have been generated leading to some 'hard' impacts (e.g. joint projects and contracts). Inevitably, the early years have suffered from a significant 'lag' period between initially engaging with the network and achieving a quantified economic outcome (Frontline 2007). Understanding the role of the network, how it can be accessed and who are appropriate players have limited the amount of activity undertaken (MacRae and Wight 2011; Frontline 2007); however, Frontline (2007) estimated that the net GVA figure attributable to the Globalscot network was almost £29 million annually within five years of its launch, a modest impact but value for money and indicative of further promise.

As anticipated, the sorts of activities that Globalscot delivers are welcomed by entrepreneurs and have a significant role to play in the development of the Scottish economy, and so should be deepened and widened through continuing Scottish Enterprise (SE) engagement (Kuznetsov 2011). Nowadays, electronic forms of communication and dissemination of good practice are integral to the building of mutually beneficial relationships and networks (Samanta 2012), and consistent with the idea that trust and co-operation are central to endogenous growth and SME and clusters developments. Social and business media networking can reduce the distance virtually, and so diminish this obstruction to successful nurturing and maturing of relationships through proximity and direct contact (Moulaert and Sekia 2003; Bergum 2012).

In selecting the initial 800+ members for the Globalscot and similar networks, SE were targeting senior personnel with strong affinity connections to Scotland and crucially relevant sector skills. Spanning over forty countries and focused on the key sectors, the plan for the network was therefore implemented to be congruent with the overall economic strategy for Scotland. As these industries – Food & Drink (including agriculture and fisheries), Creative Industries (including digital), Sustainable Tourism, Energy (including renewables), Financial & Business Services, Life Sciences and Universities – are, by definition, global in their connectivity, customer base and supply linkages, the diaspora has had a natural and obvious role to play. The channels and means of the development of 'effective, mutually beneficial relationships' between Scotland and the diaspora as funders, consumers, suppliers and conduits of knowledge are often subject to market failures and so the need for SE institutional involvement has been assured.

While there are disagreements over the immediate and quantifiable impacts of specific initiatives to engage with the diaspora (e.g. contrast the evaluations on the 2009 Homecoming and associated Gathering events by EKOS 2010 and Riddington 2010), such events and activities are consistent with the good practices proposed by theory, experience and practice. Similarly, successes with attracting inward investment and in growing indigenous participation in such new industries as renewable energies, life sciences and digital enterprises offer an indication of the potential to build on these initial efforts (Ernst & Young 2012: 17).

Enlightenment Potential

In parallel with the practices of the Nordic countries, based on the concept of the triple or quadruple helix (Arnkil et al. 2010: 15), the purposeful goal of all Scots 'being-all-they-can-be' has to bubble up from all 'airts and pairts' of Scotland and from the diaspora as part of a dialogue. Through this a new 'North Star' could be defined that could transcend differences and add much better economic, social and cultural outcomes to the resilience that Scotland has shown over the last three hundred years, or indeed the last twelve hundred years as arguably the oldest nation in Europe (Ascherson 2002; Devine 2011).

To go beyond the early impacts of Globalscot, theory and the strategies of these comparable small resilient nations suggest:

- Building and maintaining the common purpose of strengthening Scotland and its relevance to future generations (following the conclusions of Ancien et al. 2009, and consistent with Arnkil et al. 2010).
- Maintaining and developing Scotland's ability to make a meaningful and constructive contribution to world affairs and wellbeing (Baird et al. 2007; ESPON 2010).
- Creating opportunities to enable the people of Scotland and its diaspora to interact and engage in the maintenance and development of Scottish culture and identity (Ancien et al. 2009; Arnkil et al. 2010).
- Creating an environment that gives each and every one of the people of Scotland and its diaspora the highest chance of fulfilment and status as worthwhile citizens of the world (Scottish Government 2011a; CEC 2010).

This set of objectives increases immeasurably the potential that better engagement with the diaspora offers and simultaneously recognises and neutralises any differences on the issue of the constitution. In particular, it lifts this 'potential' way beyond any commercial benefits that may have been the focus in the past, where some may have seen 'Diaspora Engagement' as primarily a means to achieve objectives that have been more personal than shared, more commercial than altruistic, or more about building empires than building national resilience (Martin 2010). Just as power may appear superficially as a 'big issue', the divisive and damaging issue of self-interest will always be present in the pro-bono world of the diaspora until it is explored and higher goals set.

There may be lessons here from Hock, who constantly fought against the 'four beasts that inevitably devour their keeper:

- Ego
- Envy
- Avarice
- Ambition'. (Hock 2005: 161)

Nevertheless, this next phase needs focus and clear goals, seeking to retain those who perhaps see self-interest as their primary driver: for motivated people will be critical and, as the diaspora strengthens, so will its ability to police and sanction anyone who misuses the benefit of this trusting and well-intentioned network. In addition, the diaspora can be a force for commercial good, in that it is a good place to build a sound reputation and effective networks, with whom it is safe and mutually rewarding to do business.

Consequently, it can be argued that there is a need to develop both a purposeful set of goals that elevate activity, contributions and fulfilment, while at the same time establishing principles, to which people are expected to adhere: with suitable checks and balances. Again, such purpose and principles would benefit from being the product of bottom-up discussion between Scotland and the diaspora, with the principles subject to ongoing amendment by the full active community in the light of experience and the fulfilment of the original purpose.

Undoubtedly things are changing in Scotland, beyond the reconvening of the Parliament and the constitutional debate. This may be considered a 'second Enlightenment' or as Broadie recently said, 'The completion of the first Enlightenment' (personal communication). There is a growing recognition that this is a new phase where fresh air is being blown through some still very dusty corners of Scottish life, and new ideas being unleashed to challenge old orthodoxies and tendencies to defend the way things have 'aye been'. In that endeavour, new generations of management and staff can usefully channel the insights and impatience of the diaspora and their widely held belief that a better, more effective Scotland could and should be built.

Indeed, Martlew, as a senior civil servant, planted the idea in 2008 that a Scotland that took a more effective approach to managing its affairs, studied the data, made incremental changes at all levels and took advantage of being small enough to 'hear all the voices' could become a 'Teaching Hospital' and could then help many other parts of the world (personal communication).

That same Scotland and its diaspora could also take fully justified pride in the work it has done with successive Scottish and UK Governments during this phase of managing the potential for further constitutional change in an orderly democratic way with 'no bombs, no bullets, no assassinations and no Civil War'. And the diaspora again is well positioned to help and augment both the progress of that process at home and the broadcasting of it abroad.

For, as Deming proposed, in considering the issue of improving any system, 'Knowledge necessary for improvement comes from outside' (2000: 2). His thinking was that external help and insights are less burdened with agendas, ambitions and suspicions and more likely to be aligned with the common good and able to engender trust and a true sense of a shared endeavour. And such help could increase its chances of success by following the approach that Hock took when he turned round the problematic Bank of America Credit Card system into the hugely successful manifestation that is VISA (2005: 91). He assembled the relevant people to consider four key questions that triggered alignment, purpose and principles. In a Scottish context, those questions could be phrased as:

- Where and what has Scotland been in the past?
- Where and what is Scotland now?
- What might Scotland become if current polices, behaviours, trends and trajectories are kept?
- What ought Scotland to be – where 'ought' is used in the sense of achieving a superior, preferred, ethically better condition and outcomes for all concerned.

Progressing down such a path – not only engaging the Scottish diaspora in such a conversation but also opening up the opportunities to have more people connect, identify worthy projects and challenge each other to be involved, be mentors and measure outcomes – would offer the opportunity for a significant transformation. The impact on Scotland has the potential to be significant: tapping into the goodwill and resources of the diaspora not with a begging bowl but with an understanding that there has to be something rewarding and meaningful for each and every active member of Scotland's diaspora.

Therefore, in discussing why Scotland should do this, the debate needs to be extended to how such a period of renewed engagement would benefit that diaspora and the wider world. The meaningful rewards for the diaspora start quite simply with the act of being asked to share the task of improving Scotland's wellbeing and potential for good. What is on offer is participation in a process that will strengthen Scotland and also those who participate in that process – with the long-term prize of potentially being a role model to the world – and the short-term equivalent being the knowledge that a better legacy has been promised. Participation in these wider networks, perhaps with a sense of both fulfilment and altruism, echoes Frankl's words:

Ultimately, man should not ask what the meaning of his life is, but rather he must recognize that it is he who is asked. In a word, each man is questioned by life; and he can only answer to life by answering for his own life; to life he can only respond by being responsible. (Frankl 2006: 131)

Our argument is that all those who are 'responsible' towards Scotland will get the rewards of respect and fulfilment that come from making a meaningful contribution, making new purposeful connections and building the resilience of colleagues, Scotland, its people and oneself. One aspect of that contribution will be the positive impact that this has globally, not merely in proving the effectiveness of engaging the diaspora, but in doing so with such purpose, blending many different strands of expertise and experience, that a 'role model' nation is created, with much to teach and a willingness to learn from others. This process should raise Scotland's self-esteem and self-confidence – both important factors in economic development – and, through this but also directly, generate beneficial impacts on how Scottish enterprises work. Further, this also should consolidate recent learning from nature by Johnson and Broms (2000), who would applaud any country getting its house in order as they believe that successful entities do best when they conform to the three basic principles of living systems that could be the foundations of a new era of diaspora engagement in Scotland.

Adopting these would both reward Scotland and inform the world:

- Principle 1: Creative energy continually and spontaneously materialises in self-organising forms that strive to maintain their unique self-identity.
- Principle 2: Interdependent natural systems interact with each other through a web of relationships that connect everything to the Universe.
- Principle 3: Diversity results from the continual interaction of unique identities always relating to one another.

Such an approach would be consistent with vibrancy and dynamism in Scotland through better networking and connectivity, essentials for economic and business development (Lundvall and Lorenz 2012; Moulaert and Sekia 2003; Danson et al. 2005). This promotion of openness and evolution would ensure staying interconnected and interdependent at home and abroad and befriending diversity and the insights of those who want to play a part in the positive development of Scotland and its cultures. Nordic countries and institutions such as the Nordic Council have laid the trail here, of course. For Scotland, the prize is the chance to maintain and develop our contribution to diversity for another three hundred years and beyond, to do more that is worthy of both global attention and emulation, and make this country a place which most people on the planet want to visit or at least know more about. In the process, Scotland would be better able to be a force for good that could build on a Second Enlightenment and a growing reputation as a centre for arbitration and mediation services, to be a legitimate and effective conciliatory force: building on past and recent histories and using that to generate a society which is even more ethical and cohesive at home.

Indeed, with some reflections in the quadruple helix, and especially appropriate for a Scotland with an increasingly active diaspora and a unifying worthy agenda for building the nation and being a good global citizen, Ury has argued: 'Every conflict is actually three-sided ... [with] the third side [being] the surrounding community, which serves as a container for any escalation conflict' (Ury 2000: 7). In other words, he suggests that in any conflict the holders of the opposing views are much more likely to behave well and reasonably if they feel that 'the surrounding community' is aware of the stances they are taking and willing to help broker an agreement that reconciles the parties and leaves the door open for future productive engagement.

So, Scotland could build its expertise in this arena and establish its ability to reconcile opposing views at home and between diaspora and domestic visions of what Scotland ought to be. Two Affinity Scots, Cloke and Goldsmith, offer a plan to build collaboration through a 'Hierarchy of Unity', where Scotland and its diaspora could travel to achieve transformational results and be better able to help other people in other jurisdictions. They suggest six progressive steps to address hostile disengagement (Cloke 2008):

1. Unity of Opposition – the starting point where the parties recognise and articulate their differences and different viewpoints on any matter.
2. Unity of Purpose – where a common goal is debated and agreed.
3. Unity of Process and commitment to fairness – where the principles, terms and conditions are established and accepted by all parties as being fair and in line with the 'purpose'.
4. Unity of Process and commitment to fairness – more a phase than a process, where all parties see evidence that the purpose and

principles are being honoured, people are aligned, trust is building along with a new sense of camaraderie and friendship.
5. Unity of Experience – bonded in hard-fought struggles – again a phase where, especially in challenging times, people realise that they are best sticking together to avoid dissipating energy and to increase the chance of good resilient outcomes.
6. Unity of Care and Empathy – when there is a realisation that they have a community of goodwill made up of like-minded people committed to lifting all the boats, trusting that they too will be lifted by the efforts of others – and knowing that the community has lost or converted those who could have previously abused the system, betrayed trust and succumbed to moral hazards.

To that end, Aikins and White (2011) have produced a 'Global Diaspora – Strategies Toolkit' that offers Scotland and the 196 other nations of the world a very effective guide to activating and engaging their diaspora members in purposeful and fulfilling ways, so presenting a path to help activate the diaspora and promote the potential of Scotland.

Conclusions

Scotland's significant diaspora, which has been estimated between 28 and 40 million globally (Eirich and McLaren 2008), could have an important role to play in the economic and social revitalisation of the country. As well as direct co-operation and linkages with businesses and customers, there are more subtle opportunities including improvements to management practices, widening horizons and promoting learning across the community. Lessons from other small independent nations offer the potential for all Scots to be active participants in the quadruple helix of business–state–academia–people. While Scotland has high levels of human and social capital, raising their application and aspirations would benefit from strategic and tactical internationalisation of networks and partnerships. Agencies and institutions in Scotland have already demonstrated an aptitude for such collaboration and consensus-working in the sphere of public and private organisations within European Union frameworks (Cameron and Danson 2000). Now, a period of overcoming the hollowing out of Scottish control over the ownership and management of the economy since the 1970s (Scott and Hughes 1980; Baird et al. 2007) through the diaspora promises the potential of renewal and reinvigoration. Independence need not be 'separation', therefore, but rather a resilient and pro-active integration into the global economic and social system.

In considering future engagement, there are questions over whether the attitude of the homeland to the diaspora will be an obstacle. To date, most relations have been cordial and positive and it has been argued above that this must continue to evolve if the diaspora is to be an effective source for sustainable and positive development. GlobalScot has shown some success in delivering such progressive moves but possible suspicion of the diaspora within Scotland could temper ongoing improvement.

Encouraging indigenous Scottish enterprises to do business and realise the potential of engagement with the diaspora will require a reappraisal of core–periphery relations, where the diaspora may be viewed as merely exploitative multi-national players wielding power over local companies (Danson and Whittam 2001). While there may be tensions between developing linkages and partnerships with the diaspora in North America and Australasia, on the one hand, and playing a full role in the single European market on the other, these have not presented significant issues for comparable EU countries seeking to attract inward investment (World Economic Forum 2012), encourage high levels of innovation (CEC 2012) or exploit opportunities within the common market (ESPON 2010).

Finally, there is the opportunity for nation-building, as Scotland expects and gains more economic autonomy, whatever happens in Autumn 2014, and starts the process of building that national balance sheet and converging on the wellbeing achieved elsewhere, as spelled out in *The Truth about Markets* (Kay 2000).

That process coincides with a refinement of Europe's approach to capability-building (CEC 2010). This is to be progressed through programmes like Horizon 2020, which will invest around €80 billion between 2014 and 2020, support research and innovation, and deliver more viable goods and services that improve economic resilience but also address societal and environmental challenges, blend the work of universities, multi-nationals and SMEs, and make all of Europe more connected and more international in outlook.

Taken together, this critical period and such initiatives create a great opportunity for both altruistic and commercial involvement in Scotland by the diaspora and the synthesis of ideas and experiences that can make Scotland and all Scots 'be-all-we-can-be'.

6

Scottish Politics and the Diaspora

Murray Stewart Leith

INTRODUCTION

Bulmer and Solomos point out how the study of diasporas within modern society 'has proceeded apace over the past two decades' (2009: 1301) and that during this time they have shifted from being somewhat the sole preserve of historians, an academic area within which they have long been studied, to being a core area of study within the wider social sciences and humanities as well. In this, they echo the same point as Brubaker, who pointed out that Safran's (1991) claim that scholars of ethnicity and immigration paid no attention to diasporas was 'out of date' by 2005 and that this was all part of a much greater wider interest. The term diaspora 'yields a million Google hits; a sampling suggests that the large majority are not academic' (Brubaker 2005: 1). It is true that a wider range of interest has been shown within the social sciences but, as Lyons and Mandaville (2010) point out, the focus has often been rather precise, with much of the attention in the nexus between diaspora studies and politics being on three specific areas: immigration, minority ethnic lobbying and multi-culturalism/citizenship. It is certainly true that these all have resonance within the Scottish debate, but this chapter takes in a wider arena, with a consideration of the interplay of ideas of national identity and political community.

Clearly, the awareness of the wider implications in both social and political circles of diasporas is growing; this text is itself evidence of the continuing and increasing interest in the contemporary Scottish diaspora. It is also important that such interest should not be purely academic. Governments around the world have progressively become more aware of the importance of diasporas; not only acknowledging them in some formal sense, but seeking to employ them as a resource (Sim and Leith 2013). This is very much the case in Scotland where not only the concept of engaging with the diaspora, but also of having a distinct Scottish government that can engage with it, is a relatively new concept. As Scotland has begun to develop a more international role for itself as a nation, it has begun to engage with elements of the Scottish diaspora. This is an emerging relationship that is perhaps somewhat reversed, for as earlier chapters within this work clearly illustrate, many elements of this wide and varied group have been institutionally organised for far, far longer than the Scottish Parliament itself. This distinct politically based relationship between a distinctly Scottish Parliament/Government and the Scottish diaspora is very much a twenty-first-century phenomenon.

Thus, this chapter specifically deals with the issues of Scottish politics and the Scottish diaspora, areas that have undergone significant change in the last decade and a half, and while there has been a greater increase in general academic analysis and wider activity in recent decades, the examination of the interplay between diasporas and Scottish politics remains a very limited field. Therefore, unlike other chapters of this book, this work includes a greater focus on Scotland, and particularly events within Scotland, rather than just the wider world. The discussion that follows covers an analysis of Scottish politics; the issues of identity and belonging in Scotland and among the diaspora; the relationship that the Scottish Government has sought to develop through the creation of a 'Diaspora Strategy'; and what the implications are for both Scotland and the various diasporas with which it engages. In order to provide context for this analysis, the discussion begins with a consideration of the recent political changes affecting Scotland. While it touches upon the Scottish diaspora in England, the full debate on this topic is provided by Mycock in Chapter 7. Therefore, we start by examining the political system that now provides for a more direct relationship between Scotland and its diaspora. This relationship is new because the political system within which diaspora relations are considered, viewed and created is itself new. The nature of this new relationship is very much still in the initial stages, and its success is so far unclear.

The New Political Scotland

When focusing on Scotland or, more specifically, Scottish politics, it is clear that the most significant event of recent decades has been the granting of legislative devolution (habitually and simply known as 'devolution'). Scotland long had a form of administrative devolution within the UK, through the Scottish Office, under the operation of the Secretary of State for Scotland, an office initially created as a more minor post in 1885 (Torrance 2006). Devolution as we know it came about in 1999 with the establishment of, and first elections to, the unicameral Scottish Parliament. This parliament was created by the Scotland Act 1998 (although further devolutionary powers were granted in the Scotland Act 2012). This parliamentary activity of the (still sovereign) Westminster Parliament should never be underestimated. It is perhaps the most momentous constitutional change to take place in the UK, certainly since the advent of mass voting. As political transformations are measured, it qualifies as the most significant constitutional and institutional change for Scotland since the Act of Union itself. Such statements may seem slightly dramatic, until it is remembered that, whatever else may result from devolution, and whatever further constitutional changes the future may have in store, Scotland now has a firmly distinct national voice. This voice speaks for Scotland, not as a part of the wider UK, or by an individual that is part of the UK Government, but from an elected national legislature. That voice (in the form of elected officials and leaders within that legislature) speaks for Scotland, and Scotland alone. In the Presiding Office of the Scottish Parliament there is a leader that can stand above the day-to-day fray of politics but in the post of First Minister, the head of the Scottish Government (held since 2007 by Alex Salmond, leader of the SNP), there is a political leader of Scotland, elected by, speaking from and for Scotland. (For a concise history of the development of Scottish policies from the 1950s onwards, see Leith and Soule 2012. For a consideration of the structure of the Scottish Parliament and political system, see McGarvey and Cairney 2013.) In short, Scotland is now able to speak directly to the world, and directly to the Scottish diaspora.

The creation of the Scottish Parliament in 1999 is itself the direct result of the expressed, positive public support for such a body, and illustrates the growth of national identity as a political force within Scottish/UK politics (Leith 2006). The Scotland-wide referendum of 1997 was the end result of decades of activity by groups and parties from across the socio-political spectrum (Leith and Soule 2012). A number of different routes had been previously employed as Scotland sought self-government of some form within the UK (Mitchell 1996) during the preceding decades but the creation of the Scottish Parliament was nothing less than the direct result of the expressed wish of the Scottish electorate. A modern cliché of politics in Scotland/UK is that devolution is 'the settled will of the Scottish people' (a phrase attributed to John Smith,

MP, leader of the British Labour party in the early 1990s), although it is actually clear that the issue is far from settled, given the continued drive for further devolution, Home Rule or Independence (fuelled by the electoral success of the SNP, especially in 2007 and 2011).

The fact that the Scottish electorate themselves were given this opportunity to express their wishes is a reflection of a changing political arena within the wider UK. Plebiscites have not been a common factor of the British political system. Only eleven have been held in the UK (all since 1973, and over half of these since 1997 alone) and only two of them have been UK-wide. While the Scottish Government will hold a referendum on the possibility of independence for Scotland on 18 September 2014, it had to obtain the prior permission of the Westminster Parliament specifically to ensure that no legal challenge could muddy the outcome. It must not be forgotten that sovereignty within the British political system ultimately rests with Westminster, and it has historically been very loath to share that power. Yet, the recognition that it must, in reality, do so has increased. In 1997 (and 2014), by allowing voters in Scotland to publicly pronounce their wishes, Westminster has clearly acknowledged the existence, and importance, of national distinctiveness in modern Scottish/British politics (Trench 2008). Whatever the initial objectives, the genie is firmly out of the bottle, and the call for other future plebiscites within the UK (such as for consideration of continued UK membership of the EU, or greater powers for the Welsh Assembly) illustrates the continued dissemination of political influence outwith Westminster and Holyrood (the informal name for the Scottish Parliament).

However, despite there being a clear majority in favour of the establishment of the Scottish Parliament, and of that parliament now being firmly entrenched as an aspect of everyday Scottish life, it also remains a facet of the wider British political system, and perhaps a secondary facet in the eye of many within Scotland. Voter turnout for Scottish parliamentary elections remains stubbornly low, averaging just over 50 per cent for Holyrood elections since 2003, with the first election of 1999 having the historic high of 59 per cent. Turnout for Westminster elections in Scotland, while dropping in recent years, along similar lines to that of the rest of the UK (Denver 2007), remains higher, with an average since 1997 of 63.5 per cent. Perhaps this reflects the disputed nature of the current status of Scotland and the Scottish political system. As noted above, a referendum will be held on 18 September 2014. The question that will be posed to voters is 'Should Scotland be an independent country?', with the choice of answer being Yes or No. This referendum is being championed by the SNP-formed Scottish Government, who hold a majority of the seats in the Scottish Parliament. The SNP are supported in this objective by the Scottish Greens, but opposed by the other parties represented in Holyrood, Labour, the Conservatives and the Liberal Democrats (often referred to as the 'Unionists' or Unionist parties). While the SNP gained a majority of seats in the 2011 Scottish parliament election, they did not gain a majority of votes cast. This is conceivably one of the most ironic outcomes of Scottish politics, as avoidance of a nationalist majority is the very reason that the voting system employed was adopted in the first instance (Curtice and Steven 2011).

Nonetheless, despite the majority MSP status of the SNP, and their control of the Scottish Government since 2007, only around a third of people in Scotland favour independence, and this has been a fairly consistent figure across the past decade or so (Park et al. 2012). In elections, social attitudes and referendum surveys taken from 1997 through to 2011, the highest recorded support for independence was 35 per cent (in 2005), while the lowest was 24 per cent (in 2007). At the same time, aside from a handful of exceptions, the same period has always seen more than 50 per cent support devolution within the UK. Clearly there is volatility in the electorate but 'there is no evidence of a long-term increase in support for Scotland leaving the UK' (Park et al. 2012: 116).

The establishment of the Scottish Parliament was predicated upon the simple premise of 'Scottish solutions for Scottish problems' (Paterson et al. 2004) and it is certainly the case that 'identity is an important source of legitimacy for the new political institutions in the UK' (Bond and Rosie 2010: 87). National identity is also clearly a driving force within UK politics, especially inside the nations within the UK. However, while nationalism is clearly a political force and national identity plays a clear role in Scotland, the nature of that national identity is just as important. Scottish national identity has long been presented as civic, modern, inclusive and forward-looking (Keating 2001), especially by the SNP (Leith 2008) but also by most members of the political elite (Leith 2012). However, this may be liable to cause a certain conflict with the notion of a Scottish diaspora. After all, if modern diasporas are 'ethnic minority groups' (Sheffer 1986) or 'that segment of a people living outside the homeland' (Conner 1986: 16), then an inclusive, civic-based sense of belonging in Scotland causes an element of dissonance with such notions. Therefore, we turn to definitions of both Scotland and Scottishness to discuss this potential inconsistency.

Identity and Belonging in Scotland

The emphasis on membership of the Scottish nation (and potentially of any future Scottish state) within SNP documents has long been a civic one, rather than being derived from any ethnic or ancestrally based right (Leith and Soule 2012). However, the SNP vision of a civic-based, independent Scotland has been challenged with the claim that 'the SNP either does not understand or deliberately overlooks the lack of congruence between citizenship and nationality in construct-ing its version of an independent Scottish nation-state' (Mycock 2012: 64). Mycock points out the SNP's avoidance of a consideration of the wider implications of Scottish independence on a future UK and how the Scottish people have long differentiated their national iden-tity from their state identity. Nonetheless, the SNP has emphasised the civic aspects of Scottish identity, even when dealing with a diaspora that draws its membership directly from heritage, culture and ances-try. In 2007, on St Andrew's Day, Alex Salmond stated:

> That sense of inclusive Scottishness, one which does not simply tolerate diversity, but rather celebrates it, is at the heart of what I want St Andrew's Day to become. Modern Scotland is about con-tinuing that traditional welcome for those of all faiths and none, of including those from every part of the world and of every belief in our social mix. (www.scotland.gov.uk 2007)

It is important to remember that this emphasis is not purely an SNP projection. All major political parties within Scotland present a very civic and inclusive sense of national identity (Leith 2006) and upon investi-gation of individual elite perceptions, a 'majority of Scottish politicians provided a very tenuous and porous sense of nationhood and national belonging' (Leith and Soule 2012: 137) when it came to Scotland.

In addition, it has been argued by Leith and Soule that the masses hold a differing sense of belonging and identity to that projected by the political party elite within Scotland. It has shown that public nar-rative of belonging and national identity in Scotland 'tended to be non-civic in character' (2012: 119) and that the 'mass conception of Scottish national identity has restrictions that serve to exclude cer-tain groups and individuals from membership of the Scottish nation' (2012: 98). So it would seem that there is an incongruity between the mass and elite interpretations of what Scottishness is and who could be considered to be Scottish.

However, Leith and Soule also noted that such ideas among the elite and the masses were not monolithic, that context was very important and that a wider variety of attitudes and opinions existed across the political and social spectrum. Furthermore, Ichijo has noted that there 'are now many more different, legitimate, ways of being Scottish in the twenty-first century (2012: 35).

Therefore, it could be argued that there is no conflict with the notion of a civic-based national identity and the existence of a large and widespread Scottish diaspora. As we shall see below, the term diaspora itself can be sub-divided into a number of other groups. Some within these groups form/hold their membership through a familial or bloodline connection, some through a sense of heritage or cultural affiliation, and others through a sense of territoriality or residence. All of these attach, in one fashion or another, with current and existent political and wider social expressions of Scottish belonging and identity, and therefore all can connect. What is of little doubt, however, is that the mainstream political parties in Scotland consider membership of the Scottish nation in very wide terms indeed, and provide many routes for membership of the diaspora. When in office, many of these terms/routes have been formalised in government documents and the more formal definitions provided by Scottish Governments since devolution took place are outlined and discussed below.

IDENTITY AND BELONGING IN THE SCOTTISH DIASPORA

The argument that Conner's definition of the diaspora, 'the dispersal of people from its original homeland' (Butler 2001: 189), is far too broad to be useful is very apt in this particular case, as defining the Scottish diaspora is itself somewhat difficult. Like the term itself, diasporas vary significantly around the world (Leith and Sim 2012) and the connection to the homeland held within a diaspora can be as individual as the person who holds that attachment. Sheffer, when discussing diaspora as a term, emphasised the more ethnic aspects of the group identity, considering the definition as describing those of 'migrant origins residing and acting in host countries but maintaining strong sentimental and material links with their countries of origin – their homelands' (1986: 3). Yet, as outlined above, the term Scottishness itself is conceived within Scotland as a civic-based, inclusive sense of belonging. In contrast, work within various elements of the Scottish diaspora have highlighted birth, culture, ancestry and heritage as important (Sim 2011a, 2011b; Leith and Sim 2012) while also acknowledging that different elements of the Scottish diaspora operate differently depending upon their geographic location (Leith and Sim 2011).

Given both the terminological inexactitude of the concept, and the differing behaviour of the units which make up the wider Scottish diaspora, it is perhaps difficult to define identity in the eyes of that diaspora widely, but ethnic/historical and cultural elements clearly play a role, something perhaps not always appreciated by Scots in Scotland, or elements of the Scottish/British governments. Alan Bain, President of the American–Scottish Foundation, was very critical of the Scottish Government when it sought to change the name of Tartan Week to Scotland Week (Ferguson 2008) as it was the more traditional elements of being Scottish that appealed to individuals in America.

Sim (2012) has perhaps defined the issue best when he states that each diaspora 'remembers' Scotland and being Scottish differently to the homeland itself. While they seek to connect with a sense of Scotland they are not necessarily seeking to become Scottish (although they are also often seeking to be considered as fellow 'Scots'). It is more about the perception of authenticity in the eyes of the elements of the diaspora in question rather than the authentic nature of the experience itself. This is a point clearly emphasised by others (see Devine 2011). Such events as 'The Kirkin' o' the Tartan', which occurs among celebrations within elements of the diaspora, especially parts of North America, and which has never taken place here in Scotland, have more to do with their perception of the root culture than with Scotland itself.

What is clear is that for many in the Scottish diaspora, especially the far diaspora of the Americas or Australasia, culture and tradition are core elements of the diaspora, and that kinship, history and tradition are key to their definitions of being 'Scottish'. What is also clear is that there may well be some inherent conflicts between how the diaspora define themselves along more ethnic, ancestral lines and the more civic, inclusive model advanced by various political elites and entities, including the Scottish Government among them. Therefore, we shall now consider how the Scottish Government has defined the diaspora itself, and examine how it seeks to connect with it today.

DEFINING THE DIASPORA – POLITICALLY SPEAKING

In 2009 the Scottish Government held the Scottish Year of Home-coming, a celebration that was designed to coincide with the 250th anniversary of the birth of Robert Burns, Scotland's national poet and literary hero who ranks akin in the Scottish psyche to Shakespeare in the English. Along with this main theme, others were developed as part of the wider celebrations. This set of themes included golf, whisky, the inventions and innovations of the Scottish Enlightenment, and the culture, history, people and overall heritage of Scotland itself. A mainstay event of the year was 'The Gathering', held in Edinburgh in July 2009. This involved a gathering of clan associations and groups, a Highland Games event, a parade up the Royal Mile, attendance by royalty and celebrity alike, and a number of other activities. While it was been argued that 72,000 additional tourists and £53.7 million was raised by the event (Ekos 2010), the company running it went bankrupt, the Scottish Government had to step in to keep the issue solvent, and the overall effectiveness of the event has been questioned in the popular press and beyond (Sim and Leith 2013).

More importantly for the issue of diaspora politics, the same time period saw an almost frenetic level of activity in terms of research, reports and plans involving the Scottish Government and the diaspora. In the years just before and just after Homecoming 2009, the Scottish Government commissioned several documents discussing, defining and considering the nature of its relationship with the diaspora. As a result of 'desk-based' research in early 2009, a report was issued that sought to do just those three things, providing a rationale and a framework for engagement (Rutherford 2009). This was followed a year later by the *Diaspora Engagement Plan*, which sought 'for the first time' to outline 'the Scottish Government's ambitions for harnessing the power of Scotland's Diaspora' (Scottish Government 2010: 1). These and similar documents have provided insight into how the diaspora is viewed and framed, and how the SNP-led Scottish Government in particular seeks to interact with it and employ it as a resource.

Rutherford provided eight areas of possible value that the diaspora represented to the Scottish Government: investment, transfers, trade, tourism, knowledge transfer, international influence, immigration and circular migration. He recognised that such assistance could be gained from general international activity and involvement (although it could be argued that this is transgressing somewhat on Westminster's reserved authority) but argued that 'the development of diaspora policy provides an opportunity to realise these benefits efficiently' (2009: 2). Perhaps most important for the political perspective though is how the diaspora was defined within this report. Rutherford provided several sub-groups within which to classify members of the Scottish diaspora, while rightly recognising that members may move between such groups at different times and circumstances. First he considered the *lived* diaspora; individuals born in Scotland who have migrated from it, or who have lived and worked or lived and studied within it. Obviously, these individuals have varying levels of experience of Scotland, as well as personal or wider family connections to Scotland and Scottish culture. Some individuals prefer the term *living* diaspora, to more tightly focus on those who were born in Scotland. This particular term/group is also closely linked to the *ancestral* diaspora; individuals who can trace their heritage and familial roots to Scotland. Rutherford noted such roots could range from second generation migrants through to more 'ancient' dates of descent. It is often the case that such individuals may not hold direct or current family links to Scotland, and their knowledge may relate simply to visiting or studying in Scotland. In ancestral terms, an internal report to the Scottish Government stated that almost 17 million people in North America and Australasia claimed Scottish descent (Eirich and Mclaren, cited in Rutherford 2009), and the significance of this group as a potential resource is clearly numerically appealing.

Also part of the wider diaspora is a group who lack any formal or direct attachment to Scotland (although they are often, wrongly it would seem, included in the ancestral group); the *affinity* diaspora. Members of this group are those who feel a connection to Scotland, who may be active through cultural or extended family groups, or who may simply be attracted to the wide heritage or specific aspects thereof, such as the art or music, of Scotland. This is the most diaphanous facet of the wider diaspora, and often the most difficult to ascertain, as individuals who participate in Scottish-styled events may not have any plausible link to Scotland other than that activity, although it has been (perhaps somewhat incongruently) argued that this does not make them any less 'Scottish' (see Hesse 2011a, 2011b).

It is clear therefore that, drawing upon such documents, the Scottish Government has sought to define the diaspora in a number of ways, and also to break up the rather monolithic term into specific sub-groups or components. Politically speaking, perhaps the most significant of these external diasporic sub-groups is that termed the lived or living diaspora. The Scottish Government has focused on the living diaspora because of the international exchange opportunities they represent (Carr and Cavanagh 2009) and perhaps because this part of the diaspora is often thought to be more aware of and positive towards Scotland

(TNS 2007). One can assume that individuals born in Scotland or into a Scottish family will have more knowledge of, and empathy towards, Scotland than the members of other diaspora sub-groups. As noted above, however, there are significant limitations of the nature, size and other levels of understanding and data of the living diaspora and the Scottish Government has sought a greater depth of knowledge in this area (Carr and Cavanagh 2009).

The most immediate individuals with a claim to being Scottish in any ethnic sense, the living diaspora, individuals born in Scotland, could (according to official Scottish Government figures) represent as many as 1 million-plus throughout the world, and the majority of these (835,000) live in the rest of the UK (rUK) (and thus they have no right to vote in the forthcoming referendum on Scottish independence). While the population of Scotland has grown in recent years (see below) this still represents a significant proportion of the Scottish-born population, and a large number of the living Scottish diaspora are currently living within the same state as their fellow national Scots, albeit they are resident in a different nation within that state. Despite the potential voting power they could hold, in relation to their size vis-à-vis Scotland's resident voters, they will not be able to have a voice in the 2014 Independence referendum that may radically alter the relationship they have with their nation and directly impact upon their relationship with the state in which they reside. At the moment they may be members of the Scottish diaspora but they remain fellow citizens and residents of the UK, into which they were born as citizens all. Should a majority of voters resident within Scotland choose the option to become independent in 2014, then that situation may be subject to significant change and the relationship to Scotland that Scottish-born rUK residents have will therefore also change. Should such events occur, then the most populous diaspora, especially the living diaspora, will be right next door.

It is clear that political involvement of the diaspora is not, and never has been, an element of thinking within any of the various administrations of the Scottish Government (which from 1999 until 2007 was known as the Scottish Executive, when it was run in coalition by Scottish Labour and the Scottish Liberal Democrats). What is clear though from the documents discussed here is that all governments have sought a relationship with the diaspora and it is to that relationship we now turn.

THE NATURE OF THE RELATIONSHIP THE SCOTTISH GOVERNMENT SEEKS WITH THE DIASPORA

Despite Schedule Five of the 1998 Scotland Act clearly stating that international relations is a reserved matter, since devolution came about the Scottish Government has actively sought to create a wider international profile. Core among this mission has been the establishment of a relationship with the diaspora, albeit with a heavy slant towards a relationship with the North American aspect in particular. In 2001 the then First Minister Henry McLeish attended Tartan Day celebrations in New York; and in the same year the aim of the government was to 'develop an international network of Scottish influencers that can assist Scottish economic success' throughout the world (Scottish Executive 2001: 2). During the next administration from 2004 to 2007, First Minister Jack McConnell continued this effort, also attending Tartan Day celebrations, and Presiding Officer George Reid also visited the US during this period.

During the period 2002–7, the Deputy First Minister, Jim Wallace, took on the responsibilities for external affairs 'including the promotion of a positive image of Scotland overseas' (European Committee Paper, EU/02/1/2, 15 January 2002) and the European Committee of the Scottish Parliament was renamed the European and External Relations Committee in 2003 and had scrutiny over the activities of the Scottish Government and its relationship with the diaspora. A key activity of the Scottish Government during this period was to halt, and reverse, the brain drain and to ensure Scotland's population did not decline. The Fresh Talent Initiative had three main goals, including 'retaining home grown talent' by attracting those who had moved abroad to return, and 'by attracting those who are completely new to Scotland' (SP Official Report, 24 February 2004, Col 5941). This aim to connect with the diaspora was part of the wider official *International Strategy* (Scottish Executive 2004). As noted in the discussion above on defining the diaspora, the SNP-led Scottish Government has only continued this emphasis, seeking to build on the ties of the diaspora, envisaging members as a potentially significant economic resource for Scotland and Scottish products throughout the world.

This reflects a diaspora strategy many other governments have followed. Brinkerhoff (2009) illustrates the importance that diasporas can have materially, socially and/or politically in their homeland. Although much of her discussion focuses on the developing world, and comments such as the ability of diaspora involvement to aid in 'democratization' illustrate such emphasis, her focus is not without applicability here. She highlights the potential economic impact and points out that a diaspora can provide a significant source of skill transfers and wider civic experiences as well. As she indicates, establishing an environment in which the diaspora can contribute to the homeland, 'even in relatively more mature democracies' (Brinkerhoff 2009: 89), requires new forms of thinking, and structures and policies need to be developed specifically for such aims. Strategically aimed targeting of those aspects of the diaspora who are already 'mobilised, willing and able' is necessary. Even where the diaspora also represents a potential source of competition, and the established economics in which many of the Scottish diaspora reside evidently do, opportunities clearly exist.

In 2010 the Scottish Government produced a document entitled *The Diaspora Engagement Plan – Reaching Out to Scotland's International Family*. As the opening sentence clearly stated, this represented for the first time the ambitions for 'harnessing the power' of the Scottish diaspora, and the document also proudly proclaimed that Scotland was the first nation in Europe to produce such a plan. What is perhaps most interesting is that, while the document spoke of a 'mutually beneficial' set of relationships, the diaspora was seen as a potential 'resource', which could 'contribute to the Government's core purpose of increasing sustainable economic growth for Scotland' (2010: 1). The three ways in which this could be achieved were identified as bringing the diaspora to Scotland to 'live, learn, visit, work and return' (2), promoting Scotland to the diaspora itself, and to 'manage' the reputation Scotland had with the diaspora, as 'an independent-minded and responsible nation' (2).

The document identified six sub-groups (Reverse, Returning, New, Lived, Ancestral, Affinity) of the diaspora and highlighted how each would be focused upon or engaged with. In terms of the *lived* diaspora, the plan was seeking to identify 'new opportunities to engage with the young, economically active "lived" members of the diaspora' (2). While it also outlined how it would work with 'Scottish Development International, the Fresh Talent Initiative and delivery agencies to encourage talented members of the diaspora to return' (2), the Fresh Talent Initiative ended in 2008 when the Westminster Government brought in new immigration rules based on a points system. The other sub-groups specifically targeted include the *reverse* diaspora ('to promote and advocate for Scotland through their contact with their home country' (3)) and the *new* diaspora (defined as Scots about to leave

Scotland), 'with a view to encouraging them to return' (4). In closing, the Scottish Government recognised that this was a long-term plan with action times that would require 'sustained commitment if they are to return measurable benefits' (4).

Although other aspects of the diaspora were alluded to, such as the ancestral or affinity (with mention of several sporting events, Homecoming 2009 and 2014, and social media), only the *reverse, lived* and *new* diasporas were specifically mentioned and focused upon. Interestingly enough, a section discussing the establishment of the Scottish Centre for Diaspora Studies at the University of Edinburgh (in 2007) was discussed with the aim to 'build capacity' as it 'offers the unique opportunity to position Scotland as a world-leading centre of excellence in this area of study' (4). The engagement plan also highlighted several organisations or agencies the government would work with as 'key delivery partners'. These included VisitScotland, the Saltire Foundation, Scottish Enterprise and GlobalScot. These would present the opportunity to 'Raise awareness of contemporary Scotland's strengths and culture' (3).

This document, the governmental action plan, clearly highlights the economic and communication aspects of engagement with the diaspora. Thus, as Brinkerhoff (2009) highlights, there are emphases on the material and social aspects of the engagement with the diaspora, but there are no discussions of any political involvement of the diaspora; not unsurprising in itself. Even where the reverse diaspora are specifically discussed, the opportunities highlighted are as advocates in the original country of origin, or simply to encourage them to remain in Scotland. The communication involvement is highlighted not only as a two-way process but also as three-way, or even a hub, that would allow interaction between the Scottish Government, key agencies, 'segments and geographies' within the diaspora, but with the government operating as a 'central point'.

THE OTHER DIASPORA

Yet there is one group not yet discussed, a diaspora that will exercise power in Scotland in 2014, one that has significant political connotations, and within which many individual members have even greater influence than those from the living diaspora in political terms. This diaspora is one that is not originally Scottish *per se*, but who nonetheless must be considered central to the contemporary political debate in Scotland. This is the *reverse* diaspora, another group that the Scottish

Government has sought to become more knowledgeable about (Carr and Cavanagh 2009). The reverse diaspora are individuals from other nations/states living within Scotland, and many of them, due to their membership of EU member states, or status as citizens of the UK, have voting rights for the Scottish Parliament. As an internal diaspora group, they are often overlooked in Scottish diaspora studies, despite their ability to have greater political impact than any group of the Scottish diaspora outwith Scotland. Indeed, many members of the reverse diaspora, due to the impending referendum debate, will have an impact upon Scotland's relationship with the Scottish diaspora. Voting rights for the forthcoming referendum will be based on the electoral roll for the Scottish Parliament (plus sixteen- and seventeen-year-olds), which means residency in Scotland, not Scottish birth, is the driving element. This illustrates better than any academic debate the political and contemporary interpretation of 'being Scottish'.

In terms of the reverse diaspora and their potential political impact, the 2011 census noted that 83 per cent of Scottish residents were born in Scotland, with 9 per cent, or 459,000 people, English- born. The rest of the UK provided 37,000 (0.7 per cent) from Northern Ireland and 17,000 (0.3 per cent) from Wales. In addition, 369,000 individuals resident in Scotland were born outwith the UK (NRS 2013). Of these, 55,000 (or 15 per cent of those from outwith the UK) were born in Poland, making them the largest element of the reverse diaspora after England. This is a massive increase since the 2001 census, when only 1 per cent of Scottish residents were recorded as Polish-born. Other significant European-born populations included the Republic of Ireland (11.4 per cent of foreign-born), Germany (9.8 per cent), France (2.6 per cent) and Italy (2.5 per cent). All of these individuals, should they meet the age requirements, will generally be liable to register and vote in Scotland for elections to the Scottish Parliament and in the 2014 referendum.

When we compare the lived with the reverse diaspora, the influence of the first, a significant number of Scots, is politically negligible in Scotland, while the second have a substantial potential influence. Such discussions are difficult, as ethnic-based discussion of diaspora connections 'causes uneasiness in many quarters' (Butler 2001: 309), and there are few adherents of an ethnic-based sense of Scottishness alone, although some calls have been made to allow Scots-born rUK residents to vote in the forthcoming referendum (BBC News 2012). These calls have been dismissed by the Scottish Government, as it clearly conflicts with the nature of contemporary Scottishness, and the idea of Scotland as a sense of place, rather than tribe.

The situation of the large rUK lived diaspora reflects the long-term drain of individuals from Scotland to other countries, and other nations within the UK. To put it simply, in 2001 one in five, or 20 per cent, of Scots-born individuals lived outwith Scotland (the average for the rUK was 5.5 per cent). Recent migration has helped reverse the population decline in Scotland, however. In Scotland in 2011, 17 per cent of the resident population was not Scotland-born, and this group has only increased in percentage terms during the last decade. Census data up to 2001 illustrates that the reverse diaspora are mainly from the rUK but by 2008 'the population of Scotland had risen to its highest level since 1983 due to an increase in births and migration from England and Eastern Europe' (Devine 2011: 288), a fact which the 2011 census clearly illustrates. This increase during the first decade of the twenty-first century (and devolution) was significantly due to the expansion of the EU, and the rights of citizens of those new member states to settle legally in Scotland. All individuals from across the EU and rUK citizens will be able to decide the relationship of Scotland within the UK, but the lived diaspora within the rUK and wider Europe will not have that privilege.

CONCLUSIONS

It is clear, and perhaps not particularly surprising, that the creation of a distinct political system within Scotland, for Scotland, has led to the emergence of a new and clear relationship between the new Scottish political institutions and (the often much older and more established institutions of) the Scottish diaspora. For the first time since the Act of Union, Scots around the world are able to look to Scotland and see an entity that is very much Scottish, rather than an appendage of the wider British Government, such as the Scottish Office. During the twenty-first century Scots-born individuals have continued to move from Scotland to the wider world, as they have done for centuries before. Today, however, unlike the past, they have a government in Scotland that seeks to establish, and maintain, a relationship with them, as they do so, and also seeks one with the descendants of the Scots that went before them. They also move from a Scotland that has a growing population, rather than a declining one. Not only that but, following political changes in Scotland, new opportunities for diaspora involvement with the homeland have also been created, yet these remain perhaps somewhat underdeveloped and very much in the initial stages.

As the Scottish Government(s) have sought to formulate a diaspora strategy, comparisons have often been made with a number of countries that have also sought to create a link with their respective diasporas around the world. Within contemporary Scottish Government documents this is often now New Zealand, which is seen as a model in terms of research and activity. Other comparisons have been made with Ireland, a nation which, like Scotland, has long seen significant outward migration and has seen those emigrants maintain a strong and significant cultural and emotional connection with the 'auld country'. However, the Scottish forms of diaspora involvement, both historically and contemporary, are significantly different from such models or other often-employed arguments. The outward migration of the Scots, despite some noticeable historical events that are often focused upon, such as the Highland Clearances, did not result from a lack of opportunity or choice. The history of migrant Scots has not pointed to a sense of victimhood. The Scots were active participants – indeed, active partners – in Empire, and Fry was able to discuss how the Scots remade the Empire after they entered into the Union with England (Fry 2001).

As political changes in Scotland continue, the relationship between Scotland and the diaspora will also need to develop, despite possible contention between them. The nature of belonging in modern Scotland is presented as civic and inclusive and this creates a certain sense of dissonance with elements of the diaspora, many of whom are connected through history/culture, ancestry or family. Such elements may struggle to balance their conception of being Scottish with that presented in Scotland. Yet such a conception also allows Scottishness to flourish in a variety of elements and settings. Individuals within Holland can delight in attending Scottish Highland Days and dress in kilts, despite lacking any clear familial connection with Scotland (Sim and Leith, forthcoming). Furthermore, given that outwith the living diaspora many individuals hold Scottishness as a 'symbolic identity' (Gans 1979) while holding another more immediate national identity, it may well suit many elements within the diaspora.

However, further possible changes may also result in personal and political disruption for the diaspora itself. The largest and closest segment of the living diaspora, resident within the UK but outwith Scotland, are disempowered from any changes taking place to their own country, despite being part of the same state. Such a pattern fits with the above conception of Scottishness, but again, how does one connect with a diaspora that is disempowered? In addition, the reverse diaspora, a significant aspect of the Scottish population, are a part of the discussion on diaspora engagement and are politically empowered, but are often absent from the wider academic and political discussion. Diaspora conversations, it seems, need to be larger and much more inclusive.

It is clear that the emerging relationship that the Scottish Government has with the diaspora is very much an evolving one, but one that points to a positive reception in the first instance. Yet to maintain this positive reception and build upon it is the challenge that awaits future Scottish governments. The action plan on the diaspora connects with those with a lived or living connection, and those already resident in Scotland. Yet the wider affinity and ancestral portions (much larger as overall numbers go) are often considered without specific reference for development and engagement and only economically. Yet informal discussions and documentary evidence from ancestral groups indicate that such individuals within clan organisations want to be seen as more than tourists and as more than simply visitors to Scotland. They consider themselves Scottish, a point Scotland needs to contemplate upon.

For the Scottish Government it would seem that economic benefits are the key and sometimes overly emphasised objective within the homeland–diaspora relationship. There is often very little to no real mention of social or non-economic improvements in the government plans and objectives produced in the last few years. Therefore, a period of greater investigation and discussion is necessary as we move into the twenty-first century and seek to engage more fully with the Scottish diaspora. As Scotland further establishes its relationship with the wider 'family' of Scots, and with the wider Scottish diaspora in all its forms, it needs to establish more open lines of communication with and perhaps a better understanding of not only what Scotland wants and seeks from that relationship but what the diaspora – and the various elements within it – seek too.

7

Invisible and Inaudible? England's Scottish Diaspora and the Politics of the Union

Andrew Mycock

INTRODUCTION

In March 2013 the Scottish Government published the Scottish Referendum (Franchise) Bill, stating that eligibility to vote in the 2014 referendum would be determined by residency in Scotland for UK citizens. This principle was also extended to qualifying Commonwealth, Republic of Ireland and other EU citizens resident in Scotland. Service and Crown personnel serving in the UK or overseas in the Armed Forces who were registered to vote in Scotland would also be allowed to apply for a 'service vote'. The franchise regulations were not seen as particularly contentious as they had been previously utilised in Scottish parliamentary and local elections as well as the devolution referenda of 1979 and 1997. As such, there was widespread agreement from the respective Independence and Unionist campaigns that this was the fairest approach to determining voter eligibility in the referendum.

For most, the Referendum (Franchise) Bill was noteworthy principally for its plans to extend electoral registration to 16 and 17 year-old voters who were resident in Scotland. That 800,000 Scots who live in other parts of the UK would not be able to vote while 400,000 people from other parts of the UK and elsewhere who live in Scotland would was, by comparison, seen as relatively uncontroversial. However, one newspaper questioned why 16 and 17 year-olds were being given special provision while 'thousands' of Scottish service personnel stationed in other parts of the UK, who may in future be asked to risk their lives for a separate Scotland, might not be able to vote for or against its establishment (Johnson 2013a). The UK Scottish Affairs parliamentary select committee also raised concerns that while EU citizens were not eligible to vote to elect the UK government, they would be able to vote on whether or not to break up the UK itself (Scottish Affairs Committee 2013). They noted that, under franchise eligibility terms agreed, ten Scottish Olympic medallists at London 2012 could be excluded from voting on the future of their country.

The franchise remit for the Scottish independence referendum did though raise important questions about the potential reform of British and Scottish citizenship and nationality, particularly for the largest Scottish diaspora within the UK who live in England. This chapter seeks to provide some commentary on the plight of this diaspora and the extent to which it is invisible and inaudible when compared to 'overseas' diasporas. It will first consider how the concept of 'diaspora' has been understood by scholars and will argue that Scottish 'internal diaspora' within the British pluri-national state should be understood to possess distinctive relationships with the homeland that limit group formation and identity. The chapter will then briefly consider the historical development of the Anglo-Scottish diaspora, exploring its organisation and resonance. Finally it will assess the extent to which the Anglo-Scottish diaspora has been engaged in the Scottish independence debate.

Diaspora, State and Nation(s)

Chapter 1 in this volume discusses how defining the Scottish diaspora is 'somewhat difficult'. Macdonald (2012: 17) has gone as far as to claim she has 'sought in vain for a definition of the Scottish diaspora'. This is in part due to the widely acknowledged conceptual difficulties in defining who or what a diaspora is and under what criteria membership should be understood. Diaspora is most commonly associated with the migration and dispersal of people from an identified 'homeland' and the subsequent formation of integrated ethnic or national groups in another nation-state. It typically involves the simultaneous recognition and self-identification of common ancestral or cultural connections with a former 'homeland' through a range of formal and informal channels and the concurrent preservation of diaspora boundaries allied with a resistance to wholesale group assimilation within the country of settlement.

The consequences of migration, often associated with experiences of victimisation, racism and exclusion, have encouraged dispersed communities to adopt strategies whereby resources are mobilised through the politics of multi-cultural recognition realised through the assertion of minority rights and free expression of diasporic identities. Political, cultural and social dislocation and marginalisation caused by migration can strengthen diasporic nostalgia for a real or imagined 'homeland', informing romanticist constructions of diasporic nationalism. Ethno-communal consciousness plays an important part in retaining a sense of belonging and longing, founded on distinctive patterns of language and/or culture that are both inherently national and transnational. Thus hybridity and fluidity in identity terms means that boundary-maintenance and boundary-erosion are simultaneously experienced in multiple forms (Brubaker 2005).

Safran (1991) argues diasporas need to retain collective memories or historical narratives about their homeland that diverge from the new country of settlement combined with a belief they will never be fully accepted into their new country. This idealisation of the homeland is essential, with the promise of their or their descendants' return underpinning the maintenance of diasporic identity and group cohesion. However, Faist (2008) suggests diaspora groups do not always seek to return and often maintain dense and continuous links with the homeland while remaining in their host country or even undertaking further migration. This suggests a variety of forces determine the nature of diasporic relationships with their respective host and home societies, related to the extent to which transnational claims are positively or negatively framed and expounded. If claims of a shared transnational community are largely overlooked or rejected by the homeland, diasporas may well adopt confrontational approaches such as seeking to influence politics, with some even supporting ultra-nationalist or terrorist groups to encourage recognition and change (Sheffer 2003). A more positive reception of diasporic transnational claims may encourage the development of institutional and policy frameworks that enhance cultural, economic or political ties.

The extent to which a host country views diaspora relationships as positive or negative is dependent on the nature of overarching state-to-state relations. Fractious or confrontational relations between the homeland and host states may well encourage victimisation, exclusion or even expulsion. Conversely, migration can free diaspora from social, cultural and political constraints they may have experienced in their homeland and allow for more expansive identity framework and enhanced citizenship rights. Fractured diasporic ties may encourage individuals or groups to assimilate or integrate into the host community to such an extent that they disperse entirely. Alternatively, groups might establish bilateral bonds that both complement their original culture while concurrently accommodating the culture of the host society. In such cases, dual citizenship arrangements may well be established that recognise the transnational dynamics of group membership and identity.

The formation of diasporas has been traditionally linked with forced removal of expelled groups such as Armenians and Jews and those who migrate to seek asylum to escape persecution or enforced hardship. Increasingly though, diasporas are formed through voluntary migration, particularly economic migrants seeking a better life in another country. Some groups, however, can become diasporas without physically migrating. Barna (2010: 60) describes these as 'internal diaspora' who live in the same location despite changing political circumstances. For example, the break-up of European empires during the twentieth century saw new states created in central and eastern Europe after the First and Second World Wars and after the dissolution of the Soviet Union and Yugoslavia. Internal diasporas were created when communities found themselves separated from their majority national group through the establishment of new political borders. These internal diasporas have frequently been isolated through the application of exclusory citizenship laws and concurrent ethnicised nation- and state-building projects within their new host states. In response, Barna notes that diaspora groups have adopted dissociative strategies, thus limiting the immersive linguistic or cultural assimilation or integration within the host state national culture and society.

Their depiction as 'internal diaspora' is however open to question as their diasporic status is defined by the tensions and intersections between 'host' and 'homeland' citizenship and identity. Each of the formations outlined above would appear to support Faist's (2000) assertion that diaspora should be commonly understood as a consequence of transnational migration crossing the borders of at least two national states. Such a view is founded on the assumption that the formation and maintenance of diasporas can only be understood as the product of the interactions between two distinctive forms of national citizenship and identity, thus overlooking migration within states. Intra-state migration is a common phenomenon and is typically understood in terms of population transfers between rural and metropolitan areas or intra-regional movements. Sizeable shifts in population location are primarily economic in their causation but can also be a product of political factors or more banal reasons such as higher education study, retirement or familial reunions. This would suggest there is scope for 'internal diaspora' to exist within the territorial boundaries of a single state as a result of significant patterns of internal migration that encourage citizens to layer political and cultural citizenships and identities.

This raises a number of dilemmas that might challenge established approaches to conceptualising and identifying diaspora. Those writing about diaspora often frame debate on the assumption that the nation and state are synonymous. Such an approach privileges statist claims both to homeland nationhood and external diaspora. However, intra-state migrants who might form national diasporas within pluri-national states such as the UK are not expected to change their citizenship, and thus typically retain established sovereign political, social, economic and cultural rights regardless of their physical location. As migrants are not leaving their host state, they also have the opportunity to maintain established forms of connection to both state *and* sub-state cultures and identities, most likely without fear of state-sponsored victimisation, exclusion or expulsion. Transnational links founded on a shared nationality are thus maintained through a complex series of state and sub-state bi-national institutions, networks and familial links.

Furthermore, the interconnected relationships between state and sub-state nationalisms within pluri-national states can highlight the conflated and mutually constitutive nature of shared cultures and identities. For some, intra-state migration may well lack sufficient constraints in terms of identity rights and expression that potentially engender the sense of common grievance or group injustice often needed to motivate diaspora formation. A lack of such drivers to stimulate a sense of difference between internal migrants and their new host nation might therefore encourage integration and dispersal, thus overlooking the opportunity to form a national diaspora.

This noted, the formation of an internal diaspora within a pluri-national state may also be retarded or motivated by the reluctance of the 'homeland' nation to interpret migrants as a legitimate diaspora, as the act of migration itself is not seen to meet the criteria for diaspora recognition. Conversely intra-state migration may be seen as an act of disloyalty by some in the homeland, particularly by nationalist groups who might seek secession from the overarching state. A sense of diasporic difference may also be reactively stimulated by the differentiation of citizenship rights through the creation of distinctive state and devolved sub-state national forms of governance that benefit or penalise internal diasporas moving from nation to nation. Internal diasporas within pluri-national states thus

highlight that the identity hybridity and fluidity that complicate plu-
ral forms of boundary-maintenance and boundary-erosion can be
easily politicised. As the boundaries of membership and connectivity
are imprecise and fluid, the existence of internal diasporas – like all
diasporas – should therefore not be understood as a bounded entity
but as a cultural or political stance or claim (Brubaker 2005).

In the UK, about 1 in 10 citizens undertakes some form of internal
migration during their life, mostly moving within each of its nations rather
than from one nation to another (Dennett and Stillwell 2011). However, significant numbers of UK citizens have undertaken transnational
forms of migration within the overarching British state, thus offering the
potential of the formation of internal national diaspora. The following
discussion will focus on the largest national group of internal migrants,
the Scots in England. It will seek first to understand historical patterns
of migration and the potential existence of a Scottish internal diaspora
before considering the extent to which they have been acknowledged by
protagonists and participated in the forthcoming Scottish independence
referendum.

An 'Invisible Ethnicity'? The Scottish Diaspora in England

Armitage (2005: 238) states that no history of Scotland could be complete without an account of the Scottish diaspora. But although this
might suggest Scottish history is inherently transnational, rather than
discretely focused on the nation, it has been typically framed in terms
of those Scots who went overseas rather than to other parts of the
UK. As McCarthy (2007: 211) notes, 'within the historiography of
Scottish migration, movement within the UK has attracted relatively
little attention'. In her volume exploring the 'great Scottish exodus',
Harper (2003) notes that between the 1600s and the 1800s England
was the main recipient of Scottish emigrants, who quickly became a
prominent feature of English life. They were, though, exposed to anti-
Scottish prejudice, lampooned for consuming the wealth of England
by taking the best jobs or drawing on more generous poor law provision than that provided in Scotland (Langford 2005). This noted,
during the nineteenth century emigration flows from Scotland both
grew and altered dramatically, with many more Scots settling across
the British Empire or in the United States.

The overseas diaspora networks established by Scottish emigrants
during the nineteenth and early twentieth centuries were (and remain)
substantial and interlocking, strengthening Scotland's national pride

and esteem in the achievements of its distant sons and daughters (Landsman 2001; McCarthy 2006). During this period, Scotland not only provided the human capital to expand the Empire, it also supplied a substantial number of internal migrants who powered the British industrial revolution. Devine (2011) suggests that nearly half of those who left Scotland went south of the border as the economic opportunities and rewards were typically higher. Estimates of Scottish internal migrants in the UK are uncertain but McCarthy (2007) suggests between 1841 and 1939 an estimated 750,000 Scots moved to other parts of the UK – mainly England. During the twentieth century this flow further intensified, particularly after the Second World War, as Scots migrated in what Armitage (2005: 233) describes as 'one of the greatest continuous but least-heralded periods of Scottish migration'.

Harper (2013) argues this migration helped reconfigure the industrial landscape of inter- and post-war Britain, with significant social, economic and cultural repercussions. Many Scots worked in heavy industries and were attracted to towns such as Corby in Northamptonshire by a combination of established social networks and the promise of housing and employment (Dyer 2002). The cultural legacy of this period of intra-state national migration was a plethora of Scottish associations and clubs in areas of dense Scottish migration. These included numerous branches of the Scottish Association, the Scottish Society, the Grampian Society, the Caledonian Society and the St Andrew's Society where members met regularly to affirm and celebrate Scottish identity and cultural ties (Burnett 2007). Such organisations supplemented transnational familial ties, establishing events such as the Corby Highland Gathering that, since the 1960s, has sought to celebrate Scottish cultural traditions in England.

Devine (2011) argues that the influence of the Scots overseas diaspora has proven considerable both in the development of the countries where they settled and in the export of Scottish political, cultural, economic and social values, ideas, practices and identities. Miller (2005) suggests that, in comparison, the resonance and impact of Scotland's migrants to England is less marked, proving more isolated and invisible within a much larger and diverse host population. The comparative lack of resonance and acknowledgement of the Scottish diaspora in England is a product of at least three significant and interconnected factors that have retarded its formation and recognition in either the host or home nation.

First, the drivers for diaspora formation outlined above, to form an intra-state national diaspora, have proven less powerful in terms of organisation when compared to their overseas compatriots. Leith and Sim (2012) note that although there are over one million people in England who were either born in Scotland or who claim Scottish ancestry, their expatriate identity has not proven a sufficiently galvanising dynamic in encouraging the formation of a national diaspora in England. This is partly due to the relatively unproblematic identity relationships between Scots in England and their English counterparts in terms of cultural dissonance. Although clearly divergent in a number of ways, English and Scottish national identities draw on many common historical, social, cultural and political reference points that often merge within overarching constructions of Britishness. This would suggest that the Anglo-Scots diaspora can express their sub-state Scottish national civic and ethnic identities without constraints while also expressing solidarity with their English counterparts through a shared British national identity.

Moreover, the close proximity to Scotland has ensured that the romanticisation of Scottish identity that is evident among the overseas diaspora is considerably muted among Scots in England. Issues of overly nostalgic connectivity with Scotland, particularly comprehension of its historical and contemporary affairs, often identified with overseas Scottish diaspora are not as pronounced for those Scots living in the rest of the UK. As Sim and McIntosh (2007) note, Anglo-Scots migrants have ready access to Scottish media and other cultural resources, thus ensuring that romanticised notions of the homeland are tempered by a more realistic comprehension of Scottish current affairs and society.

The Anglo-Scots diaspora's affiliation with British forms of national identity may though be somewhat tactical, suggesting a desire by Scottish migrants to avoid identity conflict with their English counterparts. However, Leith and Sim's (2012) research suggests that second and subsequent generations of Scots appear to readily adopt an English national identity, suggesting their diasporic Scottish identity is either less attractive or lacks sufficient cultural or political potency to encourage alternative forms of identification. Of potentially more importance, Harper (2013) notes there is evidence that Scottish identity among the diaspora based in places such as Corby has been overtaken by a more cosmopolitan ethos. Scottish identity is thus increasingly viewed as only one of a multitude of identities available to Anglo-Scottish settlers.

A second factor relates to the fragmented organisation structures that are required to maintain a cohesive Anglo-Scots diaspora group identity and membership. As previously noted, Scots in England share many ethnic and civic traits that inform a common British citizenship and identity. Moreover, they typically see themselves as constituting part of the 'host' society rather than affiliating with the experiences of other overseas migrant groups. Unlike other migrant communities, there has been no perceived need to gain recognition or redress perceived or actual diminutions in identity or minority group rights vis-à-vis the host nation. Scots in England have not found their citizenship rights compromised or curtailed due to their ethnicity or suffered persecution, discrimination or exclusion beyond seemingly durable English cultural and political myopia or arrogance combined with often rudimentary anti-Scottish 'humour'.

The Anglo-Scots diaspora has also lacked formal state recognition or party political engagement on a national scale in England, though there is some evidence of the local political impact of Scottish migrant communities in Corby, Hull and Merseyside (Harper 2013; McCarthy 2007; Sim 2011). The Anglo-Scots diaspora is instead predominantly understood as a component of a wider multi-cultural, multi-ethnic civic Britishness. No national diaspora organisation has been formed either to represent their community interests, as is the case with many overseas Scottish diasporas, or to provide an umbrella framework for the various Scottish associations and societies. Indeed, there is evidence to indicate that the Scottish associations and societies in England are steeply declining both in terms of numbers and membership (McCarthy 2007; Leith and Sim 2012). Public celebrations of Anglo-Scottishness such as the Corby Highland Gathering are also struggling to find sufficient financial or popular support (BBC 2013).

The third influential factor limiting the development of a distinctive Anglo-Scottish diaspora and identity has been its lack of recognition in Scotland. Although the largely economic motivations for Scots migrating have been sympathetically understood and articulated, the act of migration itself has not been viewed as entirely positive. The migration to England of large numbers of Scots in particular, allied to concerns about a so-called 'brain drain', has been cited by some to have had detrimental economic and social ramifications in Scotland (Carr and Cavanagh 2009). In the post-war period, the Scottish National Party (SNP) sought to draw attention to the need for fundamental political change to ensure that an independent Scotland could create the economic conditions to stem emigration to

England and elsewhere. Such narratives sometimes drew on elements of Scottish victimology located in nationalist interpretations of the causes of previous overseas migrations in the wake of Jacobite defeat or the Highland Clearances (Macdonald 2012).

This noted, the SNP, as well as other parties campaigning only in Scotland and who seek independence from the UK, have historically neither campaigned nor sought election in England. Furthermore, they have not attempted to agitate the Anglo-Scottish diaspora to adopt a more confrontational nationalist approach to identity politics. Indeed, the extent to which the SNP and other Scottish parties have overlooked or ignored the Scottish diaspora in England is significant, particularly in light of recent constitutional reforms in the UK. The re-establishment of a Scottish Parliament has seen successive administrations seek to re-engage with Scotland's diaspora (Sim and McIntosh 2007; Sim 2012). This has, however, revealed a range of tensions regarding how Scottish national identity and citizenship are framed and realised.

As Leith notes in this volume, popular constructions of Scottish nationality have tended to focus on ethnic constructions of belonging and identity that reach out to diasporic groups of Scots settlers in preference to migrant groups within Scotland itself (including those from other parts of the UK). This has been increasingly contradicted by political constructions of Scottish nationality that have sought to prioritise a territorially bounded Scottish civic nationalism. The central role of ethnicity in defining diasporic group boundaries and identities has though compromised claims by those who have invested considerable political and cultural capital in framing twenty-first-century Scottish nationalism as 'wholly civic' (Mycock 2012). For those who seek to redefine Scottish identity on the principle of the congruence of an independent Scottish nation and state, connecting with Scottish diaspora who display strong attachment to ethnic Scottishness has thus required careful framing.

The failure to fully understand the implications of diaspora recognition were apparent during preparations for 'The Homecoming' in 2009 where the SNP minority government initially sought to encourage 'blood' or 'ancestral' Scots, predominantly living in Australia, Canada, New Zealand and the United States, to 'come home'. Sim (2012) argues the Homecoming was an element in the SNP government's strategy to propagate a sense of Scottishness and build overseas support for Scottish independence. Critics noted, however, that it appeared to prioritise ethnic constructions of Scottish nationality, thus avoiding engagement with those diasporic communities who might draw attention to the darker legacy of Scottish imperialism, particularly in the

Caribbean, or the largest Scottish-born diaspora based in England who highlighted links with the Union and a shared Britishness (Mycock 2012). Subsequent reform of the criteria of Scottish diaspora sought to redress the ethnic profiling of diaspora, acknowledging the claims of 'affinity diaspora' who do not have any direct ancestral connection with Scotland but who have lived there or hold a strong emotional connection (Scottish Government 2010).

Research commissioned by the Scottish Government (Rutherford 2009) seeking to assess the extent of Scotland's diaspora suggested a figure of about 40 million lived 'overseas', including the ancestral and Scots-born diaspora who lived in England. The diaspora strategy developed from this research argued that the Scottish Government needed to stimulate inward economic investment from these 'overseas' Scots to enhance Scotland's economy, together with better diaspora communications to encourage Scots to return home (Scottish Government 2010). By depicting the Anglo-Scots diaspora as 'overseas', the Scottish Government overlooked their existing contribution to the Scottish economy through the payment of UK taxes or the deep network of established social and cultural connections with Scotland. The researchers also claimed that Scottish Government diaspora policy was most often framed in terms of an inclusive Scottish civic nationalism, thus suggesting that the Scottish overseas and intra-state diaspora are not merely an extension of a Scottish cultural community and are seen to possess political capital within Scotland. However, the research also acknowledged that the vast majority of the overseas diaspora understood their connections with Scotland in ethnic terms. This is partly due to the lack of transnationalist forms of Scottish citizenship founded on shared civic institutions available to most overseas Scottish diaspora. However, the fact that Anglo-Scots diaspora do share common forms of British political citizenship, and are able to maintain some influence in shaping political developments in Scotland through participation in the UK parliamentary system, was overlooked. The largest Scottish diaspora would appear to remain largely invisible both in their homeland and host country.

An 'Absent Voice'? The Anglo-Scottish Diaspora and the Scottish Independence Referendum

On forming a majority government in the Scottish Parliament in May 2011, the SNP reiterated their intention to hold a referendum on whether Scotland should become independent from the rest of the UK. The terms regarding the referendum question and franchise terms were subsequently agreed by the UK and Scottish governments and formally published on 15 October 2012. The so-called 'Edinburgh Agreement', signed by UK Prime Minister David Cameron and Scottish First Minister Alex Salmond, continued the established practice of utilising permanent residency as the principle that dictated franchise eligibility for the Scottish independence referendum to be held on 18 September 2014. As with previous referenda affecting Scotland alone, such as the 1979 and 1997 devolution votes, diaspora Scots in the rest of the UK would be excluded from voting.

If independence was to follow the pathway of devolution, being what the late John Smith claimed was 'the settled will of the Scottish people', it would similarly require the caveat that it would be the 'settled will' of the Scottish people resident in Scotland. Indeed, only two out of the eleven referenda since 1973 have been held on a UK-wide franchise. By applying residency as the key determinant for inclusion or exclusion in the Scottish independence referendum, over 400,000 people from elsewhere in the UK, the European Union and the Commonwealth who live in Scotland would be eligible to vote. The exclusion of the 800,000-strong Scottish-born diaspora who live in other parts of the UK has though produced some heated political and public debate about the terms of the franchise.[1]

Some members of the Anglo-Scots diaspora have sought to publicly challenge their exclusion. In Corby, councillor Rob McKellar began a campaign to ensure 'anybody who is entitled to hold a Scottish passport under the Scottish National Party's (SNP) regime should be allowed to vote' (BBC 2012a). He argued that it appeared somewhat contradictory that ancestral and Scottish-born diaspora in the rest of the UK would not be able to vote but may well be eligible to claim citizenship rights in an independent Scotland, thus meaning the referendum would have significant ramifications. An Edinburgh law graduate, James Wallace, sought to draw attention to the plight of those Scots whose employment made their residency patterns more fluid. Wallace, who had lived in Scotland all his life but was required to move to London because of a new job, began a 'Let Wallace Vote' campaign in January 2012. His campaign attracted media coverage both in England and Scotland, with Wallace arguing for 'the basic right to vote on the most important vote I will ever have in my life' (BBC 2012b).

A number of pro-Union politicians took up Wallace's cause. Former Scottish Conservative leader, David McLetchie, noted the franchise terms prioritised the rights of Republic of Ireland citizens, whose ancestors 'voted for independence and breaking away from the United Kingdom', and other EU and Commonwealth citizens living in Scotland over those born in Scotland who retained a 'substantial Scottish connection' (*Daily Record* 2012). Labour MSP Elaine Murray led a debate linked to Wallace's campaign in which she argued it was 'massively unfair' that Scots living in other parts of the UK, potentially for a short period of time before returning to Scotland, would not be able to vote in the referendum. She noted that Scots working outside Scotland were allowed to vote in UK general elections and suggested the franchise be extended to the Scottish diaspora in the rest of the UK. In both cases though, there was no attempt to define whether the terms of the inclusion would be based on birthplace alone or if ancestral Scots born in other parts of the UK would also be allowed to vote (BBC 2012b).

Responding on behalf of the Scottish Government, Bruce Crawford acknowledged 'Scotland as a whole benefits hugely from the fact that so many people with ties here, but who live elsewhere, maintain a deep and abiding interest in this country' (*Daily Record* 2012). He went on, however, to argue that the inclusion of Scots-born voters elsewhere in the UK would greatly increase the complexity of the referendum. He argued that evidence from the United Nations Human Rights Committee indicated that a franchise based on criteria other than residence could have implications regarding international recognition of the outcome and would also be considerably more expensive. Lord Jim Wallace, a former Liberal Democrat Deputy First Minister of Scotland, went further, raising the potential that if Anglo-Scots were given the vote, it might be resented by voters within the homeland, particularly those seeking independence who might feel their aspirations were being thwarted by others, including diaspora Scots, across the UK (BBC 2012b).

Lord Wallace's assertion does raise interesting questions about the changing nature of political relationships between Scots in England and those in Scotland. There was scant support for the inclusion of Anglo-Scots, as well as other Scottish diaspora in the UK and overseas, by both supporters and opponents of independence in Scotland. This would suggest Scots in Scotland of all political hues do not see Scottish diaspora in the UK as components of competing constructions of civic-orientated Scottish nationality. This may well be due to the subdued response from much of the Scottish diaspora across the rest of the UK to their exclusion. The lack of sustained campaigning or emotional appeals for inclusion in the referendum franchise would suggest that ties with the homeland are seen as predominantly cultural. Indeed, the most noteworthy dimension of James Wallace's campaign was the lack of support from the Anglo-Scottish community in England and elsewhere in the UK. Even after considerable media coverage, the petition he set up gained only 811 signatures before being closed six months later. Other campaigns, such as the one in Corby, have proven similarly unsuccessful in motivating the Anglo-Scots diaspora to agitate for the terms of the franchise to be extended.

It may also reflect the limited nature of engagement of the Scottish diaspora across the rest of the UK by the protagonists fighting the Scottish independence referendum. The Scottish First Minister, Alex Salmond, has made a number of keynote addresses to audiences in England, seeking to canvass support for independence by arguing it would build a new egalitarian relationship between Scotland and England while also creating opportunities for the English to radically redefine their political relationships with Westminster (see, for example, Salmond 2012a, 2012b). He has stressed that relations between an independent Scotland and England would be founded on a social rather than political union that drew on established networks of family and friends that underpinned shared British cultural links. It is noteworthy though that the post-independence relations with Northern Ireland and Wales have been frequently overlooked, thus giving some substance to those critics who have argued Scottish nationalists supporting independence view the Union in myopically Anglocentric terms (see Mycock 2012).

However, the remit of this social union has proven ambiguous and increasingly open to redefinition regarding the maintenance of economic, military and institutional ties with the rest of the UK after independence. Moreover, pro-independence supporters have not sought to engage directly with or address the concerns of the overlooked Anglo-Scottish diaspora, or even acknowledge their predicament or interests in the outcome of the independence referendum. This oversight may well reflect a pragmatic investment of political capital in those who can vote in the referendum in Scotland. But some Anglo-Scots have suggested that the decision to limit the referendum franchise to those resident in Scotland is underpinned by a desire by the pro-independence movement to create the most opportune conditions for a 'yes' vote as Scots living in other parts of the UK may well be more predisposed to see the benefit of the Union and thus vote 'no' if they were included in the franchise (Miller 2013). Such a view may well have some merit but fails to acknowledge fully the support of the UK Government in agreeing the electoral terms of the referendum.

The campaign supporting the maintenance of the Union, 'Better Together', has sought to establish some limited engagement with the Anglo-Scots diaspora in England. For example, Better Together held a campaign event in Corby in November 2012, with the support of local Conservatives, Labour and Liberal Democrats. Campaign activist Ross Macrae commented, 'We want people in Corby to get involved and talk to their family and friends, join the debate and help keep Scotland a part of the United Kingdom' (*Northamptonshire Telegraph* 2012). Better Together has also established a London branch. At its launch, Better Together chair, Alistair Darling, sought to address directly the Anglo-Scots diaspora, noting, 'you may not have a vote in the referendum, but you do have a voice. You have a right to have your opinion heard and you have a right to play your part in keeping Scotland in the UK.' Darling argued that the independence movement would not seek to engage with Scots in England because they had chosen to live in another part of the UK (Johnson 2013b), thus implicitly suggesting that the Scottish nationalists had rejected their Anglo-Scottish compatriots.

Scots in England appear to have been overlooked by both the pro- and anti-independence campaigns, even when compared to the overseas diaspora. This is somewhat surprising when considering the continued strength of links between Scotland and England and the extent to which diaspora communities are interwoven in the national lives of both nations. The traditional patterns of migration have been reversed over the past decade and the numbers of English moving to Scotland exceed those moving in the other direction. However, younger Scots move to England while older English citizens are heading north of the border, thus suggesting the 'brain drain' will not be stemmed completely in the near future. The implications of migration to England and other parts of the UK will continue to have significant political, social and economic ramifications for Scotland whatever the outcome of the referendum.

CONCLUSION

This chapter has sought to explore conceptual and empirical dynamics of intra-state diaspora when compared to their inter-state counterparts. It has revealed that the Anglo-Scottish diaspora is structured and operationalised in divergent ways from diasporas in other nation-states. The maintenance of strong connections with the homeland is an important factor in the reluctance to romanticise the Scottish nation and national identity by Anglo-Scottish diaspora. This ongoing contact, both physical and emotional, appears to prevent tendencies to adopt a myopically rose-tinted view of Scotland. Moreover, this reduced disconnection, often associated with inter-state forms of migration, means that issues of identity politics and minority rights have also proven to be desensitised. The absence of state or popular discrimination, persecution or exclusion, allied with the maintenance of universal forms of UK citizenship and Britishness that are not problematised by intra-state migration, would appear to encourage the layering and integrating of identities, particularly of second and subsequent generation Scots in England.

The Anglo-Scottish diaspora has maintained a significant presence, expressing pride in its Scottish heritage and identity. There is an affectionate if still sometimes patronising reception from English neighbours and friends. But the absence of a dynamic group identity or activism that demands public or state recognition at a national level either in England or Scotland has ensured that the Anglo-Scottish diaspora remain fragmented and largely inaudible. Those societies and associations that endure tend to focus on cultural rather than political expressions of Scottishness. Widespread political apathy among the Anglo-Scots diaspora does not appear to have been significantly redressed in the wake of recent constitutional reforms and emerging dilemmas associated with the independence referendum.

Some Scottish commentators have complained with some justification of ignorance in England regarding the referendum (see, for example, Hassan 2012). Many politicians and media commentators in England appear ill-informed and disengaged, unable or unwilling to grasp the importance of the independence referendum in determining the future of the UK. Indeed, a sizeable contingent, particularly on the political right, appears more concerned about relations with the European Union than Scotland. But to dismiss all those living in England as being oblivious to the potential ramifications of the independence referendum can also be considered patronising. Many people in England and across the UK, including Scots diaspora communities, are keen to engage and care passionately about the outcome but find themselves denied significant opportunities to contribute to the referendum debate or to be consulted about the potential implications of independence.

So far at least, protagonists on both sides have been guilty of running often insular and exclusory campaigns, rarely looking southwards to engage with the disenfranchised Scottish diaspora in England and the rest of the UK. Those supporting Scottish independence have sought instead to exemplify differences in socio-economic, political and cultural values between citizens in Scotland and England, arguing Scottish society is nationally bound by a 'common weal' that is more Europhilic, communitarian, welfarist and egalitarian when compared to their English counterparts (Salmond 2013; Sturgeon 2013). Such claims lack evidential substance, as research indicates that divergence between English and Scottish citizens is negligible (Curtice and Ormston 2011). The notion of a national 'common weal' that binds Scottish society also rejects the potential that Scottish nationality is transnational, suggesting UK-based diaspora do not retain, adhere to or conduct distinctive Scottish national values and attitudes within their new host nation. Conversely, those seeking to defend the Union are guilty of assuming that most Anglo-Scots support their cause without recognising that devolution has problematised citizenship for national diaspora communities within the UK. There is a clear need for both campaigns to acknowledge the dilemmas and interests of the Scottish diaspora in the rest of the UK and to develop policies that address potential changes in citizenship in the event of independence or the maintenance of the Union.

The absence of a sustained campaign to extend the referendum franchise to Anglo-Scots would appear to suggest most are either resigned to their exclusion and/or accept the principle of residency in determining the electoral register in Scotland. It would be short-sighted though to assume that the Anglo-Scottish diaspora in England will remain fractured or politically docile. The potential implications of the Scottish independence referendum for the UK-based Scottish diaspora are significant. There has, as yet though, been a lack of emphasis or developed thinking from those seeking independence on the citizenship status of Scottish diaspora who would have it radically altered with regard to the homeland. If Scotland votes for independence, they could find like other 'internal diaspora' in Eastern Europe that their citizenship and identity are redefined without their input and they find themselves formally separated from the majority national group.

The SNP-led Scottish Government (2013) has stated its intention to define the precise terms of entitlement of Scottish citizenship on 'independence day'. However, a draft constitution published by the SNP stated citizenship would be determined by residency but also include 'every person whose place of birth was in Scotland or either of whose parents was born in Scotland' (SNP 2002: 10). If such terms are realised in the wake of a vote for independence, most of the Anglo-Scottish diaspora would be eligible to become Scottish citizens – if the Edinburgh and London governments agreed to extend the principle of dual citizenship in a similar fashion to arrangements with the Republic of Ireland. Agreeing terms of dual citizenship could prove controversial though, and UK Home Secretary Theresa May has suggested that reciprocal arrangements underpinned by dual forms of citizenship are not assured (Maddox 2013). But even if terms are agreed, dual citizenship arrangements could still stimulate tensions between Scotland and its UK-based diaspora. If the terms are too inclusive, Anglo-Scots could be resented by their homeland counterparts if they are perceived to exploit differences in welfare provision between an independent Scotland and the rest of the UK or are seen to be health or higher education 'tourists'. Alternatively, restrictions imposed by an independent Scotland regarding the eligibility to some social rights could see resentment build among the Anglo-Scottish diaspora if they believe they have become 'second-class citizens'.

A vote to remain in the Union may also stimulate tensions that could facilitate a strengthening of Anglo-Scottish diaspora group cohesion and identity. It is likely that, in the wake of a 'no' vote, Westminster will seek to significantly extend the devolution of powers to the Scottish Government, further fracturing universal forms of citizenship. Anglo-Scots may become increasingly vocal about growing disparities in social rights available in Scotland if the Scottish Government seeks actively to exclude them. Devolution and the independence referendum have also revealed questions about the legitimacy of Scots in Anglo-British political life, highlighting the possibility that perceptions of Anglo-Scots as an 'invisible ethnicity' may well be faltering. For example, during the Labour party's period in UK government accusations were prevalent among the right-wing press that a Scottish 'mafia' or 'raj' led by Tony Blair and Gordon Brown now governed England (see Watson 2005). Research suggests that a growing number of people in England have also become increasingly resentful towards Scotland, arguing that English taxpayers are funding more generous welfare settlements north of the border (Institute of Public Policy Research 2013), and some opinion polls suggest a majority in England now support Scottish independence (Curtice et al. 2013).

The tone of some commentary in the London media has adopted an increasingly strident anti-Scottish tone. One commentator has gone as far as to suggest that the English hold a vote on whether

Scotland should leave the Union, adding 'many Scots don't much like the English' (Heffer 2013). This would suggest that 'Scotophobia' has the potential to become a more prominent feature of political and wider public discourse in England, regardless of the outcome of the independence referendum. It is clear that, although the Anglo-Scottish diaspora lacks structure and agency, the scale and scope of potential changes in their political, social and cultural environment in the wake of the Scottish independence referendum could finally provide the momentum to encourage a more visible identity and audible voice.

8

Scottish Diasporic Identity in Europe

Murray Stewart Leith and Duncan Sim

INTRODUCTION

Research on the Scottish diaspora(s) within Europe is not well developed but the Scots in Europe nevertheless represent an interesting group for study. Firstly, there have been long-term and close connections between Scotland and Europe for centuries, with significant numbers of Scottish traders and merchants settling in northern European countries. As well as trade, there were also academic links with European universities, and political alliances, notably the 'Auld Alliance' with France (Ichijo 2004).

Secondly, there was a significant wave of emigration to Europe following the accession of the UK to the European Union (then the EEC) in 1973. Business links have been developed, through North Sea oil and EU-related organisations like Scotland Europa, while there are also Scottish MEPs and officials linked to the European Parliament. The present SNP Government advocates a policy of 'independence in Europe', suggesting that Europe is crucially important for their vision of a future Scotland.

Thirdly, the result of this relatively recent migration is a group of Scots within the EU which essentially comprises a 'lived' diaspora, being born and/or educated in Scotland prior to moving to Europe. There is a general absence of the 'ancestral' diaspora more commonly found in North America or Australasia. As a result, a fourth aspect of the diaspora in Europe is the relatively recent establishment of the Scottish diaspora organisations – Caledonian societies, Highland games and dance groups – which are generally to be found elsewhere in the world.

This chapter describes the origins of the Scottish diasporas in mainland Europe and uses recent research to explore the nature of these diasporas and how they relate to diasporas elsewhere in the world.

SCOTLAND AND EUROPE

Prior to the Union with England in 1707, Scotland was a significant European trading country, with most of its activity focused around the North Sea. As early as the twelfth century, wool and hides were exported, primarily to the Netherlands and France, and by the seventeenth century, grain, coal and cloth were being exported to Rotterdam and other ports (Lynch 1992). There was also a sizeable trade in herring to Scandinavia, ships then returning with cargoes of Swedish iron (Smout 1985). At the same time, Scotland imported brandy and wine from Bordeaux (Murdoch 2007), timber from Norway, consumer goods from the Netherlands and rye and flax from Poland (Ichijo 2004). Some ships returning from Holland carried pantiles as ballast, later to be used on the roofs of many Scottish east coast towns (Sked 2005).

This extensive trade led to a considerable Scottish presence in many north European countries. Emigration to Poland was recorded from the late fifteenth century onwards, reaching its peak in 1621, when there were about 30,000 Scots in Poland (Ichijo 2004). The commercial links with Scandinavia, the Baltic and the Low Countries led to the growth of Scottish mercantile communities in Rotterdam, Veere, Copenhagen, Gothenburg, Hamburg, Bremen, Danzig and Königsberg (Devine 2011), while Brock (1999) refers to a Scottish presence in Malmö and Bergen. Devine also estimates that the Dutch marine employed 1,500 Scots in 1672, while Scots were also active in the Dutch East India Company.

A second important connection was the intellectual one and significant numbers of Scots studied at European universities, particularly in France and the Netherlands. Leiden University was founded in 1575 and Scots went there to study law, divinity and medicine. Between 1575 and 1800, 1,460 Scottish students matriculated at Leiden (Smout 1995), while others studied at Franeker, Groningen and Utrecht. Graduates from Leiden helped to found the Medical School at Edinburgh (Guthrie 1946). In France, the University of Paris had seventeen or eighteen Scottish rectors prior to the Reformation (Broadie 1990). John Knox himself, of course, studied in Geneva.

Thirdly, significant numbers of Scots entered military service abroad. In the sixteenth century, Scots soldiers fought for the kings of both Denmark and Sweden (Ichijo 2004), while in the fifteenth and sixteenth centuries, Scots acted as mercenary soldiers in the Low Countries and in France. During the Thirty Years' War (1618–48), many Scots fought in the Scots Brigade and subsequently settled in the Netherlands (Harper 2003). By 1745 there were 5,000 men in the Scots Brigade (Devine 2011) and it was common for men to move between military service in the Low Countries and in the British Army. Military alliances were also hugely significant and perhaps the most famous of these was the 'Auld Alliance' between Scotland and France, first signed in 1295.

These European connections are still evident today, for example in the presence of Scots' Kirks in places like Paris, Brussels, Rotterdam and Amsterdam, a total of twelve Church of Scotland congregations in all. Many of these kirks are long established; for example, by 1700 the Rotterdam church had around 1,000 communicants and the 'merchants and seafarers who belonged to it were well placed to benefit from Rotterdam's emergence as a vibrant Atlantic and Asian trade centre with global connections' (Devine 2011: 28).

The European connection has enabled a number of writers to claim that Scotland is a particularly Europe-focused nation. Thus:

Scots were not a remote, insular people sitting on the fringe of civilisation, but a cosmopolitan people exceptionally prone to emigrate in order to seek their fortunes in another country, and with a reputation for competence whether their trade was learning, killing or buying and selling ... More than England, Scotland was a European country, more at ease in, and less suspicious of, other cultures. Possibly this legacy left the Scots less afraid of modern Europe than the English appear to be at the present day. (Smout 1995: 116)

Things tended to change after 1707 when entry to the British Empire led to a trading focus on other parts of the world, notably the Americas.

While the Scottish–European connection therefore had a very long history, and while it led to substantial Scots settlement within many European countries, these diasporas appear not to have survived intact. It is inevitable that its members would have intermarried with local people, their children would cease to be fluent in English (or Scots), and over time the Scottish connection would have been lost. In exploring the present diaspora within Europe, therefore, we are essentially dealing with migrants from Scotland in the later twentieth century and this raises the question of whether we can consider it a genuine diaspora.

POST-WAR MIGRATION

Following the Second World War, emigration from Scotland was significant, with 753,000 Scots leaving between 1951 and 1981 (Devine 2011); of these, 45 per cent went to England, almost all the remainder moving overseas. Given Scotland's total population was around 5 million, the loss was significant.

It seems highly likely that, following the UK's entry into the European Union (then the EEC) in 1973, many Scots would be attracted to jobs in Europe, although it is very difficult to disaggregate migration statistics which are generally compiled at the UK level. Certainly, the discovery of North Sea oil and associated investment by European companies like Shell and Elf led to movement of workers between the north-east of Scotland and Europe, while there was an increasing Scottish presence in Brussels itself. Mitchell (1995), for example, describes the establishment of Scotland Europa, a lobbying office in Brussels representing Scottish interests. Following devolution in 1999, it moved into the newly opened Scotland House, the Brussels office of the Scottish Executive (Sloat 2000).

Estimates of the current numbers of Scots living in Europe are difficult to obtain. Sriskandarajah and Drew (2006) compiled estimates of the numbers of UK citizens living abroad at that time, on a country-by-country basis, and they show that there were 1.66 million UK citizens living within the EU but outside the UK. Assuming that the Scottish proportion was similar to their proportion within the UK, then we may estimate that there were 150,000 Scots living within the EU. Some later figures were compiled by Carr and Cavanagh (2009) for selected countries, and using a similar measure of proportionality to estimate the Scottish element; their figures are broadly in line with the earlier study.

So it seems reasonable to estimate a European Scottish population of around 150,000 and, importantly, this 'diaspora' is essentially one made up of individuals who have been born and/or brought up and educated in Scotland. In this sense, it is a *lived* diaspora in Rutherford's (2009) phrase, as its members have first-hand experience of living in Scotland. It contrasts with the Scottish diaspora in North America, which is primarily an *ancestral* one, spread over several generations.

This difference suggests that the diasporas might function in quite different ways. We know, for example, that in North America and Australasia, the relationship with Scotland is strong but often based on heritage and sentiment. In England, the Scottish diaspora appears to be weakening (McCarthy 2007b, Leith and Sim 2012). But what about the Scots in Europe? If this is a 'lived' diaspora, then its relationship with Scotland might be expected to be closer and less sentimental than the 'ancestral' diaspora within North America. And in contrast to North America, how might a Scottish diaspora function within non-English-speaking countries?

This chapter draws on research carried out by the authors within three northern European countries in 2011 involving interviews with a range of diaspora Scots. It also draws on research carried out by others, notably Hesse (2011a, 2011b). These research studies are discussed below.

THE CURRENT SCOTTISH DIASPORA IN EUROPE

The authors' research explored issues of identity and the continuing connection with Scotland within diasporas in France, Belgium and the Netherlands. Initial contacts were made through Scottish social organisations, Scots kirks, international schools and institutions where Scots were known to work, as well as diaspora blogs and websites. This led to a snowballed sample of interviewees, comprising 40 individuals in France, 11 in Belgium and 19 in the Netherlands – 70 in total. Interviews lasted around 45 minutes and included questions on family history, identity, continuing links to Scotland and personal future plans.

Of the 70 interviewees, 58 (83%) were born in Scotland, the remaining 12 all having a Scottish connection; only five could be considered 'ancestral' Scots. The average age was 49 and the average time spent abroad was 19 years. This suggests a group who moved around age 30 from Scotland in order to work in Europe and a range of jobs were specified, including pharmaceuticals, computing, engineering and science research. Three people were ministers of religion, while others were lawyers, teachers or accountants, and four people were involved in hospitality and tourism-related business. A significant number (17 in all) were working in jobs associated with either European institutions (Parliament, Commission, Council of Europe) or with British embassies. Britain's expanded role within the EU since the 1970s has therefore opened up job opportunities in Europe.

A sense of identity

As most members of the diaspora were native-born Scots, we anticipated that they would retain a strong sense of identity and this proved to be the case, with most interviewees able to talk at length about the importance of their Scottishness. Many people reflected on markers of identity such as accent, education, culture and even tartan.

It's a pride and you kind of look for it when you are outside as well. I look for it now more than I ever did, you know when you hear a Scottish accent, you do get this pull and I think I am getting pulled back now. That's why I don't consider myself resident here. (Female, 31, France)

Being Scottish is being born and raised there, thus having a deep and genuine appreciation of its entire culture and language and not being able to conceal it from anyone whom you meet – usually because of the very distinct accent! It probably also means you've got at least one tartan item of clothing in your wardrobe (often a kilt) which you feel proud to wear at any gathering. It's 'comforting' to touch base with our roots every once in a while … perhaps it's an inherent human need for stability or security in knowing who one really is at the 'roots' and standing still for one moment in an ever-changing world and feeling happy with who one really is. (Female, 42, France)

It means to wear the sun in your heart and thus never worry that it's rainy outside. It means eating haggis every week and loving the poems of Rabbie Burns. It means caring about Alex Salmond, even if you disagree with him, because he is our Prime Minister more so than David Cameron. It means identifying to the Scottish flag rather than the Union Jack. It means being happy in Scotland and caring about Scotland because it's your home (Male, 30, France)

It was recognised by many that their sense of Scottishness had been affected by time spent living abroad, with the result that they had tended to adopt a slightly sentimental view of their homeland and their identity.

In my experience, one is far more Scottish when not in Scotland. I do go back fairly often, and I went to one of those souvenir shops and got a Scotland cap, Scotland flag and this and that and the guy said, 'You live abroad, don't you?!' (Male, 41, France)

It creates images for me which are, I'm afraid to say, a wee bit like the Scottish bull standing with his horns in the hay. You never see it in practice. The Scottish music and various things like that. Highland Games, tossing the caber ... Remember, I have been outside of Scotland since I was 20ish so I actually have a slightly romantic image of Scotland and Scottishness. (Male, 70, France)

Several interviewees reflected on the extent to which they felt British or Scottish, and a range of views were expressed.

I would always say I am Scottish, am willing to accept British. I do feel that European is a good description too, having lived in Scotland, Ireland and Netherlands. I never accept being described as English. (Female, 64, Netherlands)

I feel a mix of Scottish, British and European. I also feel part French because I feel I have roots here now [but] my Scottish identity is most important to me. (Female, 42, France)

I would always write down Scottish and think, 'Oh gosh, there isn't an option, do I have to put British, really do I have to?' (Female, 33, France)

In this context, we asked interviewees to be more explicit about their sense of identity, based on the format derived by Moreno (1988). Almost everybody responded and the results are shown in Table 8.1 below; they show that by far the largest grouping (52 people or 74.2%) placed their Scottishness as being greater than or at least equal to their sense of being British. But a sizeable minority also expressed a European identity, reflecting the length of time they had lived in mainland Europe.

Table 8.1: Identity: the 'Moreno' question

Identity	No.	%
Scottish, not British	20	28.6
More Scottish than British	14	20
Scottish and British	18	25.7
More British than Scottish	2	2.8
British not Scottish	1	1.4
Scottish and French/Belgian/Dutch	3	4.3
Scottish and European	9	12.9
Other	2	2.8
Missing values	*1*	*1.4*

Some researchers have noted how frequently individuals explain their sense of a Scottish identity in negative terms, by defining themselves as 'not being English' (Devine and Logue 2002). Our interviewees were no exception, suggesting that this was related in part to the different ways in which Scots and English people were viewed in many European countries.

> On the one hand, part of my brain feels that national identity is constructed. But of course, you can't escape from it. It is something that's there, so for me, I don't think that I'm British. I definitely feel that I'm Scottish. And I do think that a big part of Scottish identity is not being English.
> Q: That's quite a negative thing, isn't it?
> It is. But in Brussels, if I'm speaking French, someone can always tell that I'm Anglophone and will say, 'Oh, you're English'. And I say, 'No, I'm actually Scottish'. And I suppose it doesn't really matter if they think I'm English. But I'm not English and so I have to correct them. (Female, 24, Belgium)

> The local people here don't speak French – they speak Alsatian and they can relate to the Scottish/English thing because it's like the French/Alsatian thing. If you tell them you're English, they will probably go 'mmhmm' but if you tell them you're Scottish, you'll get a warmer welcome. (Male, 49, France)

Scottish organisations

In the older ancestral diasporas of North America and Australasia, Scottish identity is frequently expressed and maintained through a range of social organisations and activities. Indeed, diaspora Scots have a reputation for establishing Scottish societies across the globe. Some are focused on music, dancing and the arts; some, like Burns clubs, may have a more literary focus; others are purely social in character. There is often a romanticism about many of them. As Finlayson (1987: 95) has suggested:

> There is no difficulty whatsoever in assembling a room full of sentimental Australians, Canadians, North and South Americans or Africans for a Burns Supper or a St Andrew's Day dinner. Their hearts are, for that moment, in the Highlands, though their physical presence is in Sydney, Toronto, Boston, Rio or Nairobi. Their emotions, rallied by haggis, whisky, sherry trifle and a piper

in full ceremonials, conjure the cry of the whaup in the heather and sunsets over Arran and the Western Isles.

Such organisations may not therefore encourage a view of Scotland itself which is accurate or realistic but they have an important social function in gathering together people with a Scottish heritage or connection.

In America, many Scottish organisations date from the late eighteenth and nineteenth centuries. But in Europe, with its 'lived' and relatively new diaspora, Scottish organisations are of very recent origin. Hesse (2011a, 2011b) notes that Scottish festivals and Highland Games were virtually unknown in Europe until the 1990s but he estimates that there are now over 130 Highland Games held annually on the European mainland. The trigger for this enthusiasm, he suggests, was the release in 1995 of the Hollywood films *Braveheart* and *Rob Roy*. Other Scottish groups are also of recent origin. The St Andrew's Society of the Netherlands, for example, dates from 1985, and many of the European branches and affiliates of the Royal Scottish Country Dance Society date from the 1970s onwards.

It may be inferred that these recent developments are a reflection of the growing numbers of Scots working and living in Europe but, in fact, membership of such organisations among our interviewees was very variable. Some Scots had embraced activities like country dancing very enthusiastically, often having had experience of dancing back in Scotland.

Shortly after I moved here and started work [there was] an email about the Scottish country dancing group and I thought, 'Oh why not, I can dance, it's a way to meet people' and I did enjoy it. When I was in Scotland, I did Scottish country dancing until I was eighteen and I danced in the Edinburgh Tattoos. I had a break for about ten years but I was quite happy to start back again. (Female, 31, France)

The dancing is a big part of my life here and I've loved dancing since I arrived here. I met my husband through Breton dancing. I later moved on to all sorts of traditional French dancing, and to Scottish dancing. It has been one of the main ways in which I have met Scottish people and retained contact with Scottish ideas and thought. (Female, 56, France)

But many Scots believed that it was more appropriate to integrate within the communities in which they were now living, rather than joining diaspora societies.

Maybe I'm a bit snobbish and shun these organisations but I kind of wanted to be where I am rather than harping back. If I want to be in Scotland, I will go back to Scotland for a holiday. I have never really been interested in reminiscing with our regular Scottish faces just for the sake of it. (Female, 37, France)

I wanted to integrate completely in France so I avoided British organisations. I have not joined the Caledonian Society or the France Scottish. (Female, 52, France)

I didn't feel the need to find out other Scots. I think the point of living in Amsterdam is that you meet everybody, from all different nationalities. That's the fun part, you learn about so many different people. So why stick to one group, just because they're Scottish? (Female, 30s, Netherlands)

One of the striking aspects of many Scottish diaspora organisations in Europe is their domination by non-Scots. In North America, for example, membership of organisations tends to involve those with a connection to Scotland, albeit may exist over several generations. But in parts of Europe there seems to be a widespread interest in Scotland as noted earlier (Hesse 2011a, 2011b) and this has manifested itself in significant numbers of non-Scots joining Scottish diaspora organisations.

Only four including myself are Scottish; the rest are French. A few are interested in Scotland. Most love dancing and in particular Scottish country dancing, because it's sophisticated, complicated and a challenge physically and mentally. (Female, 59, France)

The funny thing is that we don't have that many Scots. There's only about three of us in the group. The rest are Danish, German, Italian, Hungarians. For some people it's a way of learning English because we always teach in English. And a lot of them have done folk dances in other countries and they find there are a lot of similarities. (Female, 60, Belgium)

At a typical event, if there were fifty people there, I would say maybe three Scots. The rest are anything – English, American, mostly Dutch.
Q: So why would they come along? What would be the attraction?
I think because it's unique. Scottish dancing is unique. And it's also quite colourful if the guys come in their kilts.
Q: So they'll buy kilts?
Oh yes, they'll buy kilts, they'll turn up in the full rig, you know, for the Ball. The ceilidhs are obviously more casual but still kilts. But for the Ball, they've all got the full gear on and there's Dutch voices everywhere. (Male, 40s, Netherlands)

It's a weird thing. They think it's Scotland but it's not really – it's their perception of Scotland ... But there's not many Scots. In America, it's much more roots and ancestral connections, isn't it? (Female, 60, Belgium)

Hesse (2011b) describes the activities of the Red Rose of Lochbuie Pipe Band which, despite its name, is based in the Dutch town of Rijswijk and none of whose members have any Scottish roots whatsoever. Yet the band travelled to Scotland for the 2009 Year of Homecoming and took part in the clan parade up Edinburgh's Royal Mile. Hesse believes that there is an apparent interest in 'Celtic' culture, with the Scots viewed as guardians of a European 'Celtic' past (whatever that may be) and as an embodiment of an attractive rebellious spirit. He suggests that many European countries have turned against their own cultural heritage (sometimes because of its association with Fascism) and so have embraced an alternative and available culture, which may be seen as somehow nobler and more attractive. Our research findings here could certainly be seen to support Hesse's conclusions.

For many Scots in Europe, therefore, diaspora organisations were perhaps not necessarily viewed as important in maintaining a sense of identity and interviewees spoke of significant informal networks. Several had organised their own Burns Night celebrations involving friends and neighbours and this had been a way firstly of celebrating 'Scottishness' and secondly of transmitting Scottish culture to non-Scots.

When I started here, because there was such a large number of Scottish people – colleagues – we had our own Burns Night. (Female, 64, France)

There is an English-speaking community in Alsace and, as part of that each year, we organise a Burns Supper in this village for 200 people and a Celtic evening which is a mixture of Scottish and Irish. We have a mixture of live musicians, whisky-tasting and so on. More than half of the people that come to that are French. (Male, 49, France)

I do Burns Nights myself, one for people at work and one for a group of friends, because Dutch friends all love haggis and Burns tradition. We do the whole formal thing, we do the Address to the Haggis, we do the Toast to the Lassies, somebody does 'Holy Willie's Prayer' or 'Tam o' Shanter' and they're all Dutch people and they enjoy it. (Female, 40, Netherlands)

There were also numerous other occasions when Scots working abroad socialised and some interviewees in Paris were members of a group of women who met regularly as 'Lassies who Lunch'.

Finally, an important role was played by university alumni organisations which have European branches and which provide a means whereby graduates can keep in touch with each other. In a number of cities, there are also Scots kirks, part of the Church of Scotland community, which have been important, particularly for newly arrived migrants from Scotland.

I am a member of the Scots Kirk in Paris. When I first got here, I was desperate to meet people first of all and I couldn't speak French properly so I wanted to speak English but it was having the Scottish connections at the Kirk that made me continue to go to that church. (Female, 29, France)

The Scots Kirk ... it's just a nice place to go and listen to Scottish people. (Female, 33, France)

LOOKING TO THE LONG TERM

Within many diasporas, particularly those resulting from forced movement or exile, there is often a continuing belief that, one day, individuals might be able to return to their country of origin, and this 'myth of return' is powerfully held (Anwar 1979, Safran 1991). When members of a diaspora have voluntarily migrated, then return is much more realistic, although its likelihood may diminish through the generations; second and third generation members of diasporas will have a much hazier knowledge of family homelands. The Scottish diaspora within Europe, however, being mainly first generation migrants, may realistically think about a return to Scotland, with the likelihood of such a return being dependent primarily on personal circumstances.

Key to such circumstances may be the position of children of the diaspora. Of our 70 interviewees, 45 had children, many of whom had been born in mainland Europe and were being brought up and educated there. Although children would have had a strong awareness of their parents' origins and heritage, researchers have suggested that the children of migrants sometimes experience difficulties in integrating where there are clear cultural or linguistic differences between the country of origin and the country of settlement (Alba 2005). They therefore find themselves caught between two cultures and may try to secure a distinctive identity of their own, possibly an amalgam of their own and their parents' cultures (for example, Walter et al. 2002, Ullah 1990). We therefore asked interviewees about their children's sense of identity and the extent to which they might influence a decision on a return to Scotland.

In most cases, interviewees believed that their children felt primarily Scottish, although they would also be aware of living in another European country.

My children consider themselves both Scottish and French, but that's because of how we've educated them. We think it's important for them to have a sense of both cultures, since they are perfectly bilingual coming from a Scots mother and French father. (Female, 42, France)

Visits back to Scotland also provided opportunities to reinforce identity and some interviewees spoke of their children's enthusiasm for buying kilts or Scottish football and rugby material.

My son bought a 'Wallace Lives in Me' T-shirt when he was in Scotland this year and he said to me, 'Mummy, what do I buy with my money from Granny, for my Birthday', and I said, 'You buy what you think is right for you – it's your money, you decide'. And he said, 'I am going to buy a kilt' and he came back with a kilt on. A Royal Stewart kilt, a Wallace Lives in Me T-shirt, a Celtic cross and he was just really proud. (Female, 45, France)

At the Stirling Highland Games, there was a stand, and he pointed at one and I think it was a Gordon tartan, it was a very green one, and I thought it was a lovely colour ... Back in Paris, I said 'Leo, where's your kilt?' and he said, 'Oh, I need my kilt, I am going to school and I need to speak in front of the class and I need to take an object from the house and tell them what it is, so I am taking my kilt'. (Female, 47, France)

There was also a strong belief that children needed to be provided with a strong sense of identity, so they did not become 'rootless' or caught between cultures. One interviewee feared that her son would suffer in this way.

My children are Scottish and my son, who is four, understands that for him Scotland is home and we are in Strasbourg temporarily. I hope that he is not going to become a 'Eurokid' with no sense of identity. We hope that regular trips home to see grandparents, cousins, aunts, etc. will reinforce that. (Female, 40, France)

Thus children of interviewees did indeed appear to have a strong sense of Scottish identity and even those who had spent the bulk of their lives 'abroad' had embraced some elements of it. Some children, after leaving school, had actually moved to Scotland to attend university, although it was unclear if this would necessarily have led to a permanent move 'home'.

Many of our interviewees had thought about returning to Scotland. Continuing contact with family was important and some people still owned property in Scotland. Many people believed that they would eventually return, possibly after retirement.

Even though my kids are growing up here, I want to go back eventually. I don't want to grow old in a country where my mother tongue isn't spoken. I want to die in Scotland. That may sound bizarre, but it's important. You see so many people who've lived abroad, they've lived in an expat world and they get to retirement and they don't know what to do. (Male, 40s, Belgium)

But others recognised that moving back might be difficult.

My mother would love me to go home. She'd love me to be round the corner. But I think what happens is that you go away and there comes a time in your career that you can't go back. I think when you've been away as long as me, well ... (Female, 40, Netherlands)

So the likelihood of a return to Scotland appeared to vary across our sample. Younger interviewees stated that they would return to Scotland after they stopped working. But when the moment of retirement actually arrived, the position was sometimes complicated if their children had settled and married and themselves had children. A return to Scotland then became less likely. And there was a definite awareness of how difficult a return might be after a long period of time away.

CONCLUSIONS

Although the precise size of the Scottish diaspora in mainland Europe is unknown, our earlier estimate of 150,000 people may be a reasonable figure. This group is primarily made up of UK citizens born in Scotland and so this is an essentially 'lived' diaspora, in Rutherford's (2009) phrase. There may be some ancestral Scots with a heritage stretching back to earlier centuries but such individuals appear to be almost impossible to identify. Most migrants to Europe have moved in the post-war era and this has led to the relatively recent foundation of a number of Scottish organisations. In exploring the nature of the Scottish diaspora in Europe, we have concentrated firstly on a continuing sense of a Scottish identity – and whether this is being transmitted to children; secondly on the nature of the Scottish organisations; and thirdly on the question of whether interviewees might one day return to Scotland.

Here, we consider these issues further, while also reflecting on the nature of the Scottish presence in European countries and whether or not it functions as a diaspora in the generally accepted sense of the word.

A sense of identity?

A key characteristic of diasporas is a strong sense of identity, albeit that the identity is one that may be 'hyphenated'. In America, for example, Waters (1990) found that individuals constructed their ethnic identification using knowledge of their ancestral background. Many young people explored their ethnic roots, while simultaneously being patriotic Americans. Being American was thus a primary identity, about which people rarely had to think. But being a hyphenated American was a way of differentiating oneself from other Americans and giving oneself a more individual identity. Thus individuals were increasingly proud to be Irish-Americans, Italian-Americans and so on.

Most Scots with whom we were in contact as part of our research were first generation migrants and so most still regarded themselves as 'Scottish' or 'British' to differing degrees; many also acknowledged that there was now a European dimension to who they were. It was clear, however, that some people found it difficult to transmit their identity to their children, some of whom embraced a range of cultures, and some of whom were adopting perhaps a more international outlook.

There is research on the identities of second generation migrants, for example the cultural and identity difficulties encountered by the children of Irish migrants to the UK (Walter et al. 2002), Scottish migrants to England (Leith and Sim 2012) and English migrants to Scotland (Kiely et al. 2005). But, although cultural differences may lead to confused feelings of identity within the second generation, nevertheless in these cases migration has been within the context of the British Isles and there were no linguistic differences to contend with. But such differences do, of course, occur in a European context. Children will learn Dutch or French or German at school and in social situations. As they grow up, many will form relationships and have families and decide to settle on the European mainland, although there were significant numbers of second generation migrants who chose to return to Scotland to attend university. Scots migrants then find themselves in a difficult position, facing a choice between retiring to their homeland where they may still have family connections, or remaining in mainland Europe close to their children.

We have this big dilemma at the moment about what we're going to do. We never thought we'd be here for secondary education but my daughter started secondary school today. And now we're really dithering. My parents are getting older and if we don't go back to Scotland soon, they'll be too old to enjoy the kids ... We're thinking about building a house in Scotland to give the children some roots. (Female, 40s, Belgium)

Thus the transmission of a sense of Scottish identity to the second generation was variable and the career trajectories of that generation were likely to influence issues of family return to Scotland.

Diaspora organisations

Although it had been anticipated that Scottish organisations would play an important part in identity maintenance for Scots living in mainland Europe, this did not turn out to be entirely the case. Some individuals used informal networking while others did not see such organisations as particularly important to them. At one level, the Scottish diaspora organisations were significant not only as a link to the Scottish homeland but as a forum in which members of the diaspora would be able to use their own language. In fact, such societies were attended by other English speakers.

> I am pleased to report that some members have claimed that the group has been a lifeline – in particular for one English woman who was unhappy here. But her main interest was the dancing and the fact that we spoke English; she herself knows little about Scotland. (Female, 56, France)

But as we have noted above, many diaspora bodies – dance groups, Highland Games and other organisations – were dominated by non-Scots. Such individuals might be referred to as 'affinity' Scots in Rutherford's (2009) phrase. These are individuals who make a connection to Scotland, perhaps as a result of a tourist visit or contact with other diaspora members, but without themselves having a direct family link to the country. Hesse (2011b) suggests that this group is a large and significant one, made large by the easy availability of what he terms the Scottish 'dreamscape'. This dreamscape is appropriated because it is easily available and accessible and, importantly, because it has an innocent quality, a kind of moral integrity which Hesse suggests is important in a post-colonial context. The size of this 'affinity' diaspora has been estimated at 40–50 million people worldwide (quoted in Rutherford 2009).

A true diaspora?

Definitions of diaspora vary but there is a general acceptance that a significant element of a diasporic identity relates to nostalgia and a collective mythology of homeland, perhaps best described as being an 'imagined' past. There may be an associated idealisation of a return to the homeland and a continuing relationship with it. Perhaps a real diaspora should exist over at least two generations or needs to be truly intergenerational to be considered as such.

But the Scottish diaspora in mainland Europe appears to be different in a number of ways. First, it is primarily a first generation diaspora, comprising in the main individuals who have moved from Scotland since the early 1970s. There are undoubtedly descendants of earlier Scottish migrants but they are generally invisible and there is an absence of an 'ancestral' diaspora which comes with historical longevity and which characterises the Scottish diaspora in North America. Second, because most of our interviewees were Scots-born, many were able to speak of returning to Scotland after retirement, and many still had families in Scotland or owned property. So, for many European Scots, migration may not be permanent and return may be a realistic prospect. That said, of course, return may depend on other factors such as the decisions made by children. Thirdly, the fact that most of those interviewed were first generation Scots meant that they had a generally realistic view of their homeland and had no cause to adopt a different representation of it, although those who had been away from Scotland for a long time did acknowledge heightened feelings of nostalgia.

Of particular interest is the domination of Scottish organisations by non-Scots, as this has perhaps affected the ability of such organisations to be an effective focus for the Scottish diaspora and to assist with identity maintenance. So European Scots may not have the diaspora consciousness which seems to exist among expatriate Scots in other parts of the world. While the Scots in mainland Europe appear to form a diaspora, they do not necessarily conform to its usually accepted characteristics.

9

The Gaelic Diaspora in North America

Michael Newton

INTRODUCTION

The Scots who emigrated to North America were never a homogeneous group: the diaspora consists of distinct streams carrying linguistic and cultural features specific to their place and moment in time. Neither the source communities in Scotland nor the transplanted communities in North America have been static but have developed certain aspects of their inherited traditions, embraced certain internal innovations, resisted certain impositions and been subject to certain assimilative pressures. The ways in which the encounters between these different lineages of Scottish tradition have been portrayed, and the ways in which contests over the authority to define tradition and authenticity have been negotiated, reveal much about who has access to power and privilege, especially in formal institutions.

Scottish Gaels – the native population of the Highlands and Western Isles – are a distinctive group within the diaspora and, in particular periods, formed a significant proportion of Scottish emigrants. Although there are features which distinguish particular communities (religious affiliation, dialect, variations of vernacular culture, leadership), Gaels perceived themselves as a cohesive ethnic group in Scotland who contrasted with the people of the Lowlands. Self-perceptions of Highland distinctiveness continued in North America for as long as the Gaelic language has survived (Newton 2011). The question of language is central, for it is integral to other aspects of Gaelic cultural expression.

Some Gaelic emigrants in the eighteenth and nineteenth centuries – often from the same locale – reconstituted themselves as cohesive communities forming a strong sense of identity and rootedness to new territory in North America, at least for the first few generations. These North American *Gàidhealtachdan* later experienced large-scale outmigration triggered by economic factors. For many families whose ancestors settled those areas, the sense of belonging to Glengarry (Ontario) or Antigonish County (Nova Scotia), for example, is stronger and more immediate than the sense of being Scottish in origin.

There is a recurring motif that diasporic communities are more conservative than those of the original homeland. One of the earliest examples about Canadian Gaels comes from an early nineteenth-century account about Prince Edward Island:

> I have known many who might with more propriety be called genuine counterparts of the Highlanders who fought at Culloden, than can now, from the changes which have during the last fifty years taken place, be found in any part of Scotland. (MacGregor 1828: 70)

Similar claims have been expressed to the present, especially regarding the conservatism of Gaelic music and dance in Cape Breton (Shaw 1988; Dembling 2005; Herdman 2008). This trope of fossilisation needs to be understood critically, as it can obscure as much about change as it can reveal. There is insufficient space in this chapter to explore the complexities of tradition and authenticity in detail; for the purposes of the present discussion, the continuity of cultural expression as negotiated within Gaelic-speaking communities according to their own aesthetics and for their own purposes is central to these concepts. The continuity and cohesion of Gaelic communities in Nova Scotia in particular has enabled a strong belief in the fidelity of their vernacular forms.

North Americans wishing to be engaged in Gaelic culture – whether in its linguistic, literary, musical or choreographic aspects – are presented with a choice between 'Scottish' traditions or 'North American' traditions (with regional variants). Learning and performance experiences now happen not only physically but virtually (over the internet), and while many North Americans will automatically seek out possibilities in Scotland, others choose a North American option which may be not only geographically but also genealogically closer to them. While these divergent visions of Gaeldom sometimes coexist peacefully, conflicts around authenticity and authority can erupt when imported contemporary Scottish forms encounter vernacular forms practised in Gaelic-speaking immigrant communities, especially in Nova Scotia.

This chapter will provide an overview of the contrasting developments of selected Gaelic cultural expressions in Scotland and North

America, the settings and organisations in which these expressions have taken place and the history of contention which has surrounded them. Although this chapter is based partially on historical sources (texts and audio recordings) produced by people no longer living, it also draws from the author's experience as an observer and participant in Gaelic events in Scotland from 1992 to 1999 and in Nova Scotia from 2008 to 2013.

INSTITUTIONS, CONTEXTS AND CULTURES

The sophisticated secular institutions that supported elite Gaelic culture in Scotland were increasingly undermined from the early seventeenth century onwards and replaced by anglocentric ones controlled by the urban elite of the Scottish Lowlands or London by the late eighteenth century (Newton 2009). The pillar of vernacular Gaelic culture, the *céilidh* ('house-visit'), remained relatively resilient until the early twentieth century in both Scotland and Nova Scotia. The *céilidh* was important not just as a venue for sustaining the numerous mutually reinforcing and interpenetrating genres of vernacular culture but also as a means of maintaining communal solidarity and of mediating external stimuli.

> Storytelling, in its varied settings, has also functioned in a more practical way, serving as an effective means of affirming and maintaining distinctive cultural values, promoting social cohesion, situating the community and each individual within a larger Gaelic interior oral historical record, socialising children and teaching them about the world of adults, and maintaining the Gaelic intellectual life that had continued even after the aristocracy stopped supporting professional performers, some three centuries ago. In a culture that had only rarely received any support from formal institutions – and where physical punishment for speaking Gaelic in the schoolhouse is still recalled – oral performance in the language in an intensively supportive social context functioned as an effective antidote to cultural pressures from the English-speaking world and as a means of regularly affirming group identity while avoiding direct confrontation. (Shaw 2007: xvii)

Although native 'culture brokers' participated in the emergence of Highlandism and the repackaging of Gaelic culture for a non-Gaelic audience in Britain, these phenomena reflect the subordinate status of

Gaeldom and its corresponding inability to maintain its own cultural resources or participate equitably in its self-representation. It is commonly assumed that Highland Societies and Highland Games were established to preserve aspects of Highland culture but landed gentry orchestrated these organisations and events to enhance their own image as the natural leaders of Highland society, to project a romantic image of themselves and their estates, and to underscore their commitment to the British Empire by promoting a narrow role for Highlanders as loyal soldiers. Highland Games were crafted to highlight Highlanders as brawny rustics eager to win the approval of their superiors, to the exclusion of other cultural pursuits. In other words, these activities were part of a series of measures designed to transform selected elements of Highland tradition into palatable commodities agreeable to the tastes and fancies of the 'respectable' classes of British society, and to orient Gaels toward meeting the demands made of them by the British State and away from their development as a separate people (Jarvie 2005; Newton 2010).

Throughout the nineteenth and early twentieth centuries, the anglophone elite, whose social status gave them *de facto* authority to define tradition and repurpose it according to their own agendas, compartmentalised cultural expressions extracted from Gaelic culture and assigned them to formal institutions. Their activities, informed by the norms and aesthetics of urban anglophone culture, inevitably decontextualised genres and broke the connectivity between them (as illustrated by case studies in the sections below). Of course, not all departures from tradition were due to such external impositions.

The Highland Society of Canada was founded in Glengarry in 1818 (Fairney 2010) and some form of Highland Games may have been held as early as 1836 in New York (Redmond 1971) but such institutions and activities did not become widespread or prominent in North America until after they were embraced by Queen Victoria. In other words, few Gaels who migrated to North America before the later nineteenth century had any acquaintance with Highland Games.

From the 1860s onwards, Highland Societies and Highland Games, and the associated pageantry and iconography, were imported to North America, waxing and waning according to social conditions. While no longer constrained by the British elite and their agendas in the 'New World' setting, they continued to act as conduits for new Scottish formulations of Highlandism and their proponents. Such developments have resulted in the widespread misrepresentation of Gaelic culture in popular anglophone culture, and have also undermined the perception of the legitimacy of vernacular forms in their native communities: 'We need only look at the previous century to see that Gaeldom has been vulnerable to varieties of runaway cultural engineering which have deeply affected its concept of itself' (Shaw 2003: 46).

An Comunn Gàidhealach was founded in 1891 in Scotland. The organisation has a range of aims, including the teaching of Gaelic in schools, but since 1892 it has been best known for organising the Royal National Mòd. Modelled on the Welsh Eisteddfod, the Mòd consists of competitions of Gaelic song, poetry, music and dance, held at regional and national levels. An Comunn Gàidhealach was deliberately apolitical, compromising its ability to lobby on behalf of Gaelic and its native community from the outset (Hutchison 2005). In a bid for 'respectability', the Mòd adopted the

> musical tastes of polite drawing room society of the late Victorian age. The entire event was conducted through the medium of English, and the Mòd spared no effort in encouraging the adoption of quasi-operatic singing styles with pianoforte accompaniment or, occasionally, the accompaniment of the newly revived harp. (Kennedy 2002: 137)

The Mòd model was adopted by the Scottish Celtic Society of New York in 1893 and taken over by the Scottish Gaelic Society of New York, which held them until at least 1897. Discussion about creating a North American Mòd circulated in 1902 but came to naught (Newton 2003). The Vancouver Gaelic Society established a Mòd in 1934 which continued annually until 2007 and several other Mòds have been established around Canada and the US since the 1980s.

A. W. R. MacKenzie founded the Gaelic College in 1939 in Cape Breton, four years after emigrating from Scotland. Despite its name, the college's commitment to Gaelic and local traditions was weak; language instruction was offered but it tended to be a marginalised option until the late twentieth century.

> Unfortunately, MacKenzie had a very poor understanding of what those traditions were and was far more interested in the romantic, theatrical aspects of Highland culture that he had absorbed in his native Scotland. Through the 1940s, '50s and '60s, the College

gradually turned away from the natural expression of Gaelic Culture found in Nova Scotia and toward imported stereotypes. The
focus shifted from local Gaelic cultural development and education
to attracting visitors to a romanticized presentation of a largely
imaginary Highland culture. (Kennedy 2002: 247)

The Gaelic College formed a Mòd on the Scottish model; some
Gaels were supportive of this effort to raise the profile of and support
for Gaelic (Dembling 1997) but the imported musical forms did not
find fertile ground (Kennedy 2002; Sparling 2011).

The ideological landscape for minority languages such as Gaelic
has improved with the gradual loosening of the anglocentric hege-
mony and appreciation for multi-culturalism and multi-lingualism
but only after the core Gaelic community in Nova Scotia has reached
a critical state. There are positive signs of renewal, albeit on a small
scale. The Office of Gaelic Affairs (in Nova Scotia) was established
in 2006, the first governmental office to support the language in
North America. In 2011 the Gaelic College came under new management with greater dedication to Gaelic than in the past, although
proposed changes to the curriculum have stirred controversy
(as discussed below).

LANGUAGE

As a disenfranchised minority subsumed within assimilationist states,
Gaelic has survived best in the most self-sufficient communities at
the furthest remove from official institutions. In Scotland, the islands
of the Outer Hebrides and the associated dialects of Lewis, Harris,
the Uists, Barra and Skye (as well as Islay, Tiree and Lismore of the
Southern Hebrides) have fared best to the present. A majority of
those employed in the infrastructure for developing Gaelic which has
emerged since the 1990s – primarily Gaelic-medium education and
mass media (BBC Radio nan Gàidheal and BBC Alba) – come from
just a few regions of the Outer Hebrides. Gaelic revitalisation has
made significant strides across Scotland but there are concerns that
register and dialect variations are being displaced by a pan-dialectical
form of the language (Lamb 2011).

Gaelic died as a community language in the Carolinas in the fourth
quarter of the nineteenth century; in Prince Edward Island, Newfoundland, Glengarry County (Ontario), Bruce County (Ontario)
and the Eastern Townships of Quebec it seems to have given way

to English during the first half of the twentieth century. The conclusions of Lori Cox's 1994 article are specific to Cape Breton, but formal institutions have played a similar linguicidal role in many communities:

> Gaelic in the Cape Breton schools has been discouraged on three different levels: exclusion of the language as a medium of communication; exclusion from the curriculum of both the language and the culture which it embodied; and, in taking these actions, transmission of negative attitudes concerning the value and usefulness of the language and culture to the community at large. Without doubt, negative attitudes like these have been entirely responsible for the shift to English in the last fifty or sixty years. (Cox 1994: 36)

Intergenerational transmission of Gaelic in Nova Scotia plummeted sharply in the late nineteenth century (Dunn 1991; Dembling 2006), causing mainland dialects to become effectively extinct in the 1980s (Campbell 1999), but a small number of native Gaelic speakers in Cape Breton still exist.

The high proportion of Catholic emigration from regions such as Lochaber and Western Inverness-shire to Nova Scotia was one factor which produced a range of dialects unlike those now remaining in Scotland; in fact, some are effectively extinct in Scotland. While dialectical differences do not cause serious communication barriers for fluent speakers, they can be a source of confusion and frustration for learners. As in Scotland, how to negotiate the desire to maintain local distinctiveness and the need to facilitate wider communication in Gaelic is an unresolved issue.

Although Nova Scotian dialects are derived from specific communities in Scotland, some features have spread beyond their original usages. The best example of this is the *glug Eigeach*, a broad L which is pronounced as [w] (Watson 2010). On top of intrinsically divergent trajectories, Gaelic dialects are subject to influences of lexicon and idiom from the different varieties of English spoken in Scotland and North America, engendering further mutual departures (Campbell 1936).

Gaelic literacy may have been more common in previous generations than many now realise, despite its neglect in formal education (Dunn 1991; MacLellan 2000; Nilsen 2002). The creation of Gaelic resources is instrumental for the modern revitalisation of the language and culture but orthography is an additional complication in the interface with Scotland. The reform of Gaelic spelling conventions was initiated in 1976 and the first recommendations for Gaelic Orthographical Conventions (GOC) were published in 1981. Despite some protests, educational and publishing authorities in Scotland have adopted and require the use of a narrow interpretation of them (Black 2010).

Writers in Nova Scotia, by contrast, have continued to use a more conservative orthography that, among other things, preserves important vowel distinctions. Sìol Cultural Enterprises has been prolifically publishing new books and revised editions of older material as well as reprinting books long out of print. The University of Cape Breton Press has printed several Gaelic volumes and is planning several more. Nova Scotian enterprises are under pressure to adopt GOC, given that grants from Scottish funding agencies and acceptance in the Scottish market require it.

Literacy is a low priority for many adult Gaelic learners in Nova Scotia, however. In 2004 Scottish language activist and leader Fionnlagh MacLeòid visited the province and initiated 'Total Immersion Plus', an informal, conversational approach to teaching Gaelic conducted in homes. This has encouraged the participation of community members at a grassroots level, usually concentrating on local dialects. The more intensive *Bun is Bàrr* master–apprentice programme was initiated in 2011, modelled after a method for revitalising Native American languages (Hinton 2001) created by University of California at Berkeley linguistics professor Leanne Hinton, who visited that year.

Adult learners of Gaelic are not confined to vestiges of immigrant communities. An Comunn Gàidhealach Ameireaganach (ACGA) was established in 1981 by Dr Ian Cameron, a native of Kingussie, Scotland. ACGA began in the greater Washington, DC area but it acts as an umbrella organisation for local initiatives all over North America. It holds an annual immersion weekend which features Gaelic teachers from Scotland and Nova Scotia, and an annual Mòd judged by the winners of the previous year's Royal National Mòd in Scotland. One of the most dynamic Gaelic organisations is Slighe nan Gàidheal of Seattle, Washington, which holds regular immersion weekends and a biennial gathering that spotlights tradition-bearers from Scotland and Nova Scotia (Newton 2005). The Atlantic Gaelic Academy was founded in Nova Scotia in 2007 but holds online classes for students around the world.

Song

The Gaelic song traditions of North America remain under-researched, although field recordings exist in many archives (Nilsen 2000; Conn 2012). Immigrant communities, regardless of their location, were never completely disconnected from developments in Scotland: songs composed in Scotland in the late nineteenth century (such as those by Màiri Mhór nan Òran and Niall MacLeòid) can be found on 1914 studio recordings of Duncan Angus MacRae of Glengarry, Ontario, in Helen Creighton's recordings from Cape Breton (between the 1940s and 1960s) and in Sidney Robertson Cowell's fieldwork in the San Francisco area from 1938 to 1940. While printed books and periodicals may account for some of these importations, travel and human contact must have been more consequential (MacLellan 2000). Some themes, subjects and motifs may have resonated more strongly in some locales (or particular audiences within locales) than others but there were no impermeable boundaries preventing the sharing of songs and styles between regions, however far-flung.

Traditional Gaelic singers are knowledgeable about the origins of the songs they sing and make distinctions between 'old-country' songs (originally composed in Scotland) and local songs. Nova Scotian communities have been important repositories for tradition originating in Scottish regions which have been despoiled by depopulation or language loss (particularly those of the mainland or Inner Hebrides). There is little evidence, however, that repertoires diverged until very recently in more robust communities, such as those in the Outer Hebrides, as John Lorne Campbell observed:

> There were quite a few old songs our Cape Breton friends sang to us that we had not heard at home; but on going through them with my Barra friends, I find that most of them had heard them at some time or another. There were some songs of which the better versions came from Cape Breton and others of which the Old Country versions were better. (Campbell 1999: 26)

Old-country songs were not preserved in aspic but have been subject to the 'domesticating' influences of the immigrant context. A choral song in praise of Ailean Mùideartach composed no later than 1715 and transcribed in the Hebrides in the mid-nineteenth century, for example, contains twenty-six lines and is purely aristocratic in orientation (Newton 2009). A variation recorded in Cape Breton in

1975 contains a lengthy ten-line interpolation about a man's sweetheart leaving him for another, mentioning her linen apron, hair and ribbons (MacLellan 2000). While instances of conservatism of the Gaelic repertoire of Nova Scotia can be cited, revisions such as these demonstrate a living tradition adjusting itself to a new environment.

Gaelic songs belong to different genres with distinct origins, literary registers, social associations and functions (Newton 2009). The range of active genres and the size of individual repertoires of Gaelic singers in Scotland diminished during the twentieth century (MacInnes 2006): in general, the high-register songs of elite origin (especially those in the *dàn* and *iorram* metres) have given way to lower-register choral and/or lyrical songs of popular origin with a greater emphasis on musical form than literary content.[1] This shift is at least in part due to the linguistic demands of high-register songs and changes in musical, literary and social fashions.

High-register song genres have also weakened in Cape Breton for similar reasons (MacLellan 2000; Sparling 2005). The *céilidh* has survived in Scotland, albeit in modified form, but the *luadh* 'milling frolic' is now the primary social context for the sharing of songs in Nova Scotia, a transition facilitated by the inclusion of men in a previously female practice (Sparling 2005, 2011; Conn 2012):

> Cape Breton Gaelic culture is defined both in relation and in opposition to Scottish Gaelic culture. Thus, Cape Breton Gaels conceive of milling frolics as related to and evolved from Scottish waulkings while taking pride in the uniqueness of their milling practices. (Sparling 2005: 200–1)

Some compositions that did not originate as milling songs have been altered to fit the milling style. The strong preference for the 'lift' associated with social dance music has also affected song aesthetics in Nova Scotia (MacLellan 2000; Sparling 2005).

INSTRUMENTAL MUSIC

Highland bagpipe tradition emerged in the ranks of the Gaelic professional classes and in the context of Gaelic music and song traditions (MacDonald 1995; Cheape 2009; Newton 2009). It was later co-opted by the British military and bagpiping organisations which imposed new standards in the training of bagpipers and the judging of competitions (Gibson 1998; Donaldson 2000), effecting a shift away from Gaelic musical aesthetics and aural transmission to an intentionally obfuscated and anglicised musical style and written notation. Although the older Gaelic form survived in some enclaves into the mid-nineteenth century and beyond, it was increasingly marginalised by the 'improvers' whose social clout enabled them to define musical standards as they saw fit. As Donaldson notes,

> The commentators who shaped the official view came from a highly but conventionally educated professional elite so deeply conditioned by 'modern' society that they assumed its cultural conventions to be axiomatic. They knew little of oral transmission or what it might imply, and failed to appreciate that the simultaneous co-existence of multiple variants might be a normal and healthy condition. They interpreted it as a sign of disintegration and decay, and concluded – quite wrongly – that the tradition was at risk and that they must intervene to preserve it. (Donaldson 2000: 463–4)

Bagpipers trained in the non-Gaelic style began encroaching on the aesthetics of Gaelic immigrant communities, even in rural Nova Scotia, by the late nineteenth century, especially as teachers of young bagpipers and judges at Highland Games competitions (Kennedy 2002; Shears 2008):

> Scottish pipers (mostly from the Lowlands) trained in the new non-Gaelic style began to appear with surprising consistency in Canada, including Nova Scotia. They were granted almost instant authority over piping matters virtually from their first arrival in the province. (Kennedy 2002: 176)

Ironically enough, the Gaelic College itself promoted the non-Gaelic style. The most (in)famous imported 'authority' was Seumas MacNeill of the Glasgow College of Piping, whose misconceptions still mislead the unwary (Kennedy 2002; Shears 2008). Although traditional Gaelic bagpiping more or less came to an end in Nova Scotia in the middle of the twentieth century, some pipers are now working to reconstruct it.

Cape Breton is renowned for its fiddle music. It is often portrayed as a relic of the eighteenth century, uncorrupted by modern external influences (Dembling 2005; Herdman 2008), but such claims ignore hybridisation before and after emigration. The fiddle and associated social dance music were brought to the Highlands in the late seventeenth century during an era of cultural flux and evolved in tandem, and interacted, with related musical forms in other parts of Western Europe (Dunlay 1992; Newton forthcoming). *Puirt-á-beul* (mouth music) was the response to this new musical stimulus, a reflection of the assimilation of Gaelic speech rhythms within instrumental dance music. Other genres of Gaelic song were transferred to the fiddle, although some musicians disdained the new instrument (Newton 2009). As the fiddle music tradition has been intertwined with other aspects of Gaelic culture, including song and speech, it is little wonder that Gaelic speakers in Nova Scotia have strong opinions about the impact of the loss of the language on the fiddle style (Shaw 1992–3; Kennedy 2002; Graham 2006).

Traditional Scottish fiddlers were not recorded until the 1930s – over a century after the earliest immigration to Nova Scotia and after many changes had already occurred – so it is not possible to have a detailed understanding of early Highland fiddle tradition. Puritanical religious attitudes in the Highlands attenuated dance and dance music traditions in the later nineteenth century and musical 'improvers' such as James 'Scott' Skinner (1843–1927) altered dominant styles (Dunlay 1992; Kennedy 2002), leading some to doubt if a distinctive and continuous Highland fiddle style has survived in Scotland.

Although rural Nova Scotia enjoyed some isolation from outside influences, there is evidence of innovation and hybridity in the late nineteenth and early twentieth centuries as Gaels travelled between home and New England, bought and played commercial records, began using written musical notation, embraced the tunes of Skinner (and his peers), and introduced jigs into the fiddle repertoire (Graham 2006; Herdman 2008; MacKinnon 2009). The keyboard – first the organ and then the piano – began to accompany fiddle music in the early twentieth century (Kennedy 2002; Graham 2006; MacKinnon 2009). The piano technique must owe something to contemporary American music, especially 'stride piano', a bouncy Afro-American style popular on the east coast in the 1920s and 1930s.

In short, social dance music has been cultivated by fiddlers in a continuous line of evolution in Gaelic immigrant communities in eastern Nova Scotia from the era of emigration to the present, largely in line with Gaelic musical aesthetics and the requirements of dancers but incorporating many external stimuli.

DANCE

The French court was the dynamic innovating centre for elite fashion in late medieval and early modern Europe, not least where dance was concerned. The Scottish court was closely connected with and influenced by the French court, and over the course of three centuries French dance forms were transferred to Scotland, including Gaelic regions, displacing the medieval forms that had existed previously (Newton 2009, forthcoming).[2] Probably the first French dance style to impact Scotland was the *hay d'Alemaigne*, which arrived in England and Scotland around 1500. It came to be known as the 'reel' in Scotland and was the most popular form of social dance (in many variations) in many Scottish communities into the early twentieth century (Flett and Flett 1972).

By the early eighteenth century, French-trained dancing masters were teaching French dance fashions, as well as manners, etiquette and the French language, to those who aspired to ascend the social ladder. Along with the dances themselves came music, played on portable fiddles brought into the Highlands in the late seventeenth century, often played by the dancing master. By the mid-eighteenth century, dancing masters had established themselves in virtually all the major towns of the British Isles and made at least passing visits to smaller villages, even in the Highlands. One of their new specialities was choreographed solo dance stressing agile and exact foot and leg movement (Flett and Flett 1996; Newton forthcoming).

In nineteenth-century Scotland, these choreographed dances were increasingly subsumed within Highland Games as standardised athletic competitions. The Maclennan brothers of Fairburn, Ross-shire, were instrumental in this process; William studied ballet in Paris and Rome, and Donald, who called himself the 'Professor of Dancing', studied ballet in London. Complaints about changes to dances recur throughout the second half of the nineteenth century. The appropriation of Highland Dance tradition by non-Gaels was complete in 1925 when the Scottish Pipers' Society met in Edinburgh to regulate the dance form. The resulting dance form – regulated, ossified, freed of local variations, limited to performance or competition – is the antithesis of the vernacular folk dance, although pseudo-historical tales have been fabricated to validate its authenticity (Kennedy 2002; Newton 2012).

Gaelic dancing masters were among immigrants to Nova Scotia and some formal dance schools survived into the early twentieth century

(Kennedy 2002; Melin 2012). In general, however, formal choreographic structures were broken down and modern step-dance is the result of ver-nacularising the component parts. Wooden floors and hard shoes, luxu-ries beyond the reach of most Gaels in Scotland, facilitated the genre as well (Newton 2009; Melin 2012). Some steps have been borrowed from dances in North American popular culture: twisting leg movements, for example, were taken from the Charleston, the first international dance fad (1926–7). Popular tap dancers (such as Gene Kelly and Shirley Temple) in Hollywood films also inspired steps.

In the early 1900s, Nova Scotians returning home from New England introduced 'square sets' and these quickly took the place of the reel as the most popular form of social dance. Square sets were 'Gaelicised' as travelling steps were adopted from step-dance and tra-ditional musicians accompanied the dancing – although jig tunes had to be imported or composed to suit them (Kennedy 2002).

Contrary to popular belief, Gaelic dance traditions of Cape Breton are more innovative than conservative (no currently popular forms pre-date the later eighteenth century) and have absorbed much North American influence. Regardless, the common roots of Irish and Scot-tish step-dance from the French dancing masters in the late eighteenth century on Gaelic soil has caused some modern observers to believe that Cape Breton step-dance was borrowed directly from Acadian or Irish neighbours in North America (Graham 2006; Kennedy 2002; Melin 2012). As absurd was the lament of the founder of the Gaelic College that immigrant communities had allowed Highland Danc-ing to die out. MacKenzie immediately set about hiring teachers to 'revive' the 'lost' art, leading to resentments which smoulder to the present (Kennedy 2002; Shears 2008).

Conclusions

This chapter has briefly surveyed some of the most celebrated forms of Gaelic cultural expression and their divergence from the homeland in the diaspora. Some changes, such as the spread of dialect features and the accentuated 'swing' in the Nova Scotia song style, are due to processes entirely internal to Gaelic communities; some changes, such as the holding of Mòds, the replacement of reels with square sets, the formation of step-dance, the integration of the piano in social dance music and the narrowing of Gaelic song genres, represent the commu-nity's response to external factors; other changes, such as the replace-ment of Gaelic bagpiping by non-Gaelic forms and the prominence of

Highland Dancing, indicate the imposition of external standards on Gaelic communities, especially via Highland Games. Divergent developments in Scottish Gaeldom itself can be seen as parallel processes of conservation, hybridity and assimilation.

Although Gaelic cultural expressions could be found in communities scattered across North America at the beginning of the twentieth century, the hegemonic pressures of anglo-conformity have taken their toll over the last few generations and Nova Scotia is now the only region in which they can still be found as integrated aspects of a folk culture. The strong and enduring sense of belonging, and the embedded social networks through which knowledge and skills have been transmitted and embodied, allow Nova Scotia to offer a diasporic Gàidhealtachd to which many families feel as attached as others do to Scotland.

Nova Scotia's traditions, especially fiddle music, have enjoyed widespread popularity since the 1990s. Performers and tradition-bearers from the province now have a salient presence at events in Scotland and North America and are usually perceived as having as much legitimacy as their Scottish counterparts, if not more. In the wake of many attempts to correct the presumed error of their ways, however, Nova Scotian Gaels have become wary of 'experts' making pronouncements about the quality or authenticity of their vernacular cultural expressions. Misguided notions of authenticity and a lack of familiarity with the development of Gaelic cultural forms have allowed differences between modern Scottish and Nova Scotian traditions to be misinterpreted as archaisms or as foreign borrowings. A knowledge of the Gaelic language and of the wider body of tradition is needed to understand the origins, meanings and functions of the cultural expressions of Gaelic communities, native Gaelic aesthetics and the means by which Gaels have negotiated between their inherited repertoire and the creative possibilities offered in North America.

The vernacular cultural expressions of Gaelic communities in Nova Scotia are not stuck in a 'deep freeze' that allows them to be restored to Scotland, but are local variants of a region which has constantly evolved under its own sets of influences. The recent movement to 'repatriate' fiddle and dance tradition to Scotland on the assumption that they are emigration-era fossils is naive at best; the most extreme interpretation is that 'non-Gaels are using Canadian Gaels to tell Scottish Gaels how to be Gaelic' (Dembling 2005: 191).

There are renewed efforts in Scotland to reclaim and reassert the Gaelic language and culture after centuries of repression and stigmatisation. Universities and cultural organisations draw American and Canadian students who want to learn about, participate in and contribute to Gaeldom in the 'Old Country'. Despite this, the many millions of North Americans who have Gaelic-speaking ancestors and the groups teaching and promoting Gaelic, some Scottish diplomats have shown surprising ignorance about and even disdain for the language.

At the same time, Gaelic institutions in Nova Scotia are being reinvigorated and are also wooing the descendants of the Highland diaspora. On 23 November 2012 the Gaelic College in St Ann's, Nova Scotia, unveiled a strategic plan to rededicate itself to the Gaelic language and the vernacular cultural expressions of the region. This commitment is not appreciated by all, however. In response to the possibility that some subjects might be discontinued, the president of the Federation for Scottish Culture in Nova Scotia is quoted as remarking,

There is an isolationist element in the Gaelic community that is disavowing cultural traditions like Highland dance and competitive piping that borders almost on xenophobia. We are one people with one common culture and, while it's important to focus on language, it shouldn't come at the cost of Highland dance or piping. (Macintyre 2011)

Such basic misunderstandings of the complex relationships between Gaeldom and Scotland, and the denial of the cultural sovereignty of the Gaelic community, on the part of those who claim authority to define and represent it is troubling but fits a long-standing pattern. Other similar reactions suggest that immigrant communities will continue to be challenged over the legitimacy of their cultural expressions.

Scotland and Nova Scotia offer differing visions of Gaelic culture that appeal to different audiences: Nova Scotia is in North America, presents a (real or imagined) rural, egalitarian, pioneer ideal, and has in fact absorbed many modern influences from Anglo-American popular culture; Scotland, by contrast, has many visible layers of European civilisation (Neolithic monuments, medieval castles and so on), is still strongly affected by the legacy of the aristocracy and is directly influenced by European issues and concerns. Gaelic is currently buoyed by a nation-building exercise in Scotland, providing a social rationale not ideologically feasible in former British colonies. These distinctions may consciously or unconsciously influence where North Americans choose to go to learn about and experience Gaelic culture as much as any claimed notions of tradition or authenticity. Geographical and genealogical proximity, however, may also prove to be prevailing factors.

ACKNOWLEDGEMENTS

Thanks to Stephanie Conn, Catrìona Parsons, Heather Sparling and Lynda Harling Stalker for comments and suggestions on an earlier draft of this chapter. Any remaining shortcomings are the author's own.

10

Ancestral 'Scottishness' and Heritage Tourism

Jenny Blain

INTRODUCTION

This chapter explores how diaspora members, as family history seek-ers, create identities both as 'hybrid Scots' and as practitioners of par-ticular skills in researching family history. The growth of the family history movement, combined with developments in internet technol-ogy and in heritage tourism, has created a web-based industry focused on ancestors and, to some extent, places and meanings.

The development of email fora and lists, and partly interactive internet sites, provides a stage on which seekers perform understand-ings of Scottishness, family and self. For diaspora Scots, this begins with what they already know – often the symbolic representations gleaned from tourism brochures and websites, the tartanry, golf, whisky, Burns (though they have not necessarily read his poetry or know much of his history, other than through exposure to the idea of Burns Suppers), of the 2009 Homecoming and Gathering, promotions of the 2014 Homecoming, imagined misty Highlands and Islands, and the notion of Scots as victims, oppressed or even conquered as part of a seemingly 'authentic' Scottishness.

The stage is therefore set for some contestation and confrontation with those who have other versions of Scottishness, different under-standings of authenticity or deeper knowledge of history. This chapter extends the existing work of Paul Basu (for example 2005, 2007), with greater emphasis on the internet as a vehicle for communication and education as well as information, and a particular focus on the contested knowledges arising when the idea of the romantic Highlands is applied in contexts of Lowland history. Particularly when dealing with family histories of Lowland Scotland, diaspora Scots may find themselves re-evaluating their understanding and developing interests which lie beyond simply 'going back' or claiming a clan, into explorations of local and social or political history. Through internet sites and through physical visiting, Scots at home and Scots abroad are able not only to communicate but to learn, to develop shared understandings and give speculative, narrative life to ancestral bones, hopefully to the profit of all through negotiated understandings and more detailed and nuanced expressions of both locality and Scottishness.

This chapter therefore outlines and discusses the doing of Scottish family history, particularly by diaspora members, involving internet explorations and presentation of self through these, roots tourism visits and places explored both physically and virtually, and the kinds of expressions of belonging that family history seekers create. Within these are areas of contestation, differences of meaning and emphases that may result in knowledge claims which conflict with professional genealogists within Scotland, including issues of clan, of DNA testing, of 'true' history and 'true' line. I discuss in this chapter how such contestation, rather than being seen only as problematic, may hold the potential to open up lines of approach to ancestry and authenticity, and enable the development of a deeper grasp of Scottishness; and present some examples of debate, challenge and educative process that emerge through the pursuit of family history.

But who are these diaspora Scots who engage with family histories? Firstly, they are not homogeneous, either in their relationships with Scotland or in their constructions of identity. The Scottish diaspora is not one thing or event, and diaspora members do not necessarily make the same claims, indeed, even to be members. Not all would see themselves as Scottish, or even identify as hybrid Scottish-Australians, Scottish-Canadians or Scottish-Americans – though some do. Many hold no membership of clan or other Scottish societies – though some do. Some are first generation emigrants, others the children or grandchildren of such, though for others the connection with Scotland may be several centuries in the past. Some have a connection based in 'grandma's stories', others have retained direct connections with cousins in Scotland or elsewhere, and some seek such connections through their involvement with family history websites and visits. Some have pursued their family lines in other directions, finding through this search that they have Scottish connections. The question becomes how they then relate to these, begin to explore the connections, and possibly come to think of themselves, at least in part, as 'Scots'.

CONTEXT: EXPLORING ANCESTRY

This chapter has a basis in my own family connections, their importance for me and the work I have done to explore them. It is in part, therefore, auto-ethnographic, supplemented with more deliberate virtual ethnography, research visits to places which I would otherwise have visited for my own purposes (local family history centres, the National Records of Scotland and so forth) and discussion, on- and off-line, with family history practitioners.

I grew up in Scotland with various family stories, occasional visits to aunts and uncles, hearing my parents and my much older brothers talk about their lives and experiences; and also surrounded by concepts and stories from Scottish history and politics of the past, of industrial Scotland, of social class divisions and changing expectations. Woven within this was the romance of the Highlands, rivers, mountains and misty glens, the 'Scott-land' (Kelly 2010) created not only by Walter Scott (and indeed ignoring much of the Scotland which Scott did describe) but also by the emergent tourist and traveller industries of the eighteenth and nineteenth centuries (Grenier 2005), possibly the most visible part of Scotland to those outside the country. Eventually, though, two of my brothers became part of the diaspora, moving to England, and I headed for Canada, returning much later to Britain and taking a job in England. I was, therefore, for more than half of my life, a member of the diaspora, a 'Scot abroad'. On my father's sudden death in 1984, the brother who telephoned me indeed gave me this title, together with history and context for my being elsewhere at the time.

The association with family history may have begun with my parents' stories, but it was given shape and impetus during my PhD programme, through the Advanced Seminar on the Family in the School of Education at Dalhousie University. The assessment for this module was to trace 'family' back for around three generations, and to contextualise and discuss this. Through a series of letters exchanged with my mother, I discovered that many of her relatives had emigrated to the US and to Australia in the late nineteenth and early twentieth centuries, and that connections had been maintained through first her mother, later her eldest sister and finally herself. Through her network I received stories and genealogical trees from cousins in New England, others from my mother herself and from my brothers, including a copy of a letter sent by my father to a cousin some years previously. This was before the advent of internet genealogy but access to the microfiches of the Church of Jesus Christ of Latter Day Saints, through their family history centre in Dartmouth, Nova Scotia, enabled me to start to fill in some of the blanks, and a visit to Scotland in 1987 enabled an extended life history interview with my mother and a trip to explore birth and marriage records at Register House in Edinburgh.

Copies of the document I produced were circulated through the family network and its material has since become part of family histories created by others. This work had opened up as many mysteries or questions as it had answered but then was set aside while I completed the PhD, sought lecturing jobs and dealt with the exigencies of bringing up a young family, with only occasional dips into the past. In the early 2000s, now based in England, I became aware how much more material was now available through the internet and my explorations of pasts gained momentum. There was a connection, too, with my academic work on sacred sites, 'visiting' and how people related to place (Blain and Wallis 2007).

Through internet exploration, and through web-publishing part of my initial 1980s family history paper, I started to make connections with other family members, so that the network which I first inherited from my mother has developed and grown, with 'cousins' in England, New Zealand, Australia and Canada, and those remaining in Scotland, in addition to those New England ones with whom I began. Much of the growing of my family tree has been done in association with others, both kin and non-kin, and connections made through the various family history fora and email lists that have developed around this area. This, then, gives context and personal location for my discussions of how people 'do' Scottish family history, and what this means for constructions of identity of diaspora members and their relationships to the landscapes and populations of Scotland.

DOING FAMILY HISTORY: DIASPORA AND THE INTERNET

Here I am seeing 'identity' as something people do and as something which is multiple and complex (see, for example, Jenkins 2008): not something that is given but something that is attained and which changes as people, whether as individuals or as part of a group, place emphasis on what matters to them within a particular context of location, time or relationship. Identities are developed within sets of embodied practices and discourses through which people craft how they come to feel about themselves in relation to others, through creating and sharing representations of self, group, community and history and adopting positions in relation to these. Identity in this view is created, invented and, in particular, performed as both individual and collective action with referents in others – performance here relating to the concept of 'behaviour heightened, if ever so slightly, and publicly displayed, twice-behaved behaviour' (Schechner 1993: 1) with therefore a deliberate and a transformatory element. People seek to accomplish something and to effect change in themselves and others, and they do this through many means, some conventionalised, some apparently spontaneous, some becoming routinised for the doer. So here I explore performances of identity through practices of family history, and examine some of the arenas in which meanings are accomplished and which contribute their part to the performative and relational identities established.

Identity, then, becomes intersubjective (see, for example, Bottero 2010) and identity practices or narratives are also contested, as will be shown here. People 'do' family history and talk about it, share, assist, challenge, comment, teach and learn, sometimes through face-to-face interaction (such as in family history society meetings) but increasingly on web-fora, social networks and email lists. The identities discussed here include not only representations of Scottishness, but expressions of insertion in the communities of those who do the work of family historians – identity therefore of being 'a family historian', of having ownership of particular skills, or having and using particular kinds of knowledge.

This includes knowledge of how to go about doing family history and where to seek and find resources. For many members of the diaspora (as for myself in my 1980s explorations) a first port of call may be the family history centres of the Church of Jesus Christ of Latter Day Saints (hereafter LDS or Mormon Church), where people can look through microfilmed records from an ever-increasing variety of countries. Indexes to the LDS records, though, are online at this church's *Familysearch*[1] website, accessible and free, though sometimes incomplete or of doubtful quality. Television advertisements point to pay-for-use sites, in particular *Ancestry* and *Find My Past*, holding differing sets of records.[2] The various *Ancestry* sites make up the Ancestry.com global network, claiming to have around two million subscribers as of May 2013, and to hold 'the world's largest online community of people interested in their family histories'; the base of Ancestry.com is in the US. *Find My Past* is a British-originated site, owned and run by the internet company Brightsolid Publishing Ltd, which also owns *Genes Reunited*, and which specialises in digitising records. Brightsolid has a registered address in London but is owned by the publishing house of D. C. Thomson in Dundee.

However, the records of these much-advertised companies may hold little material which is directly relevant to Scotland or those seeking Scottish relatives, and in the case of *Ancestry*, transcriptions of Scottish census records have often been made without knowledge of Scottish names or place-names, so that transcription errors abound. (I found 'Nickmoudse' as a rendering of the Wigtownshire parish of Kirkmaiden in a transcribed extract from the 1851 census.) Both *Ancestry* and *Genes Reunited* enable paying subscribers or registered members to upload family trees, to contact other members who may be related, and in the case of *Ancestry* to add 'ancestors' from another member's tree to one's own – which can be problematic as that other member's tree may be based on guesswork or on someone else's poor information.

Family historians seeking Scottish connections on the internet, though, may find discussion fora and lists such as *Rootsweb*[3] – a free spin-off from the *Ancestry* network. If they find a list that suits them, relevant to a geographical area or to a name, often the first queries regard differences in doing Scottish family history, where to go for missing records and the cost of certificates. For others, the *Scotland's People* website holds many extant records, and a 'certificate', or more accurately certified extract, is a legally verified document which is not what is needed, because from *Scotland's People* they can download a replica of a register page. *Scotland's People*[4] is hosted and organised by Brightsolid in partnership with the National Records of Scotland (formed from a merger in 2011 of the General Register Office for Scotland (GROS) and the National Archives of Scotland) and the Court of the Lord Lyon. It therefore represents one way in which the devolved Scottish Government and its associated government offices are engaging with the diaspora, as well as with home-based family history seekers.

Internet fora and lists therefore become part of an educative process, where people find out how to go about doing family history within Scottish contexts, and also where they might find information directly related to their own search. There are also queries about how much trust to put in these trees on *Ancestry*, with standard responses being 'always check the sources for yourself' and 'look to see what sources the other tree uses, and how they fit in with your own knowledge'. How to find or check items is not the only issue, though, as illustrated by recent posts to the Perthshire *Rootsweb* email list.

The query:

I have a name in a handwritten marriage/banns extract that I can't read because it's abbreviated (or whatever) – is there any way/anywhere I can post part of the extract so that the list can see it and, perhaps, help read it?

An 'old hand' diaspora member responded:

Ask the good folks at the GROS to help. They have access to the original books not just to film and fiche. They are pros at reading old writing and are soooo nice. True ambassadors of their nation ... You'll see how little I know, but we are all on the same learning curve, and you've come to the right place. Hope you find your folks and you get to Scotland. (Both via perthshire@rootsweb.com, June 2013)

Similar queries may lead to direct offers to help read a piece of scanned text; responses may be off-list or on-list and not everything is therefore publicly visible. However, fora such as *Talking Scot*[5] and the various *Rootsweb* fora (accessed online rather than through having email messages come to subscribers) can enable uploading of small pieces of scanned text. Further frequent queries relate to why records took the form that they do, findings that might appear anomalous, similarities of names, searching records using 'wild cards' or issues of different forms of the same name (Patrick/Peter, Ann/Agnes, Jane/Jean, Elspeth/Elisabeth/Isobel being in older records alternative forms rather than different names), or why a couple might apparently marry in two different parishes. (This relates not to the actual marriage but to the records of 'proclamation' or banns.) Throughout the queries and discussions, forms of sharing emerge and more detailed discussions develop, on contexts of Scottish history, splits in the Kirk, changes in the legal system, marriage conventions, occupations and issues of quality of life and social class, through exploration of specific stories of list members.

The virtual environments, too, form points of contact between those who are physically present in Scotland, who have visited recently and who plan to visit. Where should people go and what should they do? Importantly, what could be available only in Scotland, and particularly in local contexts? A querent to the Angus *Rootsweb* forum[6] asked on behalf of relatives who were soon to travel to Scotland:

[My relatives] will be traveling to Scotland in the next few months and I wanted to ask some advice on how best to prepare [one] to collect information while she is there. Our lines include; Mc/MacDonald from Kirriemuir and Perthshire, Barrie also from Kirriemuir and Perthshire, Sommerville which appear to be from all over, and McCulloch from Lanarkshire.

What I am hoping to learn from all of you is where to send her, what to send her with, and what information I should ask her to focus on (what can only be obtained in Scotland).

Advice which followed began with a caution from another diaspora member to gain as much information before leaving as could be got online, to leave the opportunity to see places rather than look for records while in Scotland.

So many genealogical records can now be accessed on line from www.Scotlandspeople.gov.uk that you should certainly do as much as possible from home before they leave. What can't be done from afar is seeing the places they actually lived. Make sure they take a good camera.

Have you, or they, done much research already?

This advice was partly contested by an 'old hand' diaspora member pointing out that many records were not online, and some were available through visiting the National Records of Scotland in Edinburgh. She however concurred in the importance of place, experiencing this, being there:

Enjoy seeing all of the country and don't do research first trip. Enjoy Scotland's legacy as an heir to everything she was and is.

She however advised making use of places 'where records are likely to be free', including local family history organisations, and pointed to the etiquette of travelling – the country code ('use common sense, don't leave gates open') and the importance of staying in local bed-and-breakfast establishments and, where possible, consulting local people as guides.

DOING FAMILY HISTORY: HERITAGE LANDSCAPES AND FAMILY VISITORS

The virtual environments of the internet therefore connect individuals, in various ways, with the heritage landscapes of imagined or (following Basu 2005, 2007) imagineered spaces, pointing to where to go and what to do there. Roots tourism is promoted strongly by the official

VisitScotland website, which invites people from around the world to come to the 2014 Homecoming to 'return to explore their roots, their clan heritage and discover more about how and where their Scottish forebears lived'. An area of this website, *AncestralScotland*, is billed as 'official ancestral tourism site' and features a videoed range of people stating 'I am a Scot because...', such as: 'I am a Scot because my ancestors came from this country, and everything that Scotland is, you know, means a lot within me', and 'I am a Scot because the sound of bagpipes brings tears to my eyes'. People are encouraged to 'research your roots' and, says the website, 'From the meaning of surnames to the jobs our ancestors did, this section of ancestralscotland.com will help you explore your Scottish roots. Then it is a small step to making your own ancestral journey home to Scotland.'[7]

The promotion material, whether as physical brochures or online, is of course carefully constructed. Scarles (2004) has documented some of the processes of market research, design, image sourcing, staging and repackaging Scotland in ways that catch the imagination of potential visitors, and Basu (2007) points to differences in tourism marketing to England and to the US. The material needs to be fresh but also needs to fit the existing discourses of 'Scotland', notably the romance of the Highlands. People with Scottish ancestry are therefore encouraged, via *AncestralScotland*'s manipulation of images and signifiers, to think of themselves as Scottish, so see themselves as a diaspora with connections to one another through all things Scottish and through the landscapes and buildings imaged on the website. Tourist promotions both acknowledge and exemplify tensions between the Scotland of diaspora imaginings and a Scotland of contemporary arts, drama and creative industries.

> Scotland has always been seen as an idyllic land, where ancient castles nestle amidst majestic mountains; where world-class heritage sites come alive with a rich, turbulent history. The soul-stirring landscapes of the Highlands give way to a rugged coastline, and beyond to Scotland's magical isles. Of course, this romantic, heather-hued backdrop exists, but it does so alongside a vibrant, contemporary new voice. (http://www.ancestralscotland.com/explore/)

Some elements, though, seem missing from these presentations. Where on the *VisitScotland* or *AncestralScotland* websites are the stories of sweat and grime of industrial Scotland, or of the poverty of weavers through growing industrialisation and their emergence as a radical voice? These websites likewise show a tension – not always acknowledged – between, for instance, emphasising the diversity of regions, displaying short pieces on notable Scots (again by region) and recommending itineraries linked as 'Follow in the footsteps of your ancestors' – which, when clicked, turn out to be 'Clan Tours'. The experiences of actual family history seekers may be more varied. While they may begin with a name and a place, they frequently discover the history of family to be a history of movement from place to place, from one parish to another, from cot-toun or mill-toun to village, to town or city, from one town to another, in the generations before emigration of a particular diasporic line.

Being there, being in place, is important. Angus Baxter, a US-based writer on doing family histories, presents it as a goal desired and attainable:

> One day we want to stand where they once stood; to walk the fields they ploughed and the cobbled streets they trod to work; to stand silent for a moment by a graveyard on some lonely hillside; to visit the old stone farmhouse or the tiny cottage where they lived and died – or perhaps the great castle or baronial mansion ... All things are possible, all dreams can become reality as you trace your family back. (Baxter 1991: 1)

The above passage has been repeatedly posted on internet fora and lists (a recent poster making a later comment that 'it's much the best way to explain to my kids why I "chase dead people"'). Destinations, though, may differ from those evoked by Baxter; field organisation changed notably during the eighteenth to twentieth centuries, houses have been demolished and cities rebuilt. As one example, two of my own ancestors were married in Dundee in 1774; they would have known its High Street with the townhouse on the south side and steep streets sloping south to the harbour. Today the streets run more directly south, after the pattern of later eighteenth- and nineteenth-century developments, down to a further half mile of reclaimed land which has been in turn harbour, docks, railways, and now roads and (currently in building) a new waterfront of hotels and cultural industries. Discussing this, McKean et al. (2009: xxi) point out that 'Dundee has neither built heritage nor its setting to act as anchors for memory', and while this seems more true of this city than others, serial changes have affected many of the heritage landscapes to which roots tourists turn in search of that prize of roots tourism – authenticity.

Equally, rather than a lone hillside stone, the burial place sought by roots tourists is likely to be a crowded town or city one. Stones with inscriptions were, until the mid-nineteenth century, rather rare unless the family had money and importance, and many inscriptions are illegible or indeed stones may have been removed or laid flat for safety reasons. However, Baxter's words point to a key factor not only in how people research but in which 'lines' they choose to pursue and which they feel themselves most connected to. What is available to see? How do they come to know about this?

Following tourist directions, particularly to clan territories or monuments, may be one means of finding places where people feel they belong. The UNESCO website identifies a 'cultural landscape' as one which has importance beyond the personal, which pertains to the condition of being human, or a sense of history and emergence of particular cultures.

> Cultural landscapes – cultivated terraces on lofty mountains, gardens, sacred places ... – testify to the creative genius, social development and the imaginative and spiritual vitality of humanity. They are part of our collective identity. (UNESCO, n.d.)

Thus the Edinburgh New Town is a cultural landscape; however, for the imagineered Scotland, particular areas of country associated with specific clans may be presented as such. Basu (2005, 2007) has described journeys with diaspora tourists and their expressions of belonging, and discusses the 'clanscaping' through which their journeys may be constituted. This may include the presentations of clan visitor centres juxtaposing general stories or narrations, sometimes from the far past, with specifics of movement from or to a particular place, drawing on legends or accounts of leading figures such as Cluny Macpherson 'of the '45' (Basu 2007: 136). Clan territories become, in these journeys, ancestral landscapes for particular individuals, spaces within which diasporic visiting and clan membership are performed. As Basu indicates, this performance is not enabled only for the sake of the visitor, and the connection between diasporic Scot and clan organisation or heritage trust is such as to encourage financial contributions. This is part of the clan industry. Rallies, gatherings and clan walks enable mapping of the legends to the landscape, and visitor participation in these almost requisite performances becomes physical performance of identification, later remembered and narrativised as authenticity. Basu (2007: 139) quotes an organiser of walks to specific sites connected with Macpherson history as saying that these have 'become *totems* to go and visit' (his emphasis).

There are, though, other ways in which places feature within personal performance and memory, the less 'official' or organised means where again the internet fora and networks of connections come into play. As an example, resulting from my personal web discussions of a piece of my own explorations, I was contacted in 2011 through the *Ancestry* website with a query about graves in the 'wrights' ground' of the burial ground of South Leith Parish Church. 'We are from Australia and doing family history ... Any clues on where we can find this ground?' The querent and her spouse, a distant cousin, were in Edinburgh for only a few days as part of a three-month-long journey seeking ancestors in Scotland, Ireland and England. I sent directions and a photograph, as of course there are no markers for the wrights' ground, where ship carpenters were interred, and no stones for the family members buried there. The Australians were able to find the 'ground' and stand in the approximate area where our mutual ancestors, Mary Bell and her husband James Philip, were buried in 1826 and 1836.

Graveyards are one of the examples Foucault and Miskowiec (1986) give of heterotopic space; graveyards have histories and imbued meanings, and these meanings are complex, contradictory, changing over time. South Leith burial ground holds pointers to belief and understandings of culture and community, accrued over centuries; it holds evidence, in those stones that are decipherable, for patterns of social class, skill and belonging, here less through family lairs (or plots) than through the division of the space between craft organisations. Hence the wrights' ground, the tailors' ground and so forth; and it holds the echoes of disease and loss even while it holds the sacredness of 'ancestral' bones. It surrounds the parish kirk, which is not in the same form that it held for James or Mary, due to extensive rebuilding in the 1840s.[8] This particular graveyard now holds another set of meanings, becoming through my own narrations on websites a point of connection between homeland and diaspora, within networks including the cousins on their extended vacation/quest from Australia, and others in London, the US and New Zealand.

Heritage sites for visiting diaspora members may be found through many means, whether as part of the heritage industry based within Scotland, outside it (as are many clan organisations), through personal networks or internet connections. For the members of the diaspora who hope to find relatives in the landscape, all means are important. One question is how to give more access and information on places and histories which are less mythologised on the official roots tourist websites. Exploring what kinds of information family history practitioners seek may be a way in which the Scottish Government can reach out to those diaspora members who want more than romance in their imaginings or rememberings of place and people.

HIGHLANDISM, LOWLAND ANCESTORS AND THE LURE OF DNA TESTING

This section takes further the tensions between Highland imaginings and the uncovering of Lowland ancestors by many diasporic Scots. Indeed, unless their Scottish ancestors all emigrated directly from Lewis or Badenoch, Sutherland or other places seen as Highland or Island, there is a Lowland connection. During the period of the Clearances, the most common moves were to the burghs and ports of the Lowlands; and the movements from country to town, in the eighteenth and nineteenth centuries, were not all of Highland people but instead show a steady drift from areas such as Angus, Fife, Galloway or the Border counties. However, my focus in this chapter is not to document the ways in which migration occurred but to explore the meanings for diaspora members who attempt to trace their families and who may find themselves faced with weavers, carpenters and farm labourers in Fife rather than the expected Island crofter or Highland clansman.

One 'line' of my explorations moves from Angus and Fife, through the marriage in Dundee previously mentioned and birth of children in Fife, to the Leith docks and shipbuilding industry in the late eighteenth century. From there in the 1830s, the story of the Philip (Philp, Phillips – there is no consistency in spelling) line moves to Greenock and Glasgow, and then beyond to Australia, Canada, England and New Zealand, through the sons of James Philp and Mary Bell, James and John, both ships' carpenters in Leith and then Greenock. Their descendants have come to their stories – and to that Leith cemetery previously mentioned – in diverse ways. One cousin in England told me that she 'started to research my London ancestors and found myself, almost immediately, transported over the border'. Since then she has acquired considerable expertise in pursuing her Scottish family history, drawing on archival newspaper and other sources as well as the more obvious *Scotland's People* records. A cousin in New Zealand drew on different knowledges, stating that 'My mother had a little book of Scottish tartans which she brought out from time to time. She showed us the Macdonnell

(Keppoch) and the Macmillan tartans claiming them as her clan connections. All I know is that the Philip, Macpphilip, Mckillop, Mcgilp, Philipson were clan septs of the Macdonnells of Keppoch.'

These examples raise questions about how people in developing family histories are finding ways to reconnect disrupted family links, and also on the difference of expression shown in this example and the assumptions that may underlie this. From a recent small-scale study of diaspora Scots within England, Leith and Sim (2012) raised questions about second generation diaspora members and differences in emphasis of their Scottishness as compared with the much more studied diaspora members overseas. My London informant does not appear to think of herself as 'Scots' – she is a Londoner, and she has explored other connections including English and French – but places great value on the details of Scottish history that appear through her research. The New Zealand cousin knew that he was 'Scottish', and his response indexes a constructed 'Highlandism' of clans. Both are endeavouring to use what is available to them to learn more about particular individuals and a possible descent from Fife.

There is, though, another set of complexities introduced to the genealogy communities, often through clan sites. The family history industry has taken up genetic tests – DNA analysis, with websites pointing to DNA studies and how these could be used by family historians. For the Scottish diaspora, clan websites now offer, along with some accounts of the meaning of clan names and short quasi-historical pieces, access to DNA testing, with negotiated discounts. Much of the DNA testing offered is focused on Y-chromosome analysis, by definition privileging male line ancestry, and some websites particularly call for men sharing a surname to have the test done.

The use of DNA testing holds several possibilities. On the one hand, it may actually demonstrate a lack of connection, enabling more understanding of diversity when male bearers of a name find that they are not all closely related. For example, bearers of the name Philp or Phillips may have descents from different men, quite unrelated, who were at some point given a version of the Biblical name Philip; some practitioner discussions indicate this. However, the Y-chromosome focus may also increase adherence to one 'real' identity, that of male line ancestry. Tyler (2009) points to a need for understanding complexity in the sociological investigation of DNA testing and 'race'. She reviews the rather sparse sociological literature on lay understandings of genetic inheritance within family history contexts, concluding that while on a simplistic level genetic tests may indeed incline toward essentialist concepts of ancestral line and 'race', there is potential for DNA investigation to expand awareness of diversity, commenting that:

> these studies challenge the argument that the search for genetic roots and origins necessarily signals a return to the idea of absolute and essential racial and ethnic biogenetic identities. Moreover, studies of laypeople's engagements with the new genealogical technologies complicate the idea that the quest to know 'who you are' and 'where you come from' straightforwardly undermines the notion of discrete biological racial ancestries. (Tyler 2008: 170)

In contrast, though, on many clan websites, the focus is on shared lines not on diversity, and it is usually Y-DNA testing that is offered. Other forms including mitochondrial DNA (mother's line) and indeed autosomal testing are available, but the cost then increases. While there is considerable potential for autosomal testing to show influences that may be surprising, these give only a generalised view of ancestry and not specifics that can link a person to a particular family or place. On clan websites, therefore, women are often advised to have a father or brother take a swab test, or it is implied that they may be searching on behalf of a husband who can therefore provide a sample. The Clan Donald USA Genetic Genealogy website[9] claims to host 'among the largest family-based genetic genealogy project in the world', urging (male) MacDonalds to 'get a 12, 37, 67, or 111-marker Y-DNA test from Family Tree DNA', and stating that the purpose is 'not simply to identify modern cousins but also to learn more about us as a clan'. The clan appears in this discourse as *authentic* descent, the one to be focused on. Yet the concept of clan as only a male-line descent is problematic, failing to recognise the complexity of family relationships, including that inheritance of name and land may be transferred through women.

Assumptions about clans as essential to Scottishness, often derived from diaspora websites, are common among newcomers to family history. A final example comes from one of the *Rootsweb* fora previously discussed. A seeker posted to the regional forum dealing with the county of Angus, requesting information about a James Elliott born 'in Scotland in 1850', and mentioned seeking information through the (US-based) Elliot Clan Society website. A response was to the point, displaying a 'teaching' function of the forum:

How do you know that he was born in Scotland, and where does the birth date come from? Did he marry in Scotland before he emigrated? In what records have you found him?

As for the Clan Elliott web site, there is absolutely no point in looking at that unless and until you have found a specific connection to the family. (Strictly speaking, the Elliot(t)s are a Border family, not a Highland clan; they have no historic roots in the Highlands.) (Response on Angus forum, 1 March 2011)

It turned out that the querent had very little information on the sought ancestry, based only in US censuses which gave a birthplace as 'Scotland'. In attempting to find more, though, this seeker was appearing to give a standard performance of assumptions about Scotland and clans. Indeed, the Elliot Clan Society website[10] plays into perceptions of tartans and chiefs, although it does state that the Elliots were from the Borders. Their website shows a tasteful blue tartan, but without explaining that the creation of these clan tartans was several hundred years after the suppression of border raiding. The respondent, with over twenty-five years' experience of doing family history, likewise demonstrated experience as both an 'old hand' and a Scot of Scotland, giving the advice most generally offered to 'newbies' by established practitioners and professional genealogists: start from what you know, and look for reputable sources. This practitioner commented to me outside the forum, 'You have obviously gathered that I have no time for Brigadoonery and especially the idea that every Scot belongs to a clan'. These performances, through website and e-list, demonstrate authenticity practices and knowledge claims, and illustrate ways in which practitioner interaction creates awareness of historical grounding while creating, imagining or imaging pasts.

CONCLUSION: PRACTITIONER VOICES

Family history practitioners of the diaspora express finding, meaning and belonging in many ways: here are a few voices. First, a practitioner in the US expresses her sense of belonging, emerging before her first visit to Scotland, and developed since over several decades. Growing up, she said, she was 'a misfit':

I was more Scottish then 'American' or whatever name people living in the States give as a handle ... I knew more about Scotland then I did about this country. I was always a misfit and realized I didn't know who I was ... In 1977 I realized that I was HOME in Scotland but we only had two weeks ...

I love history and for the first time I was beginning to know who I was. In 2004 then the children gave us the three-month trip and we started in England ... and then to Scotland to see all I could find on my families ... I knew that my families were not wealthy but also know they were not ever destitute either. My great-grandfather was a coachman and we saw all the places he worked for and the quarters for the coachman and they had a fairly good living ... Sometimes Jenny when people immigrate and circumstances happen you lose who you are. I want to know why I think differently from my brother and mother's family. I needed to belong. (Online interview, 2011)

For an Australian practitioner, the doing of family history became paramount after the death of her husband.

It's lovely to talk to somebody ... I don't know what I would have done without family history. It's kept me sane with something to do. (Emailed comment, 2011)

And finally a US practitioner already quoted in this paper:

[Through the lists and online community] we build a family of friends who share our passion, as my own sister's eyes glaze over if I begin to talk family history. They want my results, but think it is a destination, but it is really a journey.

We understand about that in each other. The family history I like best is not going just the dates that are bookends on the life, [but is] the book between. I read everything I can about the trades/occupation, regiments, and general history. You can infer your ancestors' life by looking at a person who did write down – life in a bothy, or one-room tenement. (List posting, 2012)

Family history in the diaspora holds many meanings. For those with whom I am talking, it goes far beyond a simple keeping of names and dates. It is a development of identity, a sense of 'who I am', not simply in the past connections made but in how these are made, the skills developed, the pride taken in doing the work. Practitioners say it gives a sense of where they have come from but also of what they might become, whether through the detailed pursuit of one's own 'line' through records, through immersion in history, or being in place. For members of the diaspora and those of the homeland, there may be a sense of stretching out, of connections which reach forward as well as back. Throughout the discussions there are tensions between the romanticism of Highlandism and 'Brigadoonery' with homeland meanings and the different knowledges that result but the doing of family tracing holds potential for seekers to broaden their understandings of people and history. This chapter has attempted to emphasise complexities of meanings for practitioners, and the sense of personal connection which they develop with place and people, with other seekers and with their discovered ancestors, what they did, who they were – whether coachmen in Lanarkshire, wrights in Fife or crofters on Mull.

Mass Market Romance Fiction and the Representation of Scotland in the United States

Euan Hague

INTRODUCTION

Scottish authors like Robert Burns and Sir Walter Scott have long been popular in the United States. Burns Suppers are celebrated by members of the Scottish diaspora and, somewhat infamously, in *Life on the Mississippi* (1883) Mark Twain cited Walter Scott's intoxicating mixture of historical romance and nationalism as inciting secessionist passions in the US South and promulgating America's nineteenth-century Civil War. There is also the case of Thomas Dixon's trilogy of white supremacist novels, beginning with *The Clansman* (1905), which venerated the Ku Klux Klan whose members were 'the reincarnated souls of the Clansmen of Old Scotland'. Today, however, a very different type of literature shapes Scotland's reception in the United States. Since the early 1990s there has been a rapid growth in mass market romance novels that have Scottish settings. Attracting primarily female readers, many of these are penned by women, some of whom describe ancestral ties to Scotland on cover biographies and websites. Often heroic in outlook with historical settings (a number of these romance novels use a science fiction 'time travel' element as a central plot device (Hague and Stenhouse 2007)), kilted warriors seduce women as castles, crags, heather-clad moorland and lochs form the backdrop for the action. Drawing on interviews conducted in 2013 with four popular authors of Scottish romance novels (Terri Brisbin, Blythe Gifford, Susan Fraser King and Margaret Mallory) and another woman integral to their production, historical researcher Jody Allen (who has worked with some of these writers), I explore how these authors came to write about Scotland, represent the country, and interact with readers.

THE PLACE OF LITERATURE

Literature provides insights into places and societies, both past and present. A geographical analysis of fiction, argues Withers (1984: 81), can be 'used to illuminate the features of a particular place or a region and its people' (see also Pocock 1981; Crang 1998; Kneale 2003; Brückner and Hsu 2007). From landscape descriptions to experiences of living there, literature can show an area's physical geography, explain how a location's communities are constructed and suggest how people of different racial, ethnic, gender and sexual identities, ages and religions, etc. experience the same location. Beyond the place descriptions within a work of fiction, academic analysts have uncovered the geographies of authors, asking where authors lived and how their experiences of places shaped their writing. This for Pocock (1981: 13) is the 'geography or topography *behind* literature', namely the impact of landscapes and places on authors, that is often accompanied by a 'geography *in* literature', that is, how places and/or the lives of those inhabiting them are described.

Place-centred themes like exile, home, migration, rural or urban life are common in literature, and the trope of a character moving to an unfamiliar location is often a starting point for a novel. Some authors are strongly connected with places: Faulkner's novels about the fictional Yoknapatawpha County, Mississippi, or Dostoyevsky's of nineteenth-century St Petersburg, for example, can be mapped in detail (see Bradbury 1996; Andrews 1981; Mallory and Simpson-Housley 1987). The most famous example of such literary mapping is arguably Joyce's forensically detailed path through Dublin taken by Leopold Bloom in *Ulysses*, now available on numerous websites. Others have explored the geographies of fantastical places, such as Tolkien's Middle Earth in the *Lord of the Rings* trilogy (see, for example, Habermann and Kuhn 2011).

It is within this academic context that scholars have explored the representation of Scotland and Scots in fiction (see, for example, Whyte 1995; Schoene 2007). Typically these collections focus on acclaimed authors, most of whom were either born or lived in Scotland. For Withers (1984: 82), examining such 'literature provide[s] insights into the nature of Scotland's geography past and present' and there is, he maintains, a key distinction between 'writings set *in* an area and those *of* an area' (1984: 86, original emphasis). The latter generate 'a regional distinctiveness or personality of place as it is reflected in the relationship of the occupants to their land', which demonstrate the integration of landscape and life (Withers 1984: 86). Fiction that merely uses a place as a setting or backdrop for the characters, namely that '*in* an area', fails to meet the level of authenticity necessary to offer insight into the human condition in that particular place. Although, as Kneale (2003: 39) asserts, examining literature to uncover the geographical imagination of a place is about exploring 'representations of reality rather than reality itself'. Thus, fiction is necessarily partial: it cannot be expected to capture or describe the reality of a place as understandings of these are subjective, as are readers' readings of a novel. Indeed, one challenge of such examinations is what can be considered a 'Scottish' book. University of Glasgow literature professor Willy Maley (2005: 3), in a slim volume listing Scotland's best books, concluded, 'Our Scotland is a big country and we have opted for as inclusive, elastic and open-minded an approach as possible. You don't need a Scottish passport to gain entry ... [Scottish books include] works by the major Scottish writers ... [and] mighty tomes by non-Scottish writers published in, written in or set in Scotland.' Despite such a wide net, American-authored romance fiction is notably absent from Maley's collection.

Literature is also a reference point for what McCrone (2001) identifies as competing and complementing discourses of Scottish identities, the Kailyard and Tartanry, to which others add a third discourse, that of Clydesidism (see also Nairn 1981; Caughie 1982; Craig 1982; Trevor-Roper 1983; McCrone 1989; McCrone et al. 1995). The late nineteenth-century's 'kailyard', epitomised by novels like S. R. Crockett's *The Stickit Minister* (1893) and J. M. Barrie's *Auld Licht Idylls* (1888), highlights parish gossip and exhibits a 'rural sentimentality' (Withers 1984: 86). Cultural critic Cairns Craig (1982: 7) describes kailyard literature as imagining 'a Scotland of parochial insularity, of poor, humble, puritanical folk living out dour lives lightened only by a dark and forbidding religious dogmatism'. Tartanry, replete with kilt-wearing, sword-wielding, bagpipe-playing Highlanders wandering across treeless mountains and along scenic lochsides among the purple flowers of heather and thistles, remains the dominant representation of Scotland internationally, and one that critic Andrew Ross (1995: 18) describes as 'the longest running caricature of national identity in a field of world-class competitors'. A third discourse, 'Clydesidism' or 'red Clydeside', is identified by McCrone (1989: 168) as an effort 'to break out of the mental traps of the historic myths of Tartanry and Kailyard', but one that 'risks embracing another myth based on a fast-disappearing working-class culture'. Tinged with socialist politics,

Clydesidism is founded upon depictions of shipyards and heavy engineering workshops along the Clyde in the first half of the twentieth century and is evident in novels of Scotland's industrial working class, most famously the Glasgow-set *No Mean City* (McArthur and Long 1935), to which novels like James Kelman's Booker Prize-winning *How Late It Was, How Late* (1994) could arguably be added.

Tartanry developed in the late eighteenth and early nineteenth centuries and was popularised by authors like Sir Walter Scott who transformed the Highlands into the Romantic essence of Scotland and Scottishness. Central to the majority of Scottish-set mass market romances, 'the mere fact that novels reviving tartanry constitute such a thriving subgenre of contemporary American writing ought to give pause to those who categorically dismiss representations of this kind of "Scottishness" an artistic dead end' (Hague and Stenhouse 2007: 361). Romance novels with a Scottish setting authored by American writers therefore offer the opportunity to explore what is arguably the most widely read contemporary literary understanding of Scotland.

THE ROMANCE NOVEL

Romance novels are often looked down upon as being unliterary and their readers as unsophisticated. As Selinger (2007: 308) remarks, 'disdain for popular romance fiction remains a way to demonstrate one's intelligence, political bona fides, and demanding aesthetic sensibility'. Yet a wave of scholarship is exploring romance novels from numerous angles (for example, Radway 1984; Krentz 1992; Regis 2003; Flesch 2004; Selinger 2007; Vivanco 2011; Frantz and Selinger 2012; Teo 2012b) and a new academic *Journal of Popular Romance Studies* began publishing in 2012.

The setting of a romance novel, the places it depicts and the writing '*in* an area' that Withers (1984: 86) describes is, I suggest, crucial to the success of certain romance sub-genres. Romance author Kathleen Seidel (1992: 165) concurs that 'in a romance the setting itself may be part of the fantasy'. The most popular place setting for romance novels is England in the Regency period of the early nineteenth century. Other settings, such as the American West or Middle Eastern 'desert' or 'sheik' romances, have somewhat fallen out of favour in the twenty-first century, although the latter have been reassessed through an Orientalist lens (for example, Flesch 2004; Teo 2012b). Scotland emerged in the 1990s as one of the most prominent sub-genres within romance fiction, although Selinger suggests that 'undead Highlander chick lit'

(2007: 309) is one plot device that has been pushed by romance publishers 'long past [its] time'.

The Texas-based trade association Romance Writers of America (RWA) states that a romance novel must fulfil two genre conventions. Firstly, the plot's main focus is 'individuals falling in love and struggling to make the relationship work', most commonly a heterosexual couple with a clear hero and heroine, although there are sub-genres that cater to other sexualities. Secondly, a romance novel needs to have '[a]n emotionally-satisfying and optimistic ending', in which 'the lovers who risk and struggle for each other and their relationship are rewarded with emotional justice and unconditional love' (RWA 2013a). Offering a definition of romance novels that incorporates writing from Jane Austen to late twentieth-century bestseller Nora Roberts, Regis (2003: 14) states, 'The romance novel is a work of prose fiction that tells the story of the courtship and betrothal of one or more heroines'. Many romances today, however, are more sexually explicit and racier than their courtly nineteenth-century precursors.

RWA estimate that the romance novel industry generated $1.3 billion in sales in both 2011 and 2012 and that around 75 million Americans read a romance novel in 2008 (RWA 2013a). The US audience for romance novels, RWA statistics show, is somewhat narrow: 91 per cent of readers are women; 50 per cent aged 30–54 years old; but this is a loyal audience and around half have been reading romance novels for at least twenty years (RWA 2013a). The majority of these readers are white (Hague and Stenhouse 2007). Out-selling genres like mysteries, thrillers and science fiction, romance novels have a dedicated readership who often follow favourite authors, sub-genres and characters. Although the RWA lists sub-genres of romance novels, place-centred writing is not typically noted, despite Scotland being a major focus of many writers. Indeed, within the romance category there are few other comparable locations other than English 'Regencies' set in the early nineteenth century. Another major US industry association, *Romance Times*, gives annual awards across numerous categories of romance fiction. Categories are place-based, including the generic 'urban' and more specific 'British Isles-set' and 'Scotland-set'. It is in this latter category that Margaret Mallory's *The Warrior* was successful in 2012; and in the former, the Glasgow-set *Starlight* by California-born Carrie Lofty (2012) won with its original blend of Victorian-era romance with cotton mills and labour unions, adding a dash of Clydesidism to the genre.

In the United States, Harlequin is the publisher most associated with romance novels. Typically releasing at least four titles a month, a

Harlequin romance is usually 70–75,000 words (other romance publishers accept longer manuscripts of around 100,000 words). Harlequin posted annual revenues of $42.6m in 2010, down from a peak of $51m in 2005 (Gale 2013). Employing a US staff of around one hundred people (Gale 2013), Harlequin was established in 1949 and is now part of a global company with affiliates in sixteen countries (Andriani 2009), most notably Britain's Mills and Boon. In 2012, of the 1,590 paperback positions on bestseller lists, Harlequin occupied 8.2 per cent of them, ranking fifth behind less specialised publishers like Penguin and Random House, which have their own romance imprints (Maryles 2013).[1] Romance writing is, in short, big business.

Scotland in Romance Novels

Within the growing number of studies of romance novels are commentaries on Scottish romances that discuss the conventions evident in this sub-genre of the form. Some of these accounts are by journalists (for example, Day 2002; Stenhouse 2005; English 2005; McVeigh 2005), while others review a selection of books (for example, James 2008; Romance Reader 2008) or offer analysis of Scottish romance novels (for example, Hague and Stenhouse 2007; Vivanco 2010). These assessments demonstrate that in Scottish romance novels key themes include genealogy, family and heredity, which raise associated plot lines of the legitimacy of heirs and competing claims to land, power and leadership positions in both clans and royal families. Brooding, passionate, feisty Scots are often drawn in contrast to more prosaic English or American protagonists. 'The particular narrative resources provided by a Scottish setting', Hague and Stenhouse (2007: 361) maintain, 'promises the exploits of heroic warriors, sexy and dedicated to clan and family, in a land that is mystical, full of adventurous possibilities, and emotionally charged'. Vivanco (2010) quotes Jove Books editor Cindy Hwang: 'The image of the Highlander is very romanticised ... They are seen as very rugged and independent – in terms of how Americans see the Scots, anyway. That rebellious side has its appeal'. To discover more about Scottish-set romance novels produced in the United States, I interviewed four prominent genre authors and a researcher who works within the industry.

When reviewing the careers of the authors whom I interviewed, it is apparent that the majority of them began writing in the 1990s. This was the decade of Diana Gabaldon's *Outlander* (2005).[2] First published in 1991, *Outlander* is a Scottish-set time travel novel that most interviewees cited as a formative influence. Inspired by an episode of *Dr Who*, Gabaldon's main character is Jamie Fraser, an eighteenth-century Highlander who falls in love with time-travelling twentieth-century American woman Claire Beauchamp Randall (Hague and Stenhouse 2007). Although Gabaldon's writing differs from genre romance in both style and length, her focus around a romantic hetero-sexual relationship is central to romances and likely why *Outlander* was initially promoted at a RWA conference (Stephenson 1997). Gabaldon, an Arizona-based data analyst at the start of her writing career, had neither visited Scotland nor had an ancestral or genealogi-cal connection to the country (Stephenson 1997). Yet *Outlander* and its multiple sequels established the stories and scenery of Scotland for a generation of American readers.

Other pioneers of Scottish romance fiction include Bertrice Small, whose sixteenth-century characters were Scottish in *The Kadin* and *Love Wild and Fair* (both 1978) (see Teo 2012a); Kansas author Julie Garwood, whose novels *The Bride* (1989) and *The Secret* (1992) out-lined a number of conventions that came to define the sub-genre; Susan (Fraser) King whose first Scottish romance was *The Raven's Wish* (1995) set in the mid-sixteenth century; Hannah Howell, author of at least twelve books for Zebra between 1998 and 2005 featuring the Highland warriors of the Murray clan in the fifteenth century; May McGoldrick, a husband-and-wife team whose first book was *The Thistle and the Rose* (1995); and Connie Brockway (1999, 2000a, 2000b) who published her *McClairen's Isle* trilogy set in the 1760s. All of these authors were born and live in the United States. Other prominent contributors to the Scottish romance sub-genre include Karen Ranney, originally from New Mexico, Karen-Marie Moning from Ohio, Cath-erine Coulter from Texas, and Sue-Ellen Welfonder, born Sue-Ellen MacDuffie in Florida (who also publishes under the pseudonym Allie Mackay). Ranney (2013) explains her location of romances in Scotland as 'a marketing decision I was asked to make a few years ago' following prior books set in England, but that she now 'adore[s]' nineteenth-cen-tury Scottish history as it 'is filled with fascinating events'. Welfonder (2013), in turn, describes herself on her tartan-backgrounded website as a 'card-carrying Scotophile', who 'visits Scotland often, insisting her trips give her inspiration for new books. Proud of her own Hebridean ancestry, she belongs to two clan societies and enjoys attending High-land Games [and] ... loves haggis'. Welfonder/Mackay's books include *Devil in a Kilt* (2001), *Sins of a Highland Devil* (2011a), *Temptation of a Highland Scoundrel* (2011b) and *Tall, Dark and Kilted* (2008).

One of her most recent, *Haunted Warrior* (2012), adds a paranormal element with ancient spirits being upset by a redevelopment project in a contemporary Scottish coastal village. Indeed, not all authors focus on historic Scotland: Katie MacAlister's (2003) *Men in Kilts* is set in the present day (a 'contemporary').

Drawing from information available from online booksellers, I catalogued 141 Scotland-themed romance novels published between 1995 and 2005. At that stage I lost count. MacKenzie (n.d.), a fan of Scottish romance novels who identifies herself as 'being of Scottish descent', hosts a website gallery of covers from eighty-nine Scottish-themed romance novels. Romance Reader (2006, 2008) lists forty-four Scottish-set books as favourites, and 321 authors writing within the genre, many having published multiple books. There are, in sum, hundreds of Scottish-set romance novels published since the late–1980s in the United States. The business, however, is one of rapid turnover, meaning many books have short shelf lives. Blythe Gifford (2013a), author of a Harlequin trilogy set in the Scottish Borders in the 1520s, told me, 'My books are on the shelves for four weeks – it's like a magazine!' Some authors are now seeing old titles gain new audiences as they are republished as downloadable books for electronic tablet portable readers, but the availability of an author's back catalogue depends on copyright agreements in their publishing contracts. Some companies allow copyright to revert to an author after a stipulated period, allowing self-publication of past titles in this new format; others do not.

WHY SCOTLAND?

Neither Terri Brisbin, Blythe Gifford nor Susan King had visited Scotland prior to beginning their careers as successful authors of Scottish historical romance fiction. Margaret Mallory had made two short visits and, after deciding to set stories in Scotland, returned to do research. Each of these authors with whom I spoke had different reasons for choosing to set their work in Scotland. One theme that emerged was that each wrote novels set elsewhere prior to deciding to write about Scotland. Susan Fraser King (who also writes using the pen name Sarah Gabriel), an art historian born in New York state and living in Maryland, won a competition with her first novel set in England. This gained her an agent and led to her drawing on genealogical connections to Clan Fraser for her initial Scottish historical romances (for example, King 1995). Blythe Gifford, who worked in public relations and marketing in Chicago before focusing on Scotland explained, 'I am an anglophile.

I have written four books set in fourteenth-century England ... my move to writing about Scotland was a marketing-driven move ... more than one writer who wanted to amp up her sales has gone to Scotland to do so!' Margaret Mallory (2013a), who moved from Michigan to the Pacific Northwest and pursued a career as a lawyer and then administrator in the state child welfare agency, had set books in medieval Wales, Normandy and England before turning to Scotland:

> After my first series, my editor said they would like another book proposal. She said they were open to another medieval, but if I wanted to sell more books, I should consider trying a more popular sub-genre. She suggested Regencies or Scottish historicals ... Regencies sell the most and I think what my publisher really hoped for was Regencies set in Scotland. I just laughed at that ... Scotland suited my storytelling style. It lends itself to strong heroines and heroes and colourful secondary characters. I love the legends and ghosts I come across. The least believable parts of my books are the real history.

One result is Mallory's acclaimed 'Return of the Highlanders' four-book series: *The Guardian* (2011a), *The Sinner* (2011b), *The Warrior* (2012), *The Chieftain* (2013b).

In turn, Terri Brisbin (2013) told me, 'I had not been to Scotland until 2002, so I had three or four books out before I got there the first time. I feel like I am going home when I visit, it's strange ... I feel like I almost lived there before.' Now author of thirty books, nineteen of them set in Scotland, Brisbin initially tried to publish a 'contemporary' romance but, after failing to do so, decided to write within the genre that she derived the most enjoyment from reading, namely Scottish historicals. A dental hygienist in New Jersey for over thirty years, Brisbin's first Scottish-set publication, *A Love Through Time* (1998), involved a time travel plot device that sent the hero and heroine from New Jersey in the 1990s to Scotland in the 1370s:

> I decided to send them both back [in time] because they needed to have a lesson to learn and to teach each other a lesson, and they needed to be isolated to do it. I remember a [news] report at the time about a man who was dying on Mount Everest, and the last thing he did was call his family, and that made me think that there's nowhere that you can be isolated now, so I would send them into isolation by sending them back in time, but they could still be engaged with historical elements, society and community. (Brisbin 2013)

Thus, what at first seems a bizarre plot device, time travel, is chosen as central to the emotional development of the main characters' relationship, namely the core theme of a romance novel. The technique also enabled Brisbin to ask and answer her own questions about Scotland's past, through the conduit of her characters. A determination to depict medieval Scotland authentically led to some awkward moments for Brisbin as *Once Forbidden* (2002), part of her fourteenth-century MacKendimen clan trilogy, developed. She drew on the expertise of researcher Jody Allen:

> I needed to know where the influence of the Catholic church was and the Celtic church and the next thing I know, she's posted my questions to a loop that included bishops in Scotland and got all this historical information. I learned the Celtic church had a different rule about marrying your brother's widow, so that helped me tremendously and solved the problem! (Brisbin 2013)

Such interest in being historically appropriate animated each of the authors. Blythe Gifford (2013a) put it succinctly: 'there's a difference between accuracy and authenticity', she told me, and her intention is to be 'authentic', without forgetting that 'you're writing fiction, you're not writing a history book, it's what you have to leave out. Because, after all, if you don't tell a good story, no one will care. Most writers of historical fiction, historical romance, historical mystery, we really do love history.' Brisbin (2013) described herself as an 'unofficial student of history'. 'Getting the history right is an interesting part of it', states Margaret Mallory (2013a): 'It is important ... but I am also a fiction writer. I'm not going to change when the Battle of Flodden happened ... but minor events such as the date of a marriage I will, and I'll condense years, for example, something that happened over 10 years, I've compressed into 2 years [but] I don't shift well-known events.'

Not only does the history need to be 'authentic' but the landscapes accurately described and behaviours and beliefs plausibly related. Gifford, for example, told me of her efforts to ensure she accurately represented the flora and fauna of the sixteenth-century Scottish Borders. Researcher Jody Allen (2013) often helps with such efforts and she described her advice to an author on a recent manuscript:

> Lori Handeland writes a series called 'The Night Creatures', a paranormal romance, but she had a book set in Scotland when her night creature was the Loch Ness Monster. She contacted me

because she wanted things to sound correct. There was a line, 'She could see somebody across the loch', well, no one who had been there would say that! She also had them drinking American whiskey, and Scots would of course drink Scotch!

One of the most difficult things to represent 'authentically' is language, not least because medieval Highlanders, as Mallory explained when describing her characters, would have spoken Gaelic. Across the sub-genre of Scottish historical romance fiction, Hague and Stenhouse (2007: 357–8) remark:

> the implementation of Scots language ... is idiosyncratic rather than systematic. Whenever Scots is used, spellings are rarely consistent ... the Scottish characters speak an accented English, signalled by minor changes to spellings: 'no' becomes 'nay' or 'nae', 'you' and 'your' become 'ye' and 'yer', 'yes' is replaced by 'aye', 'know' by 'ken', 'girl' and 'boy' by 'lass(ie)' and 'lad(die)', and 'does not' turns into 'dinna', 'isn't' into 'isna', 'will not' into 'willna', and so forth.

Such transliterations frustrate Jody Allen, whose ancestors came from the Kirkcudbright area in southern Scotland:

> The 'kinnae' and 'dinnae' books make me a bit crazy because it is just so 'Scottish romance', throw a little tartan on the cover, and put Highland or Highlander in the title and some readers and publishers are satisfied ... I hate the way a lot of romance writers throw in a few 'kinnaes' and 'dinnaes' and think they have a Scottish romance!

Blythe Gifford (2013a) concurs: 'I think it's more the structure of the sentences and so forth that has to convey Scottishness rather than a lot of dinnas and cannaes.' Mallory (2013a) agrees: 'To get a feel for the cadence of the language, I listened online to Gaelic speakers and to a native of Skye speaking in English. I also listen to Celtic music sung in Gaelic sometimes while I write.'

When Scotland?

Within the Scottish historical romance genre, three time periods seem to be the most popular – the era of the Wars of Independence and their aftermath in the thirteenth to fourteenth centuries; the sixteenth century from James IV to James VI; and the mid-eighteenth century of the Jacobites. What is evident among the authors I interviewed, and contrary to popular depictions of romance writing as generic, is a determination to get the history right. Details of Scotland's medieval royal and religious history can make or break proposed plots, and the authors envisioned themselves as simultaneously amateur historians and fiction writers. It is to aid with this research that Jody Allen offers her services. Initially a reviewer of romance novels and based in Wisconsin, Allen is also pursuing postgraduate study at the University of Dundee through distance learning. Drawing on Scottish library resources, Allen will read manuscripts, research historical questions and contact Scotland-based authorities to ensure novels are accurate. Margaret Mallory works with Gaelic speakers and scholars of Scottish history; Terri Brisbin, author of ten novels about the MacLerie clan, has corresponded with Scottish officials of Clan MacDougall; and members of Clan Fraser and Scotland-based historians have aided Susan King.

Blythe Gifford's research for her Brunson clan trilogy (*Return of the Border Warrior* (2012a), *Captive of the Border Lord* (2012b), *Taken by the Border Rebel* (2013b)) included reading both books and unpublished Masters and PhD theses on the life and times of James V. She also read widely about Border Ballads, played these on CD as she wrote to get the cadence of the area's voices and, inspired by the *Ballad of Johnnie Armstrong*, gave her Brunson clan of Border reivers a ballad of their own, adding verses across the trilogy as the characters added to their legends. The Brunson ballad, repeated in each book in the trilogy, begins:

> Silent as moonrise, sure as the stars
> Strong as the wind that sweeps Carter's Bar
> Sure-footed and stubborn, ne'er danton nor dun'
> That's what they said of the band Brunson
> Descendent of a brown-eyed Viking man,
> Descendent of a brown-eyed Viking man. (Gifford 2012a: n.p.)

The 1513 Battle of Flodden is both a turning point in Scottish history and an event that catalyses Margaret Mallory's plots. 'We have a king, nobles and chieftains die in battle', she recounts, 'the heir to the throne is seventeen months old, and the widowed queen regent is the sister of Scotland's worst enemy, Henry VIII. You have these young men suddenly become chieftains, there's a lot of turnover, there was conflict on all levels and transitions, and that is just a huge opportunity for a historical fiction writer' (Mallory 2013). In Gifford's trilogy for Harlequin, Johnny Brunson has grown up with James V and, in *Return of the Border Warrior*, returns to his ancestral home in 1528:

> John had not set his eyes on his family's brooding stone tower in ten years. Not since he'd been sent to the court of the boy king. Now that king was grown and had sent him home with a duty to perform ... John would tell his brother what must be. 'I'm sent of King James, fifth of that name'. (Gifford 2012a: 9, 11)

Gifford (2013a) makes clear that the books she writes 'do have to be authentic ... It has to hang together as true ... [*Return of the Border Warrior*] takes place in the reiver era and, of course, my reivers are nicer than they really were, so there is that myth, ... we do write fairy tales to some extent, so there's some of that gloss that you do want to put on it. But at the same time I do try to be as accurate as I can.' The line between a Scottish romance novel and historical fiction is a fuzzy one, and many authors straddle these genres which overlap as publishers categorise books. Although the authors with whom I spoke sought to generate historical authenticity in their writing, the first wave of successful Scottish historical romance novels of the early 1990s set conventions that came to define the genre, much to the frustration of some. Themes like genealogy, heredity and legitimacy of offspring are common in many romance novels, but other elements were added to the Scottish-set ones, like securing a clan truce with a marriage, as in Julie Garwood's *The Wedding* (1996), or hand-fasting, a pre-modern betrothal ritual where the couple live together as husband and wife prior to marriage, as in Virginia Henley's *A Year and a Day* (1998). Jody Allen (2013) thus felt that some 'American Scottish romance writers [have] created their own Scottish history, which I am sure a Scot would not recognize as Scottish history!'

A plot device like hand-fasting in a Scottish romance novel set after 1200, Allen suggests, is almost certainly historically inaccurate. The result is that 'There is real Scottish history and there is romance Scottish history [and] if you try and write a little outside that [romance Scottish history], readers will say you've created your own Scottish history, but it's the romance books' history that has become genre and it's the American romance version of Scottish history that sells books' (Allen 2013). Terri Brisbin (2013) felt that Scotland 'is popular ... because people don't know the true history. Scotland is not as romantic as we make it seem!' Wanting to draw on her academic background, and feeling constrained by the conventions of the romance genre, Susan King (2013) moved away from the sub-genre that she helped to originate with *The Raven's Wish* (1995). 'It's more the brawny Scottish Disneyworld stuff and less the actual history that sells the romances', she said. 'That's why I began writing mainstream historical fiction, where I could really take the history seriously and explore Scotland more deeply than I could in romance ... I wanted to write historical fiction that was deeply researched and had a broader story spectrum, which was not possible in romance fiction, given the importance of the focus on the couple and the relationship.' King's acclaimed historical novels, *Lady Macbeth* (2008) and its sequel *Queen Hereafter* (2010), integrate fact and fiction. In *Queen Hereafter*, for example, the opening page has a family tree detailing the genealogy of Scottish and English royalty from the fifth to the fifteenth centuries, albeit with one added fictional character, Eva, a granddaughter of Lady Macbeth and one of *Queen Hereafter*'s central characters. Similarly, many Scottish romance writers provide an Author's Note explaining the history of the period and indicating where liberties were taken or events fictionalised. The determination to be as historically authentic as possible meant that *Braveheart* 'appalled' Terri Brisbin; Blythe Gifford sighed exasperatedly just at the thought of how Mel Gibson's 1995 blockbuster depicted the Scottish past, and Susan King opined, 'Anybody with historical background was "Aargh, Isabelle was 8 years old and in France!"' Yet King acknowledges that *Braveheart* was a 'phenomenon ... that impacted the publishing industry and authors'.

WHERE SCOTLAND?

The majority of Scottish historical romance novels by American authors are set in the Highlands. 'The Jacobites are why the Highland history dominates', suggests Jody Allen (2013). '80 per cent of historical romances set in Scotland are set in the Highlands. You always have a Highland hero.' The Jacobite influence comes from two sources: Sir Walter Scott, who the interviewees mentioned as the originator of Highland romance, and Diana Gabaldon, whose sexy hero Jamie Fraser is a Jacobite. Given this convention, Blythe Gifford (2013a) describes herself as an 'outlier' in the genre for her novels set in the Scottish Borders, but says her choice is both shaped by her own knowledge, namely that of medieval England, and the inspiration gained from the fact that 'the history happened on the

Borders ... what was going on in terms of where most of the population was and where the interaction between Scotland and England was, was on the Borders. For me history is important, there is a spine of history that has to be part of what I'm writing. The Highlands don't appeal to me.' Margaret Mallory (2013a), by contrast, 'picked the MacDonalds of Sleat on the Isle of Skye for my heroes' clan. The real first chieftain, who is the grandfather of one of my fictional heroes, had six sons by six different women. The discord among these six half-brothers led to two generations of murder and mayhem, which gave me a lot to work with.' In her travels to Scotland, Mallory has visited Skye, photographing locations for her website and social media communications: '[In June 2010, when travelling in] the Isle of Skye where "my" clan was based, [I] drove around and visited other areas. The trip was very inspiring, and I ended up setting scenes in a number of places I hadn't planned to include in the books before visiting them. Luckily, I had four books to work with. I had no plan, for example, to have my Highlanders go to Edinburgh.' Taking a tour of the underground Mary King's Close in Edinburgh inspired Mallory to bring her characters Alex MacDonald and Glynis MacNeil from Skye to Edinburgh in 1515 in *The Sinner* (2011b: 131, 133):

> Glynis held Alex's arm tightly as they climbed the cobblestoned High Street through the heart of the city. Edinburgh was a buzzing hive of activity with people hauling goods up and down the crowded streets ... The High Street followed a ridge through the city like the spine of a sitting dog. Between the buildings, Glynis caught glimpses of an enormous fortress rising from black rock above the city ... 'What is that horrid smell?' Glynis asked, as she wiped her eye with her sleeve. 'It's so foul it makes my eyes water.' 'Too many people living close together,' Alex pointed to one of the many narrow passages off the High Street. 'The buildings are ten and twelve stories high on these passageways they call closes. Everyone living on the close empties their waste out their doors or windows, and it all flows downhill to the loch below. The loch has no outlet, so the filth of the city stagnates there'. 'That's disgusting,' she said, wrinkling her nose.

Susan King, author of twenty-two novels, has set Scottish romances in the Highlands from medieval times through to the nineteenth century, the Lowlands in the Victorian era, and the Borders during the sixteenth century. Her *Laird of the Wind* (1998: 349), set in 1305, centres on a legend that the dismembered body of William Wallace was returned to Dunfermline Abbey for burial:

> The hawthorn tree stood in a gentle slant of dawn rain. A man in a pilgrim's coat walked past the abbey church ... A few people clustered in the arched shadows of the north door ... Over the last four weeks, Quentin and Patrick had travelled to four towns in Scotland and northern England in search of the mournful reminders of the unjust death of a great leader. They had gathered his bones into the box and brought it to Dunfermline Abbey, where kings, saints, and leaders of Scotland had been laid to rest for centuries.

Although Lofty's award-winning *Starlight* (2012: 58, 311, 92) is set amid Glasgow's 'harsh industrial architecture', 'smog', 'noisy factories and cramped tenements', it is the Highlands that remain the most popular location for Scottish-set romances. Terri Brisbin's *The Highlander's Stolen Touch*, with its Clan MacLerie residents of the village of Lairig Dubh, is described as being northwest of Crieff:

> Their route back to Lairig Dubh would take a more southerly route: to the tip of ancient lands of Atholl following the Tay to the loch, then west along Glen Lyon and north to Lairig Dubh. Once more following the drover's roads ... They would not visit Dunalastair on the way back. (Brisbin 2012: 147)

CONNECTING WITH READERS

One thing for which the romance genre is known is an interactive experience connecting readers and writers. Hague and Stenhouse (2007) note that books contain directions on how to contact authors and readers sign up on websites to receive regular e-newsletters, details of upcoming books, excerpts and events. In the past five years, such accessibility has both increased and accelerated. The advent of Facebook, Twitter and other social media means that readers can now both more easily contact authors and expect replies. A 2012 RWA (2013b) survey indicated that 41 per cent of readers visit an author's website and 5–16 per cent follow favourite authors on Twitter, Facebook or blogs. The marketing of romance novels has also changed dramatically as authors are expected to engage in blogs and produce additional online content that enhances the books. As I wrote, Blythe Gifford (2013c) released a novella, *Tempted by the Border Captain*,

in twenty daily chapters on Harlequin's website; Susan King interviewed me on-line (Word Wenches 2013); and Margaret Mallory
published a blog entry that consisted of a love letter written by Ilysa
to Connor, characters from *The Chieftain* (Mallory 2013b) (Reading Between 2013). Book tours have become 'Blog Tours', such as
Forever's February 2013 'Scottish Seduction Tour' in which Margaret
Mallory and Sue-Ellen Welfonder were interviewed on-line by fans
posting questions and comments for a limited time period (Ramblings
2013). The *Romance Times* website also sets up competitions, such as
one for readers to comment on Margaret Mallory's four-book series
and answer the question: 'With brains, brawn, and noble deeds ...
all wrapped in a kilt ... who do you think is the hottest Highlander?'
(RT Book Reviews 2013, ellipses in original).

'Facebook has made it easier to interact', comments Terri Brisbin (2013). 'In the past, a letter sender would hope that you would
respond, but now readers ... expect an answer.' This interactivity
enables authors to engage in dialogue with readers, and leads to comments such as those received by Margaret Mallory (2013a):

> One blog post reader last week told me that I'd portrayed con-
> flicts in which her ancestors participated on both sides, and that my
> books made her feel much more engaged with her family history
> and made it come alive for her. I do receive a lot of comments from
> readers about making Scotland come alive and making them feel
> as if they are there.

Mallory also regularly uploads to her Facebook page and website
photographs of places that she has been to in Scotland and that she is
writing about, generating further reader comment and interaction.

WHAT MAKES SCOTLAND ATTRACTIVE?

Heather Lobdell (2013), reviewing Margaret Mallory's *The Chieftain*
(2013b) on the *Fresh Fiction* website, enthuses:

> The Scotland described in Mallory's books is everything that
> I have ever imagined Scotland to be. I can smell the heather,
> see the faery mounds, and even the vivid colors of green rolling
> across the fields ... Mallory clearly has a very unique way of
> mixing words that create the most vivid pictures in my mind.
> She has a way with building characters that come to life on

the pages and make them real for the reader. Every single time I open one of her books I remember why I fell in love with Scotland, why I fell in love with the Highlands, and most of all I remember why I fell in love in the first place.

So just what is it about Scotland that excites America's romance authors and readers? Scotland is, Blythe Gifford (2013a) notes, the second most popular sub-genre of historical romance fiction in the United States after Regency-era England. The difference between these two genres is why Scotland is an attractive setting for romance novels. 'I like to read Regencies', explained Margaret Mallory (2013a), 'but they have too much about manners and clothes. I write adventurous romances with big politics and wars, and strong plots ... Scottish history is just rich with conflict, drama, clan wars, captured brides, returned brides, political strife.' Blythe Gifford (2013a) explains similarly, 'I think you then go to the warrior myth or the warrior archetype rather than the Duke ... people who like the Scotsmen ... strong, you've got to have a kilt, you've got to have a sword. It's a very sexy archetype, so in that case, I think it's all about the idea of the Scottish Highlander hero.' 'Scotland is hugely successful with readers', said Terri Brisbin (2013), 'and I think part of it is from Scotland's history, myths, legends, stories. It is isolated and always struggling against adversity, the elements, there was always conflict. Conflict is interesting, a good guy and a bad guy draws readers, the fact that it is a land of beautiful scenery and landscape adds to it ... the wildness and isolation of the Highlands and Islands drew me.'

The Scottish landscape also inspires Mallory, as do Scottish accents, but the idea of Scottish adversity, typically in relation to England, produces an 'underdog' theme which researcher Jody Allen (2013) finds appealing: 'Scotland as the underdog, always fighting back, still today with the "yes" vote campaign for independence.' The idea of fighting against a superior political power resonates with US readers reminded every Fourth of July about their nation's struggle for independence. A reader of romances who posted on Word Wenches (2013) concurs: 'I think we like to read about the "underdogs". Scotland is loaded with "underdogs" in history ... I read a lot of English-set novels – but for them I am usually reading for the heroine, who is the underdog. When I'm reading a Scottish one, the hero is just as important because usually he's as much of an underdog – the stakes are greater! Freedom for your entire country – a huge stake!'

Susan Fraser King (2013) offered her perspective:

Scotland is one of the most beautiful places on earth, and there's a power and a mystery in that sort of vast and ancient landscape that sets the soul on fire, that taps something deep that we can't always neatly define. It's an important element of the Scottish charisma. And there's the strong sense of romance, of nobility of character in a culture and people who fought through centuries for their independence – and their cultural identity and individuality, that Celtic and Highland character, for example, people who adapted to rugged terrain and a tough way of life in extraordinary locations ... Another attraction factor is rebellion. For me, it's a big part of the reason I prefer to write about Scotland rather than England, for example. The feisty, freedom-loving historical Scottish spirit is very appealing to Americans, I think, as we had to summon our own brand of feisty centuries ago to break free from the British.

Added to all of this, of course, are men in kilts, as King (2013) continued:

the kilted Scottish hero, that's definitely a factor for American writers, readers, and the publishing industry. To fully understand the appeal of Scotland in American publishing, marketing cannot be overlooked. Scotland sells, sexy heroes in kilts sell books in big numbers, and so the American publishing industry feeds the romantic kilted-hero character that has become, in some sense, a stereotype by now, but which works very well when handled authentically in the context of a historical era. And that kilted hero began with Sir Walter Scott ... There's a fascinating contrast between a tough guy in a kilt – the skirt speaks of earlier centuries, of traditions and pride and cultural identity, and the skirt, with its more feminine connotation, offers a contrast to the rugged masculine characteristics necessary in a Highlander. There's a perfect yin-yang in a kilted hero that makes him appear larger than life, outside of this time, and even in a historical context, outside and larger than his own time and situation. He's more than ordinary. The whole Highland kit adds metaphor, myth, history, legend, power to him, and places him on another level entirely.

CONCLUSION

In the late 1990s, writes Hague (2006: 41), members of the Scottish diaspora in the United States were depicted in the Scottish media 'as romantic buffoons or as "racist Scots" with white supremacist viewpoints'. During that decade, Scotland and Scottish identity became favoured in American political and popular culture. The US Senate inaugurated 6 April as an annual Tartan Day in 1998 (see Hague 2002a, 2002b), members of the Scottish diaspora produced hagiographic books like *The Mark of the Scots* (Bruce 1998) and, of course, in 1995 Hollywood contributed *Braveheart* and another Scottish historical film, *Rob Roy* (Hague 1999–2000). All contributed to shaping the diasporic vision of Scotland and reinvigorated the power of Tartanry as Scotland's most internationally resonant identity. The 1990s was also the decade of Diana Gabaldon's *Outlander* series of novels that arguably started the love affair with Scotland among romance readers and authors in the United States. As the glow of the 1990s has faded, for millions of American readers romance novels with a Scottish setting remain a primary source of information about Scotland. Although these novels are not written with a solely diaspora audience in mind, its members comprise both authors and readers. The sub-genres within romance fiction are numerous, ranging from Edwardian England to stereotypically sun-drenched tropical islands, the American West and beyond. That Scotland has a consistent presence in this congested market demonstrates that the country has an image and history that greatly interests US readers of romance fiction. Quite simply, Margaret Mallory (2013a) told me, 'Scottish historical readers really love everything about Scotland.'

ACKNOWLEDGEMENTS

I am grateful to Jody Allen, Terri Brisbin, Blythe Gifford, Susan Fraser King and Margaret Mallory for both their interviews and many helpful suggestions. Alec Brownlow, Eric Murphy Selinger, Carrie Breitbach and Michael Coe were sounding boards who provided welcome advice; JoAnn Breitbach and Anne Folsom read novels and sent me notes, as did the following DePaul University students who completed projects on Scottish-set romance novels as part of my class: James Cooney, Chris Eves, Megan Grochowiak, Joseph L. Kral, Rina Mangurten, Daniel McCarthy and John Walsh.

12

Who's Depicting Who? Media Influences and the Scottish Diaspora

Ewan Crawford

INTRODUCTION

In a contribution to the debate over whether Scotland should become an independent country the British Government (which of course is opposed to independence) published an academic paper which concluded that the Act of Union in 1707 had 'extinguished' Scotland in the eyes of international law (HM Government 2013). For supporters of independence this seemed unnecessarily insulting, whatever the legal arguments may be.

However, assessing much of the academic criticism of how Scotland has been represented in film and television over the years, it seems that many critics believe that the bulk of these media representations did indeed do a good job of extinguishing Scotland, at least in the sense of depicting the reality of life in the country. Embarrassment, shame and anger seem to be the dominant emotions when discussing the cinematic and television efforts which seek to bring Scotland to a wider audience. Much of the ire is aimed at the apparent evils of the concepts of Kailyard and Tartanry. The Kailyard in particular has become a critical dividing line. Derived from the term for a kitchen garden or a cabbage patch, the description was used originally to describe novelists and short-story writers who 'specialised in sentimental tales of rural Scotland and cunningly contrived to scoop a large market both in Britain and among the emigrants of North America' (Harvie 1994: 98).

If something is described as Kailyard by a Scottish cultural critic the intention is usually clear: to convey to the reader or audience that the work is, to put it mildly, of questionable quality. In newspaper and magazine reviews of films, readers will be familiar with the star rating format to give a quick indication of how good or bad the critic believes the movie in question to be. As far as output about Scotland is concerned it seems as if we should have our own 'Kailyard rating' system, where the higher the Kailyard content, the worse the film or television programme is going to be. As Sillars says, this use of the Kailyard as a dividing line 'seems ... to promote a critical culture where, to put it crudely, any work that suggests Scotland to be a shite-hole shows its own seriousness, whereas any work that sees the place as couthy (a term which makes the intellectuals tremble) is not worthy of consideration' (Sillars 2009: 132).

This chapter will discuss the impact of media texts in forming and influencing attitudes among audiences. It will then go on to look at the way Scotland has been portrayed by film and other branches of the media, and discuss the ways in which they have been said to have promoted a particular image of the country, serious, couthy or otherwise. This ground has been the subject of lively debates in academic, professional and political circles. But today there is another, perhaps more urgent, concern: not just about the way Scotland is represented but about whether there will be an indigenous media of sufficient size, particularly given developments in television and newspapers, to do the representing in the first place. A recurring theme of discussions about how Scotland has been represented has been the argument that so much of that representation has been offered to Scotland and the rest of the world by film makers and television producers from outside the country. For a time in the 1990s there seemed real optimism that more contemporary and interesting themes were emerging, driven by work from within Scotland. But today there are major debates surrounding, for example, the BBC's commitment to Scotland, and the extent to which the publicly funded broadcaster is able and willing to hold up a mirror to life in the country. As we approach the independence referendum this concern seems to be particularly keenly felt.

THE SCOTTISH IMAGINED COMMUNITY: THE ROLE OF THE MEDIA

For those who subscribe to the dominant modernist school of nationalism, the idea that Scotland, and other nations, are perennial, ancient entities which demonstrate political continuity down the ages is essentially dismissed. Nations instead are said to have originated with the modernising processes of the eighteenth and nineteenth centuries (it should be noted that I am sceptical about this explanation).

Anderson's concept of imagined communities has been influential in this regard, particularly for those interested in the role of the mass media in creating and sustaining nations and national sentiment. In

Anderson's discussion of how nations came into being, he highlights the vital role of capitalism, and in particular what he calls 'print-capitalism', in creating a sense of a shared national community.

> Nothing served to 'assemble' related vernaculars more than capitalism, which, within the limits imposed by grammars and syntaxes, created mechanically reproduced print-languages capable of dissemination through the market. (Anderson 1991: 44)

Anderson goes on to argue that these print-languages became the bases for national consciousness in a number of ways, for example by providing a unified field of exchange and communication, which meant people became aware of others who shared this written language, and of course of those who did not. Interestingly for this chapter, he also uses Scotland as an example of why this process, which encouraged political nationalism elsewhere, failed to have the same impact.

Citing Seton-Watson, Anderson says the Scottish language (not Gaelic but what is known as 'Scots') did not become a 'distinct literary language' because the Union of the Crowns in 1603 'brought the predominance of southern English through its extension to the court, administration and upper class of Scotland' (ibid.: 89). Before the modernising processes of capitalism (and according to the modernist argument the formation of nations) took hold, therefore, large parts of the country were English-speaking and had immediate access to print English. In the early eighteenth century, London and the Scottish Lowlands then collaborated to exterminate the use of Gaelic in the Highlands. Thus, through different processes 'any possibility of a European-style vernacular specific nationalist movement' (ibid.: 90) had been eliminated.

Anderson also discusses why Scotland did not see a rise of what he calls 'American-style' nationalism, unrelated to a distinctive language. Here, the fact that London did not erect any barriers to the ambitions of Scottish politicians or businessmen who wanted to access London's markets or its legislature was important. And there was a further factor at work, what Nairn describes as the intellectual migration to the south. Writing of Scotland's former intelligentsia, he says they were: 'unable ... to fulfil the "standard" nineteenth-century function of elaborating a romantic-national culture of their own people, they applied themselves with vigour to the unfortunate southerners' (Nairn 1997: 124). They therefore played a large part in formulating the British and imperial 'culture-community' rather than a Scottish one.

Whatever the reasons for the historic weakness of political nation-alism (in the sense of the demand for an independent Scottish state) at the time when other nation-states were being formed, the outcome has been that Scotland has (at least at the time of writing) been part of a multi-national or nested state (Miller 2000) – the United Kingdom – for more than three hundred years.

This does not mean that most Scots believe they have been incorpo-rated into England. Certainly, whatever their views on independence, almost all Scots believe Scotland to be a distinctive nation within the UK, rather than a region. So the processes which led people elsewhere to form a political state congruent with the nation may not have had the same results in Scotland but that does not mean the idea of a Scot-tish nation (among its citizens at any rate) has been weaker. If the nation has not been sustained by independent national political insti-tutions this raises the question of the role of culture and the extent to which cultural representations have played a part in maintaining the idea of the Scottish nation, and if it has been a significant one, what sort of nation has it imagined?

SHAPING ATTITUDES

For scholars who argue that nations (whether they have political auton-omy or not) are imagined or constructed, the role of culture and the media is indeed often presented as being important. Within the tradition of critical discourse analysis, for example, the idea of the discursive con-struction of nations has been developed (Wodak et al. 2009). The basic idea here is that language in various media and political forms is used in strategies to promote a sense of assimilation among those included in the nation and dissimilation from those – the others – who are excluded. Critical discourse analysts study language and media forms to uncover these strategies and discuss the effect they have on public attitudes.

This method of discovering underlying meanings and, in particular, the impact on how attitudes about nations, politics, economics and gender, for example, are formed by those who consume the media has its critics. CDA scholars are interested, for example, in newspa-per headlines or sentence constructions which can bury or delete the agents of a particular action and obscure processes and power rela-tions. But Widdowson (2007) makes the point that studying individual sentences in isolation from a whole text can make it difficult to justify the claim that agency is being deleted and that readers are being driven towards a particular meaning. Philo (2007) maintains that a more extensive research process, involving interviews and studying production as well as textual analysis, is needed before coming to conclusions about the impact of media messages.

More generally, the whole issue of the relationship between audiences and producers of media texts has been a source of intense debate among media theory scholars. In particular, challenges to the idea that audience members are akin to passive dupes uncritically lapping up dominant ideological messages which have a direct impact on their views, has been at the heart of much of modern media studies. Williams (2003) charts the way the focus switched to discussing whether audiences should be seen as being capable of interpreting texts in different ways. Influential work by Hall (1973) discussed the way films and other media texts were 'encoded' by producers and how audiences then 'decoded' the meaning by variously accepting the dominant meaning, negotiating it or opposing it. The issue of audience reception and the ways in which audiences interpret and take meanings from films is the subject of lively contemporary debate among scholars. We should be careful, therefore, in asserting that just because a particular image of Scotland is shown in film or in television that this will have a direct impact on the beliefs held by members of the Scottish diaspora. Nevertheless there has been extensive, often angry, discussion of those images presented by films and television programmes when they seek to depict Scotland.

REPRESENTING SCOTLAND IN FILM AND TELEVISION

Scotland has been described as 'a small country whose international literary and media profiles dwarf its size' (Bicket 1999: 4). It is important to recognise, however, that this profile, especially in relation to film, was not primarily a result of film makers in Scotland projecting an image of their country to the wider world. Petrie said of the films which featured Scottish subject-matter, 'practically all of these have, by and large, been initiated, developed, financed and produced by companies in London or Los Angeles' (2000: 15). Americans of Scottish descent are therefore far more likely to come across films representing Scotland which have been made by their fellow countrymen and women rather than writers and directors who live in the country of their ancestors.

In the influential polemic *Scotch Reels*, Colin McArthur (one of the fiercest critics of the Kailyard) argued that the way Scotland had been represented in film was 'wholly inadequate for dealing with the historical and contemporary reality of Scotland' (1982: 66). Much of these representations were, he said, produced by film makers from outside the country. The dominance of such externally produced images had two pernicious effects. Firstly it limited the range of roles on offer to Scottish actors, which had a 'cruelly stunting effect' (ibid.: 66). But secondly the power of these traditions influenced the relatively few indigenous Scottish film makers, who were lured on to the same ground.

Scottish film was dominated, says McArthur, by Tartanry – for example, films depicting Bonnie Prince Charlie or Rob Roy – and the Kailyard: titles such as *The Little Minister* or *Whisky Galore*. To press home the point, *Scotch Reels* reproduces film publicity posters featuring actors as varied as David Niven, Shirley Temple and Laurel and Hardy – all dressed in over-the-top Highland dress and kilts. However, the Hollywood film that is perhaps best known for these traditions – the musical *Brigadoon* – is praised by McArthur, precisely because its representation of romantic Scotland is revealed as a dream and a fiction. This 1954 film (which was nominated for three Academy Awards and won a Golden Globe) featured a Scottish village which appears only once every one hundred years. In the movie, a New Yorker, played by Gene Kelly, gives up modern life forever by deciding to stay in Brigadoon after falling in love with one of the villagers. Both the film and the stage musical have become a byword for Tartan kitsch (the film was shot in Hollywood because, the story goes, Scotland did not appear Scottish enough). In the 1994 Richard Curtice film *Four Weddings and a Funeral*, one of the weddings takes place in a Highland castle replete with full tartan paraphernalia, which causes one of the guests, played by Simon Callow (dressed like one of the pictures referred to earlier in *Scotch Reels*) to exclaim: 'It's bloody Brigadoon'. This exclamation could be taken as a reference to the fact that this is indeed a fantasy, comic image of Scotland and not to be taken seriously as a representation of the country.

RURAL AND REMOTE

Brigadoon is a useful example too of the dominance of the rural in the representation of Scotland in cinema and on television. Petrie says it is the metropolitan basis of British cinema which has led to this predominance of rural imagery.

> Viewed from the centre, Scotland is a distant periphery far removed from the modern, urban and cosmopolitan and social world inhabited by the kind of people involved in the creation of such images. (Petrie 2000: 32)

This perspective on Scotland emphasises remoteness, not just in terms of geography but also socially and morally, from much of modern life.

As we shall see later in the chapter, important urban representations of Scotland have also been discussed but the attachment of film makers and television producers to the rural and to fantasy remains strong. In 2012 Disney released its latest epic Pixar movie *Brave*, about the adventures of a rebellious Scottish princess, Merida, voiced by Kelly MacDonald. The familiar Scottish themes – rural, witchcraft, adventure – are all prominent here. The film's director, Mark Andrews, said: '*Brave* is an amazing magical adventure with larger than life characters – including Scotland itself. During our research, we learned that everything in Scotland tells a story – every stone, tree, mountain – which is why we are so proud that this beautiful country is the backdrop of our film' (VisitScotland 2012).

Looking at the reviews in some of the major US newspapers, much of the focus, however, is not on Scotland but on gender because Merida, according to the *New York Times*, was Pixar's first female protagonist (Dargis 2012). Unsurprisingly, in the US press at least, the image presented of Scotland as a land of majestic scenery and ancient rituals was accepted as unproblematic and it was this issue of gender that attracted much more discussion.

For those who bemoan the typical Hollywood representation of Scotland and who wish to see a more contemporary, nuanced and modern depiction of the country, *Brave*, it would seem, is further cause for despair. But is there too much such bemoaning? In a lively rejoinder to critical complaints about Scotland's fantasy image, David Stenhouse offers a defence of those movies, which he says have been categorised as 'The Wrong Type of Scottish Film' (Stenhouse 2009). These films, he says, 'have too often been seen as part of an undifferentiated mass of material – tea cosies, album covers, tartan memorabilia – which is interesting for sociological or historical reasons, but has little to detain critics of cinema for long' (2009: 174). In fact, he says films which are dismissed in this way are indeed worthy of closer study.

Stenhouse offers, to my eyes, a refreshing counterpoint to so much of the scorn heaped on traditional representations of Scotland and Scottishness. He says it seems as if there is no pleasure to be taken from the fact that audiences all over the world respond warmly to films about Scotland (although critics would say, of course, that these films are not really 'about' Scotland at all). Stenhouse, however, argues that the traditional tropes of Scottishness are not exhausted but are being reimagined by film makers (and television programme makers – he cites the appearance of a Scottish character in the US hit *Sex and the City*) keen to give their take on Scotland. Representations of Scotland from abroad, particularly those enjoyed by the Scottish diaspora, should be engaged with rather than dismissed, otherwise people in Scotland will cut themselves off 'from a full engagement with the possibilities of global national identity' (ibid.: 184).

HISTORY

Stenhouse seems to be saying that it is possible to have fun with, or be entertained by, Scotland and Scottish images rather than always being on the look-out for images that require policing. In this respect the Mel Gibson film *Braveheart* seems particularly relevant. McArthur, as well as other critics, appears to be genuinely angry at the film which depicts the life of the legendary Scottish hero William Wallace. When it was released it was accompanied by a huge political, as well as cultural, debate within Scotland, as the issue of Scottish independence was becoming important again because of the persistent rejection by the Scottish electorate of the Conservative party, which nevertheless continued to govern Scotland because of its Westminster majority. McArthur says *Braveheart* and *Brigadoon* are the only films 'to have major resonance in Scottish culture and its diaspora' (2003: 1). He describes the Mel Gibson film variously as 'aesthetically impoverished and uninflectedly derivative', containing a 'farrago of romantic clichés' and is even a 'godsend to the proto-fascist psyche' (ibid.: 4). For Stenhouse, whatever its aesthetic strengths and weaknesses it is an 'act of piety' (2009: 183) and an attempt at a tribute to someone the producer, Randall Wallace, sees as a 'pre-eminent' national hero.

Given how much has been written about *Braveheart*, it is interesting to note that it grossed 'a comparatively modest' $209 million worldwide (Carrell 2012). But because it dealt with nationalism at a time when the Scottish National Party was starting again to make a major impact on Scottish politics, it attracted huge debate within Scotland itself. For Petrie, the film was part of the Hollywood tradition of 'romantic heroes and the honourable struggle for freedom' (2000: 209). It was released around the same time as another film in this tradition, the Michael Caton-Jones directed version of *Rob Roy*. If *Braveheart*, according to Petrie, was more akin to a medieval action adventure, *Rob Roy* was interested in a more complex examination of power structures. Both films, however, relied on Scottish heroism, rugged masculinity and martial combat.

Rob Roy also 'suggests a certain affinity with the revenge western with its themes of cattle rustling, struggling communities, rivalry between powerful landowners and duels of honour' (Petrie 2000: 211). The idea therefore of the Scottish diaspora being offered a representation of Scotland which itself is derived from, or mixed with, US cultural representations is again prominent. This association of the western with Scottish imagery is taken up by Scullion in her discussion of the influence of American popular culture on Scottish writing. Like the western, Scotland is often seen as a 'frontier culture' which 'poses a space on the very edge of the civilised world, at the edge of law and order, even at the edge of consciousness and rationality' (2004: 212).

Urban Images

Scullion goes on to discuss urban representations of Scotland and links with popular US cultural figures such as the hard-bitten film noir detective. Here she discusses the interest of Scottish dramatists in the industrial cityscapes of Glasgow and other towns in central Scotland. 'In the 1970s but with roots stretching back over the century Scottish drama was all but dominated by a version of the nation, a type of narrative and a set of characters which has been described as "urban kailyard"' (2004: 216).

This narrative appears to be the tradition described elsewhere as Clydesidism, films associated with male industrial labour in the west of Scotland. Scullion places one of the most iconic Scottish television programmes, *Taggart*, in this tradition – albeit a sub-genre of the hard man idea: the hard-bitten detective. Instantly recognisable to many people in Scotland through its morbid-jokey catchphrase 'There's been a murder', *Taggart* has enjoyed a phenomenal run since its first outing on Scottish Television in 1983, and has been shown across the UK and many overseas markets. More generally, Scottish detectives struggling against the corruption and bleakness of modern cities have proved attractive characters for Scottish novelists and scriptwriters. Here again Scullion notes the influence of US cinema. 'Narratives featuring these characters are explicitly affected by images of masculinity – as well as depictions of the city and narratives – dominant within Hollywood film' (ibid.: 217).

Given the scale of the audience, it would seem important not to overstate the likely influence on the diaspora of Scottish film-making and television-programming which deal with urban landscapes. That is not to say that both Clydesidism and the emergence of a different and new style of film-making in Scotland in the 1990s have not attracted a great deal of scholarly and critical interest. Indeed, it is worth noting the real optimism that surrounded Scottish film-making with the emergence of figures such as Bill Forsyth and then the triumvirate of Danny Boyle, Andrew MacDonald and John Hodge; Lynne Ramsay, and others who set films in Glasgow and Edinburgh without having to rely on the hard-man character or detectives to drive their stories. The successes of *Shallow Grave* and, in particular, *Trainspotting* in the 1990s seemed particularly significant.

Looking back on such developments, Petrie wrote in 2009:

> The predominant screen images of the nation have been transformed: a rural and remote setting for romantic or unsettling encounters has given way to a greater focus on an urban post-industrial environment framing narratives concerned with various aspects of contemporary experience and social change. (2009: 167)

However, he went on to discuss the funding, production, collaborative and other challenges confronting Scottish film makers. With recent intense controversy over the direction of the national arts funding body for Scotland, Creative Scotland, which now includes film, this debate has become particularly lively. But although these debates about the sustainability of a Scottish film-making industry and over the screen images presented by film makers working in Scotland are clearly of vital importance to ideas of national culture within Scotland, it seems fanciful to suggest these more contemporary images could have taken over as dominant themes in the minds of much of the diaspora, used as they will be to Tartanry and traditional imagery, which as Stenhouse (2009) says, so many enjoy.

SOME THOUGHTS ON TELEVISION

The recent success of Scandinavian and Israeli drama demonstrates that the size of a country is not necessarily a barrier to producing high-quality television programmes which can be exported, or at least adapted, successfully and which can therefore offer both an interesting and popular depiction of a national culture. Scandinavian programmes in particular such as *The Killing, The Bridge* and *Borgen* have attracted a committed international as well as domestic following.

Scotland is in a different position from these countries in that it has no independent, national publicly funded broadcaster. As we shall see, this has meant there are major challenges in producing programmes about Scotland for the Scottish domestic audience, never mind an international one. If it seems unlikely that cinematic representations of Scotland beyond blockbusters such as *Braveheart* and *Brave* are likely to achieve much international popular recognition then it seems an even bigger task for television programmes under the current arrangements. Nevertheless it is worth spending time on the television environment in Scotland as, unlike cinema, there should in theory (given the commitment to publicly funded television in the UK) be a guaranteed amount of money with which to make programmes and therefore to represent the country.

Although the British government classifies ITV, Channel 4 and Channel 5 as public service broadcasters (which have certain programming obligations) these channels are funded commercially. The BBC is funded publicly through the licence fee and is the main public service broadcaster across the UK and Scotland. As a PSB it has an important role in reflecting the diversity of the country, acting as a 'mirror' on society as the BBC itself has described it (Ang 1991: 15). To this end the BBC has a public purpose 'to represent the UK, its nations, regions and communities'. But how successful is the BBC in its mission of representing 'the nations', in particular Scotland? The BBC's regulator, the BBC Trust, in its latest report accepts more can be done in this respect:

> This remains an area of concern. This year the gap between audience expectations and the BBC's performance widened, particularly the portrayal of nations and regions, even while quality scores remained high. Audiences in Northern Ireland, Wales, Scotland and some English regions felt the BBC could do better. (BBC Annual Report 2012)

How then is Scotland represented through programming on the BBC? The first thing to say is that there is not a great deal of representing going on. In recent years there have been some successes in terms of programmes set in Scotland, and which have been exported. The undemanding drama *Monarch of the Glen*, for example, enjoyed a successful run and involved a familiar rural setting and various story-lines surrounding a branch of the Scottish land-owning class. But there have been real concerns about the extent of programmes made in, and about, Scotland.

The BBC does not run separate English-language channels for Scotland (or any other UK nation or region – although the BBC does part-fund the Gaelic service, BBC Alba). Instead the BBC broadcasts nine channels across the UK. The programming on seven of those channels, including a 24-hour news channel, is exactly the same regardless of where in the UK viewers live. For BBC1 and BBC2 (the two most popular channels described as 'mixed-genre') the bulk of the programming is again the same across the UK but at certain times (most commonly during evening and lunchtime news bulletins) regional programmes, made by BBC Scotland, will replace national output.

BBC Scotland has been described as being 'very much an adjunct' of the BBC in London (Linklater 1992: 140). Twenty years on from that statement, little has changed to give BBC Scotland more autonomy. Its budget, for example, is entirely determined by the BBC in London. In its latest annual review, BBC Scotland says that in 2011/12 it broadcast 850.52 hours of original 'local' content, by which it means content for viewers in Scotland only. Of that total 504 hours were devoted to news, and 53.38 to drama (BBC Scotland 2012). Most of these drama hours would have been devoted to a regular soap opera.

Concern about the lack of BBC programming in Scotland prompted the Scottish Government to establish a commission to look at broadcasting in Scotland, which recommended a 'Scottish Digital Network'. This would be a channel which would provide up to four hours of Scottish content a day. The channel would put a 'particular emphasis on celebrating, reflecting and nurturing Scottish culture in its broadest sense, including our distinctive history and heritage and our modern diversity' (Scottish Government 2011b). However, in the absence of political change there seems little prospect of such a channel being established. The BBC insists that by 2016/17 a greater proportion of total licence fee income will be spent in Scotland, Wales and Northern Ireland. This seems to be because of a commitment to produce more network (that is, all-UK programming) from these areas (BBC Trust 2011: 10). It is important to note that producing more network programmes from Scotland does not necessarily mean many more programmes *about* Scotland. For example, BBC Scotland's 2010/11 report mentions seven 'network' dramas produced in Scotland, only two of which were set in the country (BBC Scotland 2011). The BBC's decentralising strategy often results in a transfer of existing programmes from another production base (usually London) to Scotland as well as other regional centres (examples of programmes moved to Scotland from London include the quiz show *The Weakest Link*, *The Culture Show* and the current affairs programme

Question Time) without altering their editorial agenda to reflect, for example, more Scottish content.

NEWSPAPERS

This chapter will only consider newspapers briefly as, for most of their history, their journalism will have been aimed at people in Scotland and therefore their likely direct impact on the diaspora is likely to have been limited. With the internet it is possible of course to access Scottish papers across the globe but this potential to reach a far greater readership is sadly coinciding with extremely difficult trading conditions for most titles in Scotland. Twenty years ago it could be said that 66 per cent of the Scottish population read a morning paper and 83 per cent a Sunday paper (Linklater 1992: 126). Now, as in many western developed countries, sales have fallen dramatically. The paper with perhaps the best brand with which to penetrate the diaspora market, *The Scotsman*, has recently withdrawn from the monthly system of recording circulation but at the turn of 2013 was selling just over 32,000 copies a day. Few papers have worked out at present how to make sufficient revenue out of the vast potential online readership and, as things stand, declining print circulations are likely to have a major impact on journalism resources and therefore on the ability to produce compelling content whether on- or off-line. It could be argued that Scottish newspapers, although unlikely to have influenced the diaspora directly to any great extent (in that relatively few members of the diaspora will be regular readers of the Scottish press), could be contributing to an overall view of Scotland because of their impact on (or at least maintenance of) general perceptions of the country.

There are various ways of classifying the newspaper market in Scotland. Titles are sometimes categorised as falling into one of three types depending on content style: quality/broadsheet publications, 'mid-range' papers, and popular or tabloid titles. The press can also be categorised geographically as national, regional or local. Finally, titles can be said to be indigenous or editions of UK-wide papers. It is not always easy, however, to put papers into these categories. There are two daily titles which would see themselves as quality, national, indigenous papers: *The Scotsman* and *The Herald*, but both papers have a strong regional connection (*The Scotsman* is produced in Edinburgh and *The Herald* in Glasgow). In addition, the mass-selling *Daily Record* could be classified as a popular, national and indigenous paper but in recent years it has included much more content from its sister UK-wide title the *Mirror*.

Despite these complexities there have been attempts to assess the extent to which Scottish newspapers have fostered a sense of national togetherness through the deployment of language. A number of studies, for example, have used Billig's (1995) concept of banal nationalism to examine the situation in Scotland (Law 2001; Rosie et al. 2004, 2006). Billig is interested in the way that newspapers use the routine deployment of words such as 'we', 'us' and 'our' to reinforce the naturalness and obviousness of existing nation-states. For Scotland (as part of a multi-national state) there is an obvious issue here: when a newspaper uses the word 'we' is it referring to 'we British' or 'we Scottish', and is it therefore possible to assess whether the uses of these pronouns are drivers of Scottish or British national identity or both? Petersoo (2007) is particularly interesting in this regard in her discussion of what she calls the 'wandering we', where the 'we' can have a range of associations.

The biggest-selling daily paper in Scotland is the popular tabloid *The Sun*, which is owned by the media tycoon Rupert Murdoch's News International. In 2012 Murdoch appeared before the Leveson Inquiry into the culture, practice and ethics of the British press in what was billed as one of the biggest media events of that year. One of Murdoch's newspapers, the *News of the World* (now defunct), had been embroiled in a scandal over the illegal hacking of phone messages involving members of the royal family, sports stars, celebrities and victims of crime, among others. During the course of the inquiry the spotlight had also fallen on the relationships that Murdoch had built up with leading UK politicians. In Scotland there had been much interest in particular on the relationship between Murdoch and Scotland's First Minister, Alex Salmond. When asked about this by the inquiry's counsel, Murdoch said that he was interested in Scottish independence and considered himself to be half-Scottish. In his witness statement he said his grandfather, Patrick (a Presbyterian minister) had emigrated from Scotland to Australia and had been a supporter of the free press, which he considered 'the strongest foe of tyranny' (Leveson Inquiry 2012). The media tycoon therefore considers himself to be a member of the Scottish diaspora. However, it seems unlikely that most other members of the diaspora are even aware of Mr Murdoch's Scottish titles, and the impact of these, and other papers, on views held about Scotland is difficult to assess.

A potentially interesting development occurred when a new online publication launched – *The Caledonian Mercury* – with a clear aim of tapping into the expatriate market. However, its success at present is uncertain.

CONCLUSION

It would be a mistake to assume that the Scottish diaspora receives media messages from Scotland which then have a direct impact on their views of the country. As we have seen, the dominant images of Scotland are often conceived in the US or London. Inevitably, also, given that Scotland is not sealed off culturally from the rest of the world, the portrayal of Scotland by creatives working in Scotland will also be a product of wider cultural influences. The dominance of Tartanry and Kailyard has been a constant theme in discussion of the portrayal of Scotland, accompanied by frequent despair at the way the reality of modern Scottish life has been ignored. Although there has been a lively debate within Scotland itself, and some evidence of change in these portrayals, it seems reasonable to assume such debate has not had a major influence on those who live outside Scotland. Traditional imagery of Scotland seems entrenched, and as Stenhouse (2009) says, is clearly enjoyed by millions. There will be different views on the importance of these images and the extent to which they influence meaning about what it means to be Scottish. But within Scotland itself there seems to me a more pressing debate. As we approach a decision on whether to become an independent country, should we be concerned about the capacity of the Scottish media and creative industries to produce high-quality output capable of telling compelling stories about the diversity of life in the country? Given the structure of public service broadcasting in particular in Scotland, perhaps we need to think about alternative models of ensuring we really do have the capability to hold a mirror up to the country.

13

Sport and the Scottish Diaspora

Alan Bairner and Stuart Whigham

INTRODUCTION

On Sunday, 7 July 2013, Andy Murray became the first British tennis player for seventy-seven years to win the Wimbledon Men's Singles Championship. It was his second Grand Slam victory, the first coming in the United States the previous year when, in addition, he had won a gold medal at the London Olympic Games. Arguably none of this would have been possible had he not left his home town of Dunblane as a teenager to study in Barcelona at the Schiller International School and to train on the tennis courts of the Sánchez-Casal Academy. Since his return to the UK, Murray has chosen to live in London not far from Wimbledon itself.

This chapter examines the relationship between the Scottish diaspora and sport from two different perspectives. First, we consider the contribution that Scots have made to the development of sport in other parts of the world or who, like Andy Murray, have achieved success in their chosen sport in large part by leaving Scotland. While for some of these well-known, and not so well-known, people who are discussed in the first part of the essay, their reasons for living abroad may well have been far removed from sport in the first instance, in most cases migration was directly linked to desire to pursue sporting ambitions. The evidence that is examined in this opening section of the chapter is by no means comprehensive. However, it is intended to demonstrate the extent to which Scots can legitimately be regarded as sporting pioneers or missionaries who have exerted considerable influence on the global diffusion of a number of sports, specifically golf and association football. The second part of the chapter focuses on the attitudes of Scottish exiles and assesses the degree to which their relationship with Scotland and the places in which they now live is affected by their identification with sport. This is the story not of those Scots who have achieved prominence in the world of sport but of their countless compatriots living away from home for whom sport has everyday significance in terms of the construction and reproduction of their sense of identity.

The aim is to explore the significance of sport for Scottish migrants in maintaining a bond with their homeland while experiencing life in various locations and cultures. Although this issue has received relatively little attention in academic literature in the past, in comparison to the sporting experiences of other notable diasporas, we will summarise the findings of existing studies focusing on the importance of sport to the Scottish diaspora in a number of contrasting contexts. Analysis of these findings will demonstrate variety within the Scots diaspora in terms of their engagement with Scottish sport, highlighting the influence of geographic, cultural and personal factors in creating context-specific challenges for Scots migrants. When juxtaposed with arguments made about other diasporic groups which have received more consideration in relation to sport, in particular the Irish, the discussion of these studies will assist in developing an argument that the manner in which Scots use sport to maintain links with the home nation and 'Scottish identity' is distinctive although not necessarily unique. Let us begin, however, with those Scots who have left their native shores and made a mark on sport in other countries either because that was the main reason for their migration or because of sporting activities that were pursued in the course of being exiled for the more customary reasons.

Making our Mark

Scots have played a significant part in the global diffusion of a number of different sports. Indeed, it would be difficult to decide in which sport the Scottish influence has been felt most strongly. Since both association football and rugby are essentially English inventions, it is perhaps more appropriate to begin our investigation with one of the few sports which are regularly cited as having been invented by the Scots. That sport is golf.

The history of golf includes, in Campbell's (2001: 10) florid prose, 'the Scottish golfing missionaries who took the light of their great game into a darkened world for the betterment of all'. Rather more prosaically, it is undoubtedly the case that Scottish professional golfers recognised and seized the opportunities offered abroad, not least in the United States with its burgeoning interest in golf during the first half of the twentieth century. Among them was Tommy Armour, born in Edinburgh in 1894. Having attended Fettes College and the University of Edinburgh, Armour emigrated to the United States in 1923 and turned professional the following year after highly decorated service during the First World War, during which he was blinded in one eye (Campbell 2001: 42). He won twenty-seven tournaments, including the US Open (1927), the Professional Golfers' Association (1930) and the Open Championship (1931). Armour died in New York State in 1968. He was inducted into the World Golf Hall of Fame in 1976 and some modern golf equipment still carries his name.

Another remarkable Scottish-born golfer who achieved success in the US was William Anderson. Born in North Berwick in 1879, Anderson emigrated with his father and brother in 1896 and went on to win the US Open four times (1901, 1903, 1904 and 1905). He remains the only man to have won the title in three successive years and only Bobby Jones, Ben Hogan and Jack Nicklaus have equalled his record of four victories. He died at the relatively young age of thirty-one in 1910, officially from epilepsy although one historian has claimed that he drank himself to death (Delaney 2010). Remarkable as the achievements of these golfers were, however, and had Armour not been playing in the same era as Bobby Jones he would assuredly be much better known, it is arguable that it has been Scottish golf course architects rather than the most successful players who have had the greater impact on the game. Two examples suffice to make the point.

Donald Ross was born in Dornoch in 1872. Having served an apprenticeship with Old Tom Morris in St Andrews, he left Scotland for the US in 1899. He tied for fifth place in the US Open (1903) and in eighth place in the Open (1910). He is better remembered today, however, for having designed or redesigned around four hundred golf courses between 1900 and 1948, when he died in North Carolina aged seventy-five (Campbell 2001). His most famous designs include Pinehurst No. 2, Aronimink Golf Club, Seminole Golf Club, Oak Hill and Oakland Hills. He became the first President of the American Society of Golf Course Architects and was inducted into the World Golf Hall of Fame, an honour normally reserved for those with considerably greater playing success. Although born in Yorkshire in 1870, Alister MacKenzie, another hugely influential golf course architect, was the son of Scottish parents and the family spent their summers in Lochinver. He identified strongly with his Scottish roots throughout his life, asserting on one occasion that 'being a Scotsman I am naturally opposed to water in its undiluted state' (Campbell 2001: 29–30). MacKenzie served as a surgeon in the Boer War and as an expert on camouflage in the First World War. He began designing courses in the United Kingdom, including the Portland course at Royal Troon and Pitreavie in Dunfermline. However, he relocated to the US in the late 1920s and there was responsible for such courses as Cypress Point in California and, most notably, the Augusta National Club, home to the US Masters. As one of the first golf course architects who had not been a leading player, MacKenzie also designed courses in Australia (Melbourne Golf Club) and New Zealand (Titirangi in Auckland). He died in 1934 but his name lives on in the shape of the Alister MacKenzie Society of Great Britain and Ireland, which hosts regular golfing tournaments.

Even though the English first codified the modern game of association football, there is no doubt that, like golf, the sport gave Scotland what Kevin McCarra (1984: 69) has described as 'a place in the world'. This process began in England itself with Scottish professionals arriving in large numbers to play for clubs in north-east England and in Lancashire. For example, the Liverpool side selected to play against Middlesbrough Ironopolis on 2 September 1893 in the club's first-ever league match was comprised of ten Scots and an English-born goalkeeper by the name of Billy McOwen (Forsyth 1990). As former Portsmouth captain and Players' Union activist Jimmy Guthrie put it, 'After whisky footballers have been the favourite and most expensive export from Scotland to England' (cited in Forsyth 1990: 37). This almost entirely one-way traffic (with such notable exceptions as Terry Butcher and Paul Gascoigne) has continued to the present day, although it is safe to say that, with a much-altered football power balance between the two countries, the flood has become little more than a trickle with more celebrated exports such as Alex James, Hughie Gallacher, Billy Liddell, Denis Law, who also briefly took his talent to Turin where, as Stuart Cosgrove (1991: 26) commented, with admirable understatement, 'the monastic discipline of the Italian game proved ... trying', Dave Mackay, John White, Kenny Dalglish and countless others now an increasingly distant memory. In one respect, however, the impact of Scots on English football has continued. From Matt Busby and Bill Shankly to Alex Ferguson and David Moyes, as well as the up-and-coming Paul Lambert, Malky Mackay and Dougie Freedman, Scottish managers have achieved disproportionately high levels of success with a variety of English clubs.

Perhaps even more noteworthy than all of this, however, is the role played by William McGregor. Born in Braco in Perthshire in 1846, McGregor moved to Birmingham where he set up in business as a draper and went on to found Aston Villa Football Club. By bringing together representatives of other leading English clubs, resulting in the formation of the Football League of which he was chairman from 1888 to 1891, McGregor presided over the transition of English football from an amateur pursuit to a truly professionalised sport. He was also chairman of the Football Association (1888–94) and was honorary president of the Football League (1891–4). He was elected first life member of the League in 1895 and died in 1911. He is remembered today by a statue unveiled in 2009 at the Directors' Entrance to the Trinity Road Stand at Villa Park in Birmingham (Taylor 2002).

It was not only in England, of course, that the Scottish influence on the development of football was felt. No less remarkable than William McGregor, although considerably less well known, is Alexander (Alejandro) Hutton, who is generally regarded as 'the father of Argentine football'. Born in Glasgow's Gorbals in 1853, Hutton emigrated to Argentina in 1882, having graduated from the University of Edinburgh. A teacher with a strong belief in the educational value of sport, he is credited with establishing in 1893 the first officially recognised football league outside of Britain and Ireland. Hutton died in Buenos Aires in 1936 and the Argentine Football Association library is named in his honour (Hutchinson 1996).

Innumerable stories could be told to emphasise further the influence of Scots on the global diffusion of association football. But one is perhaps especially instructive. Claims have been made, and also disputed, that Scots introduced the game to Sweden. What is beyond dispute is that one of the teams that took part in the first recorded football match to be played in Sweden in 1892 was Örgyte Idrottssallskap (ÖIS) from Gothenburg and that it soon became known as 'Skottelaget' or 'the Scottish team' with reference to the presence in the team of seven Scottish-born players (Bairner 2004). All of the Scots were employed as managers or skilled workers at the city's AB Svenska Gardinfabriken, a textile-manufacturing company. Nearly all of them returned home after their contracts ended. Nevertheless, the Swedish-born widow of one of the team, Alex Thomson, is reported to have visited Gothenburg in the late 1940s with her daughter and son-in-law. During their stay they went to Thomson's former workplace and also Balders Hage, the original home ground of ÖIS and now the site of the city's Liseberg amusement park.

Leaving Scotland, William McGregor took with him an interest in football but, like the Örgyte footballers, it was not football that took him from Scotland. Similarly, the men who formed the London Scottish Football Club at Mackay's Tavern on Ludgate Hill had gone to England to further their various careers and not primarily to play rugby union (Massie 1984). Formed partially as a way of allowing Scottish exiles in London to meet, the club nevertheless became a major force in English rugby at least until the advent of the professional era. Notable among over two hundred London Scottish players to have represented Scotland are Paul Burnell, Alastair McHarg, Ian Smith and Mike Campbell-Lamerton, who not only captained the national side but also the British and Irish Lions on the 1966 tour to Australia and New Zealand. For the Scottish exiles who made such a contribution to the club and to the game of rugby more generally, even if sport had not necessarily been a major factor in taking them to England it surely formed a significant part of their lives. An interesting offshoot of the club is the Hong Kong Scottish who marked their launch in 2011 by taking part in the Melrose Rugby Sevens.

The next section of this essay focuses, however, on those almost countless exiled Scots for whom playing sport may be relatively unimportant but whose interest in sport is nevertheless pivotal in terms of how they negotiate life 'awa frae hame'.

HOME THOUGHTS FROM ABROAD

In order to provide a more nuanced understanding of the role that sport can play for 'ordinary' members of the Scottish diaspora in maintaining a link with Scotland, it is important firstly to consider the impact of the contrasting geographical contexts in which migrant Scots reside. In particular, the distinction between Scots who live in overseas locations, as opposed to those who have migrated to locations outside Scotland but within the United Kingdom, has a potential impact on the manner in which sport acts as a bond with fellow Scots. The importance of considering Scots within the UK as constituent members of the Scottish diaspora has been explored in depth in Andrew Mycock's chapter earlier in this book. Such an emphasis is important, given that out of the estimated 1.25 million native Scots living outside of their home nation, approximately two-thirds (circa 800,000) of them live in England (Ancien, Boyle and Kitchin 2009; Sim 2011a). Although the majority of the extensive studies of the Scottish diaspora have focused on emigrants in more distant locations, such as North

America, the Caribbean, the Asian sub-continent and Australasia (for example, Devine 1992; McCarthy 2007a; Sim 2011b), a growing number of studies have also considered the migration of Scots to England (for example, McCarthy 2005, 2007b; Leith and Sim 2012; Sim 2011a). This has been mirrored in academic studies on the topic of sport and the Scottish diaspora which will be outlined below.

At the outset of this discussion, it is important to explore the reasons why sport can be said to play an important role for the Scottish diaspora. Kellas (1998) argues that sport is the most popular form of nationalist behaviour in many countries, given the lack of global conflict in the post-Second World War period and thus the conditions which historically have provided the starkest manifestation of national unity and ideology. Such arguments have been replicated in various discussions about the importance of sport for the Scots (Bairner 1996; Forsyth 1992). Drawing upon McCrone's (1992) claims regarding the importance of the Scottish civil society 'holy trinity' of independent church, legal and educational systems, many authors have attempted to illustrate that certain sports such as football and rugby union similarly operate as additional pillars of a distinct Scottish civil society with independent teams representing Scotland rather than the United Kingdom (Bairner 1994; Jarvie and Walker 1994; Duke and Crolley 1996; Moorhouse 1987).

Therefore, international sporting fixtures or events can offer the Scottish diaspora the opportunity to distinguish themselves from other migrant groups, while also providing the opportunity to maintain an allegiance with their contemporaries in Scotland. Arguments to this effect have often cited concepts such as Anderson's (1991) portrayal of the nation as an 'imagined community'. The emphasis on the 'imagined' character of the Scottish nation through ideas of cultural, social, ethnic and political bonds has been a common feature of discussions of national identity in Scotland (Trevor-Roper 1983; McCrone 1992). Bairner (2001) argues that the prevalence of sport for the expression of nationalist sentiment lies in part in the opportunity it provides to bring the 'imagined community' of the nation to life, giving both physical form and voice to a given national identity. Maguire (1999) argues that contrasting forms of sporting national identities are linked to differing national cultures which underpin the 'imagined community' of the nation. Sport therefore provides members of the Scottish diaspora with an opportunity to actively and simultaneously participate in this 'imagined community' despite their geographical displacement, whether this be through using such events as a stimulus for congregating with fellow Scots migrants, viewing televised coverage of sporting events privately or by consuming mediated information on Scottish sport to keep abreast of developments.

While academic study of the importance of sport for the Scottish diaspora is less abundant when compared with the treatment of other diasporic groups, two eminent sociologists of sport have given direct consideration to this topic: firstly there is Grant Jarvie's (1991, 2000, 2005) discussion of the spread of the Highland Games to North America, and secondly Richard Giulianotti's (2005; Giulianotti and Robertson 2006, 2007) consideration of Rangers and Celtic Supporters' Clubs in North America. These extensive studies have concentrated their attention on institutionalised forms of engagement with sport for the Scottish diaspora in North America, and it is pertinent to commence by reviewing their central findings.

Jarvie's studies (1991, 2000, 2005) offer a thorough historical and sociological account of the development of Highland Games events in North America, tracing the roots of Scottish and Highland societies back to the period of increased emigration following the Highland Clearances. These societies were established in the USA and Canada as a means of assisting the integration of the Scottish diaspora into their new home by providing a medium for maintaining a number of customs associated with Highland culture, including Highland Games and Gatherings. However, Jarvie (1991, 2005) also reflects upon the different culture of North American Highland Games compared to those held in Scotland, arguing that the North American Highland Games have retained a romantic and mythologising view of the 'authentic' traditions and symbolism of Highland and Scottish culture. Similar debates regarding the 'invented traditions' of Scottish culture have prompted extensive, and often heated, discussion elsewhere (Hobsbawm 1983; McCrone 1992; Trevor-Roper 1983), with contrasting perspectives on the historicity and authenticity of romantic cultural symbols such as tartan, 'Kailyard' culture and various Highland customs. Jarvie (2005) argues that the Games in North America actually represent what it is to be a North American Scottish Highlander, rather than an actual Highlander or a Scot in the modern context of Scotland. Nonetheless, for Jarvie, the continued organisation of Highland Games in North America demonstrates a major forum for members of the Scottish diaspora from various generations to engage with Scottish culture, regardless of whether such events are truly reflective of traditional or contemporary Scottish society. He argues that membership of Scottish or Highland societies and attendance at Highland Games and Gatherings offer opportunities for members of the diaspora to generate 'social capital' through active participation, acting as a counterpoint against a general loss of community spirit in contemporary North American society.

In contrast, Giulianotti's work (2005; Giulianotti and Robertson 2006, 2007) focuses on the role of North American football supporters' clubs for fans of the two most popular clubs in Scotland, Rangers and Celtic. His initial study (Giulianotti 2005) linked the study of the Scottish diaspora to ideas of voice, arguing that football represented a key site for 'phatic communication' and 'vernacularisation of voice', allowing members to retain their sense of identity by recreating sporting cultures from Scotland, as well as the associated styles and forms of accent, speech, debate and song. While these strategies help to maintain an identification with home, Giulianotti highlights that problems of alienation can be compounded with visits back to Scotland which undermine nostalgic memories of home. He argues that football has added importance to Scots given the status of Scotland as a stateless nation, providing the opportunity to foster national pride (as is the case with the reputation of the 'Tartan Army'), express cultural and politicised anti-English sentiment or distinctions, and to foster identities related to religious divides associated with the 'Old Firm' in Scotland. Celtic and Rangers supporters' clubs and the bars in which they tend to meet are often redolent with material reminders – in the form of pictures on the walls, the food that is eaten, and so on – of Scotland and, indeed, of Ireland and Ulster. Yet, in addition to their almost total mutual exclusivity, neither type of venue is likely to be entirely comfortable for the football-loving Scot who has no affinity with either Old Firm club.

Giulianotti and Robertson (2006, 2007) apply the concept of 'glocalisation' in their later analyses of these supporters' clubs to demonstrate how these organisations provide the opportunity to transplant Scottish sporting culture to an alternative global context. They highlight three issues which face the Scottish diaspora in terms of maintaining national identity in the face of a culturally cosmopolitan environment, arguing that such a situation results in selective identification with Scottish cultural national identity by migrants, a process of 'banal relativization' of Scottish culture vis-à-vis North American culture, and the existence of alternative translocal associations which can challenge and compete with the importance of national identity to the Scots diaspora. Giulianotti and Robertson (2007) develop these arguments to produce a typology of glocalisation projects undertaken by the Scots diaspora in relation to the supporters' clubs, analysing four identified projects of 'relativization', 'accommodation', 'hybridization' and 'transformation' according to a range of criteria relating to the sociological importance and manifestations of these projects in this context. Both studies shed important insights on the strategies used by Scottish diaspora groups in relation to ideas of sporting identity, and highlight issues regarding the maintenance of future 'glocal' Scottish identities such as the impact of increased levels of mediated sport coverage and the problems of reproducing this culture in future generations of the diaspora in North America (Giulianotti and Robertson 2006, 2007).

Although the findings of the above studies shed some light on the importance of sport for the Scottish diaspora, the lack of consideration given to locations other than North America highlights the need for wider study of this topic. Studies of Scots who have migrated within the UK to locations such as England have contrastingly argued that a more implicit, social-mental Scottish identity is adopted by members of the Scottish diaspora while integrating more fully with the local culture, rather than engaging through more institutionalised, external types of Scottish cultural association in the form of Scottish societies which have often been hampered by dwindling memberships (McCarthy 2005, 2007a, 2007b; Sim 2011a). One reason for such a contrast is the cultural similarity evident within the UK, easing the process of assimilation and adjustment into a new location and culture for Scottish migrants. Nonetheless, Scots living in England still use a number of strategies to retain a national identity and links with their Scottish home, such as the development of personal networks to maintain an association with home and with fellow Scots in England, as well as the continued use and maintenance of accent and/or dialect as a form of distinction (McCarthy 2005; Whigham in press).

In terms of engagement with sport, the relative ease of access to mediated coverage of Scottish sport often negates the need to establish collective organisations for these purposes, although numerous examples of such organisations do indeed exist, often for the purpose of travelling to Scottish international and club fixtures. Indeed, the growth of televised coverage of live sporting fixtures has important implications for the dynamics of the process through which sport acts as a means of identification with Scotland for its diaspora. Given that 'internal migrants' within the UK often have access to television sports broadcasters such as the BBC, ITV, Sky and ESPN within the comfort and privacy of their own homes at a relatively low cost, it is possible

to follow Scottish international teams, club teams and individual athletes without engaging with fellow Scots in a collective manner. By
contrast, in locations further afield, access to such televised coverage
is often limited to specialised satellite providers at a more significant
cost, given the marginalised status of Scottish sport vis-à-vis its global
rivals. Therefore, finding such coverage often requires attending public venues such as sports bars or clubs, and by its very nature this
practice results in opportunities to meet with fellow Scots communally
and to make new acquaintances through a shared interest in Scottish
sport (Whigham 2011). However, the impact of recent developments
in live internet-based streaming technology for sports fixtures and
events may yet reduce the necessity for Scots in overseas settings to
congregate in this manner.

These arguments regarding developments in media and electronic
communication echo the findings of Finch, Latorre and Andrew's
(2010) extensive study on the British diaspora, in which it is argued that
media use and social networking are increasingly acting as important
means of maintaining contact with family, friends and developments
at 'home'. This perceptible shift towards the use of individual activities, such as media consumption, personal communication and social
networking, to maintain links with home as part of everyday life can
be argued to partially reflect Billig's (1995) conceptualisation of 'banal
nationalism'. Billig offers this concept to explain how the established
nations of the West reproduce and maintain a sense of national identity
and unity, and how the existence of the nation is routinely flagged in
day-to-day society and culture through the mass media, social institutions and politics. Moving on to the specific issue of sport, Billig
(1995) identifies the prevalence of nationalist flagging in newspaper
sports coverage, highlighting the emphasis given to national teams and
individuals, the use of personal pronouns of 'I' and 'we' in relation to
the nation, and the feeling of shared experience fostered through media
consumption. Growing engagement with internet-based media sources
relating to Scottish sports, such as online versions of Scottish newspapers, websites including those of BBC Sport or Sky Sports, fan fora and
blogs, provides further evidence for Giulianotti and Robertson's (2006,
2007) arguments about the prevalence of 'banal relativization' in the
use of sport by the Scottish diaspora. Similar evidence has been found
among Scots living in England, with a notable phenomenon being the
demonstration of as increased interest in Scottish affairs and culture
after leaving Scotland, with particular reference being made to reading
books about Scotland and its history (Whigham 2011). This is argued

to be fairly typical behaviour for expatriates and exiles of all countries, and, in this instance, was frequently explained in relation to personal feelings of dislocation and detachment from Scotland.

This enthusiasm of the Scottish diaspora to engage actively with contemporary Scottish culture and events has also begun to play a more central role in the tourism strategies of the devolved Scottish Government in recent years, following the precedent of the Irish Government's diaspora engagement strategy (Finch, Latorre and Andrew 2010). One of the current tourism strategies promoted by the Scottish Government and VisitScotland, 'The Winning Years', revolves around themed years of activities and events (VisitScotland 2011). Recent years have concentrated on themes such as 'Homecoming' (2009), 'Food and Drink' (2010), 'Active Scotland' (2011), 'Creative Scotland' (2012) and 'Natural Scotland' (2013). Sport has played a role within this tourism strategy, with Scotland's status as the 'home of golf' being emphasised as a vehicle for attracting overseas active sports tourists and inward investment into Scottish tourism infrastructure (EventScotland 2008). The 'Year of Homecoming 2014' is of particular interest when considering the importance of sport for the Scottish diaspora, given that Scotland will be hosting two major sporting events this year, namely the Commonwealth Games in Glasgow and the Ryder Cup at Gleneagles. The hosting of these events in 2014 clearly has an added resonance given that they sandwich the date for the Scottish independence referendum to be held in September 2014. Hosting major sporting events such as the Commonwealth Games and the Ryder Cup provides Scotland with the opportunity to place itself on the global sporting map at what is potentially the single most important juncture in its political, economic and social future. Although these events will generate significant interest for Scots, the Scottish diaspora and sports fans from across the globe, whether attending the event or viewing mediated coverage of it, it nevertheless remains to be seen the extent to which such interest is harnessed to engage the Scottish diaspora with the political future of the Scottish nation. It is unlikely that Scottish, British and international media coverage of these sporting events will fail to allude to the constitutional future of the Scottish nation at least in passing.

While discussion to this point has largely emphasised the positive aspects of the role that sport plays for the Scottish diaspora, it is also important to reflect more critically upon some of the limitations of assigning too much importance to this particular element of Scottish culture as a means of maintaining links with 'home'. Firstly, it would be remiss to ignore the highly gendered nature of the most popular sports in Scotland, such as football, rugby and golf. Undoubtedly there has been a significant growth in the numbers of females who take an active interest in these sports, either as participants or spectators. However, the demographic balance in relation to sports spectating and participation remains heavily skewed towards males. Indeed, the work of Jarvie (1991, 2000, 2005) and Giulianotti (2005; Giulianotti and Robertson 2006, 2007) reflected this male predominance in both the membership samples of the societies upon which they based their studies and in discussion of their findings. The extent to which sport reflects the opportunity to reproduce Scottish male culture, rather than an inclusive Scottish culture which involves both genders equally, is therefore open to debate.

Furthermore, relatively little attention has been paid to the role of active sports participation as a means of reproducing Scottish culture for the Scottish diaspora. Such a reflection can be used to shed light on some of the cultural divides evident within Scotland, given that McCrone (1992) emphasises the importance of appreciating the potential cleavage between Highland and Lowland Scottish culture. While the establishment of Highland Societies in North America facilitated the maintenance of Highland Games events on a regular basis, another Scottish sport associated with Highland culture, shinty, has failed to replicate the success of Irish sports such as hurling and Gaelic football in establishing a central role in the lives of certain members of the respective diaspora (Darby 2009). This has been attributed elsewhere to the failure of Scots to follow in the footsteps of the Irish and to establish a Scottish equivalent of the Gaelic Athletic Association (GAA) which has prioritised the maintenance of Irish sporting culture at home and overseas (Bradley 1998). With reference to the sports often associated with Lowland and Central Belt Scottish culture, such as football, rugby union and golf, the historic dissemination of these sports on a global basis, due in part as we have seen to the pioneering work of Scottish migrants, has resulted in their adoption and establishment in various locations throughout the world. This provides exiled Scots with an opportunity to participate in the same sports as their counterparts in Scotland; however, participation in team sports such as these will often equally, if not even more so, involve integration and assimilation into friendship groups and networks consisting of members of the 'host' population with whom they play. Although the establishment of predominantly 'Scottish' clubs has been evident in certain locations, with examples such as the London Scottish Football Club and grassroots teams in amateur leagues for various sports, the prevalence of such organisations is negligible in comparison with other diaspora groups, most notably the Irish (Darby and Hassan 2008a). There is, of course, a plethora of Celtic and Rangers supporters' clubs and meeting places throughout England, not only in towns with sizeable émigré communities such as Corby in Northamptonshire but even in relatively small settlements such as Thringstone in north-west Leicestershire. However, like their counterparts in North America and elsewhere, these are not necessarily welcoming locales for all Scots living in England.

The limitations of sport as a means for maintaining cultural links with fellow Scots at home and overseas are further exacerbated by the challenges faced by long-term Scottish migrants, especially those who have started families in their 'host' countries. Previous considerations of the engagement of second and third generation Scottish diaspora members with Scottish culture and sport have reported a lack of interest in Scottish sport in relation to the sporting culture of the 'host' country (Giulianotti 2005; Leith and Sim 2012; Whigham in press). While the studies of Giulianotti and Whigham found that many first generation members of the Scottish diaspora actively encouraged their offspring to feel at least partly Scottish or retain connections with the country of their parents' birth, the fact that their children were of a different nationality by place of birth challenges the beliefs of both the parents and children in this regard. Furthermore, Leith and Sim (2012) argue that this lack of a Scottish 'symbolic ethnicity' for second generation Scots appears to be heightened for those living within England compared with those situated further afield. Developments such as these are indicative of recent debates about identity and 'hybridity' for members of particular diasporas (Kalra, Kaur and Hutnyk 2005), as individual members are forced to reconsider their notions of nationality, citizenship, national identity and cultural identity in light of their new surroundings. Interestingly, although Leith and Sim's study considered the identities of second generation Scots in a general sense, sport was raised frequently by their participants as a central issue in demonstrating the national identity of second generation Scots, illustrated by the national team they offer their support to. Thus it appears that sport's potential to bring the 'imagined community' of the Scottish nation to life can allow us to reflect upon the complex construction and maintenance of Scottish identity within the Scottish diaspora. Understanding the role of sport within this process adds an important strand to future academic study of this group.

CONCLUSION

Comparing the Scottish and Jewish diasporas, McCrone (2013: 6) writes, 'the Scottish diaspora, such as it is, is not obsessing about whether or not there should be a "homeland"'. Perhaps not, but the reason for this may well lie in the fact that, unlike those central European Jews who aligned themselves with Theodore Herzl's Zionist ideology, they have a 'homeland'. Former Irish President Mary Robinson made strenuous attempts during her term in office to ensure that such a sense of belonging should resonate with members of her country's diaspora. In her election address in 1990, she emphasised the bonds between the Irish at home and the Irish overseas. Moreover, as Darby and Hassan (2008b: 2): note, 'By going on to state that she viewed herself as a representative of them all Robinson was simultaneously reaching out to a diaspora that felt neglected and forgotten and challenging Irish politicians and the Irish public to adopt a more inclusive and less territorially bounded view of who or what constituted the Irish "nation"'. As we have argued in this chapter, however, the Scottish diaspora's relationship with its homeland, unlike that of its Irish counterpart, is commonly more individual – even solitary for some – rather than communal. For many, sport has been a major feature of their persistent, if relatively isolated, relationship with home.

There can be no denying that, in the world of sport as in so many other human endeavours, Scots have made their mark in various parts of the world. Yet the achievements of men such as Tommy Armour, Willie Anderson, William McGregor and Sir Alex Ferguson are for the most part personal. While they may owe something to aspects of the Scottish psyche or to environmental factors associated with growing up in Scotland, they came about despite the existence of a global Scottish diaspora rather than because of it. To that extent they contribute considerably to the pride that Scots, at home and abroad, so often exhibit in relation to their nation. They shed little light, however, on the life experiences of those far more numerous Scots who have left their native shores, not in search of sporting success but rather to make a living in a huge range of jobs, relatively few of them sport-related.

Until quite recently the ways in which Scots outside the United Kingdom used sport to maintain contact with home have been at variance with the experiences of those who have simply moved within the UK. However, not least because of developments in information technology and the communications industry, this gap between the two groups of exiles is narrowing. Thus, perhaps the most striking contrast that emerges from the preceding discussion is not that which distinguishes Scots in England from Scots in North America but the one that differentiates the Scottish and Irish diasporas. It is surely telling that, whereas the GAA ensures that sport plays a pivotal and largely inclusive role, except for the Scots-Irish, in the lives of countless Irish exiles throughout the world, the main institutions which foster (by accident or design) settings in which Scots can mix are Celtic and Rangers supporters' clubs with all that their teams are believed, rightly or wrongly, to represent in terms of what divides rather than unites the Scottish nation (Bairner 1994).

For many members of the Scottish diaspora, the main connection with Scotland, apart from familial ties, is through sport. This is often a relatively solitary relationship, however, not least if it involves negotiation with immediate family members who may have relatively limited interest in sport or Scotland or both. Nevertheless, even in such circumstances, it is difficult for members of the diaspora not to experience a sense of belonging when television broadcasts allow us to watch the national rugby union and football teams take to the field or Andy Murray step on to the Centre Court at Wimbledon for a Grand Slam Final. At moments such as these, sporting Scots abroad, just like those at home, are inclined to reach for the old but self-delusional adage, 'Wha's like us? Damn few and they're a' deid'.

14

Conclusions: The Nature and State of the Contemporary Scottish Diaspora

Murray Stewart Leith and Duncan Sim

REVISITING THE NATURE OF THE DIASPORA

In the introduction to this work, we began by considering the nature of diasporas and the theoretical literature surrounding the term itself. Drawing on Adamson (2008) we emphasised that a diaspora is as much a social construct as it is a form of belonging, among which identity, emotion, mythology, history, memory and dreams all feature (Shuval 2000). We considered Brubaker (2005) and his stress on the need for a 'homeland' to which the diaspora could connect and even long for. However, we also noted that this prominence was disputed by Cohen (1996) who was more questioning about the need for only such a locale, arguing that the need for an identity among the diaspora itself was just as important. In his work he also stressed that migration, the act of creating a diaspora, was not always a forced or involuntary act, and that several forms of diaspora could exist (Cohen 2008). Later in the introduction we considered the areas of his typology that Scots could fall into. We decided on three but given the nature of the discussions within this work we could perhaps extend it to four. As part of the British Empire, they would certainly class as imperial, serving as administrators and defenders of the extended state (see Fry 2001, for example). Yet they also served as a labour force in that empire and others, and thus could be indentured diaspora. The Highland Clearances and the expulsion of defeated Jacobites (Pittock 1998), part of the historical grievances listed against the British State, could be used to highlight the Scottish element that were part of a victim diaspora, forced from their homeland to suffer (initially, at least) exile in foreign lands. As we illustrated, Scots most certainly formed part of the trade diaspora, and the work of Fry, both in Chapter 3 and wider works, clearly illustrates this. So we began by plainly identifying that the term was very much an umbrella form, within which a wide variety of differing groups, with a variety of roots, could be found and that Scotland served as a prime example. These points have been stressed in several places within this work, and we shall do so again before we close.

In addition, we highlighted other, necessary, features for a group to be considered a diaspora (Butler 2001; Brubaker 2005). A diaspora must, it is argued, be found in more than one destination, or rather scattered across the globe. It must have that connection to the homeland, whether real or imagined, for a relationship must exist for the diaspora to exist. This also links to the third aspect of a diaspora; self-awareness of the identity of the group. As noted above, this links the group not only to the homeland but also to each other, wherever the 'each' and the 'other' are. The key addition to the wider debate by Butler, and one with which we fully agree, is the argument that for a diaspora accurately to be considered as such it must cross the generational divide and exist across time as much as space.

There is little doubt that time has had an influence on many diaspora groups. The works of Glazer and Moynihan (1963), Nagel (1994) and Waters (1990) indicate that the hyphenated, or dual, identity allowed a diaspora to exist and thrive within a host community, and where the original identities were valued in conjunction with the modern host identity. This is surely the nature of the Scottish diaspora in North America, and other similar Western-style democracies of the 'new world'. This existence of hyphenated belonging is challenged by Safran (1999), of course, who argues that lack of a homeland language, church connection or historical awareness disbars such groups from being diaspora, and such individuals from being able to claim such a dual identity. Yet America, where much of the work on hyphenated identities was based, challenges his position with their yearly, wide-ranging, Scottish-centric celebrations of a cultural idea.

Our analysis in the introduction set the stage for the understanding of the three-way relationship which exists between the diaspora, the homeland and the host society (Shuval 2000). When opening, we stressed the need to consider the relationship between Scotland and the Scottish diaspora but we also stressed the importance of the relationship between Scotland and the host societies too. One of the major reasons for the continued, and growing, focus on the Scottish diaspora is the changing nature of the relationship between Scotland and its diaspora, and among Scotland and the various host countries within which elements of the diaspora can be found. As we noted, the idea of the homeland within various aspects of the diaspora may differ markedly from that held by individuals within the homeland itself but the nature of the homeland identity has also changed. Furthermore, the homeland is undergoing significant political change. Devolution, the legislative transfer of authority from the UK level to the national level in Scotland, took place in 1999 and there have been other transfers of power to Scotland since. These have impacted upon, and in reality greatly empowered, the ability of Scotland as a distinct country to engage with its diaspora, in a manner other countries, such as Ireland, have taken for granted for much of the twentieth century. Scotland began to find its own voice and was able to speak to the diaspora in a manner it has never done in the modern era.

Moreover, in 2014 Scotland will unambiguously consider its position within the UK. While those campaigning for Scotland to become an independent country seem to represent a minority within the likely voting population (*The Scotsman* 2013), the final decision has yet to take place. Whatever happens, Scotland has become international news, and the connections with the diaspora not only will continue to change but as the power of Scotland to operate as a semi-autonomous or even fully autonomous country grows, the relationship with the diaspora will become a fuller part of that operation. At such a time, works such as these collected insights are not only timely but necessary.

WHAT HAVE WE LEARNED?

But what insights have the works presented herein brought? To say they are varied and complex is both a cliché and yet also correct. In fact, we can assert that the Scottish diaspora is indeed a complex one. As a product of the modern world, the Scottish diaspora can easily be labelled as 'culturally, linguistically, religiously, politically' complex (Werbner 2010). But our text challenges some aspects of existing diaspora theory, while reaffirming others. We argue that the Scottish diaspora, as complex as it is, illustrates the need for time as a variable within any examination. It may well be that Butler's position, that a group requires two generations or more of activity to be a diaspora, while ostensibly accurate, misses the wider nuances of time as a factor in the diaspora equation.

To be more specific, we need to compare two distinct elements of the Scottish diaspora. Our analysis in Chapter 8 illustrates that the diaspora in Europe has few extant historical roots. While the history of the Scots in Europe is extensive and varied, the Scottish diaspora that exists across Europe today is mainly a first generation, lived diaspora. Many of these individuals, born and sometimes fully raised in Scotland, express a wish to return there at some, often vague, point. Yet the evidence suggests that the children of these individuals may well see themselves as members of the host society and do not wish to 'return' to Scotland (see also Leith and Sim 2013). Thus the roots of a diaspora could be provided already. It is at this point that the issue of time becomes a wider factor.

Before we discuss that, however, we must have our comparator. The strength and activity of the diaspora across North America, and in Australia and New Zealand, as evidenced by the work of Newton, Sullivan and Blain, for instance, indicate the great interest that latter generations have about their ancestors and their 'root' culture. While the actual number of those identifying themselves as 'Scottish' is still vague and uncertain, it is clear more and more Americans, to choose an explicit example, have self-branded as such in recent years. We assert that such identification is the result of a *trans-generational dip*. It may be that the initial second generation cleaves more firmly to the host society, to the peer group in which they develop, than to the origins of their parents – even while perhaps identifying themselves as having a hybrid identity. It is, therefore, up to the 3rd/4th/5th generations to undergo a rebirth of interest in the heritage and origins of their family line, long after the family itself is fully settled within the host society. As such interest grows, with little knowledge of the homeland, they can seek an identity and a belonging that may, as many of our contributors have illustrated (not least Crawford), bear little resemblance to that of the modern homeland itself.

If our hypothesis is accurate, then the historical or ancestral diasporas within such countries as America, Canada or Australia have had the chance to establish themselves not only as a vital part of the host society but also to create a myth of identity and belonging that is different to that of Scotland; something that the more modern European diaspora has not. Thus we have divergent visions of Scottishness in various parts of the world, all fuelled by stories unique to their own settings, albeit strongly influenced by a romantic and mythic interpretation.

Again, we argue that such difference and divergence among the Scottish diaspora is perhaps due to the roots noted by Fry in Chapter 3.

He clearly makes the point that Scots emigrated as much into the early empires of Spain and Portugal as they did into the later empires of England and France. Many Scottish migrants, Fry thus notes, correlated more to Scandinavians than to the English in that they were traders rather than colonists. Such individuals left little to no trace, unlike the waves of emigrants to follow in the eighteenth, nineteenth and twentieth centuries to countries such as Canada, the US, Australia and New Zealand. It may be that such factors lead to differing visions of Scottishness that exist not only between the homeland and the diaspora but also among the diaspora itself.

Nor should we forget the impact that the Scottish diaspora had around the world (and continues to have, as it continues to grow). As Devine indicates, for a significant portion of the nineteenth century the public discourse surrounding Scottish migration into what would become the roots of today's diaspora was extremely positive. By the act of emigrating Scots were, it was felt, continuing a long-held tradition of 'maintaining and extending' the Scottish aspects of Empire, spreading Scottish-based Presbyterian ideas, educational styles and also further enhancing what would be extensive commercial networks around the world (2011: 285). Although this discourse would, during the middle to latter part of the twentieth century, become what it is today – a negative perception of one of continued loss of the accomplished, educated or young – it nonetheless clearly provided a legacy. Just as Cowan has noted in Chapter 2, these founding members of today's contemporary diaspora, even if they left only limited signs or roots, transmitted the ideas of 'enlightened social union, equality and respect for Humankind' (26) throughout many areas. It may be the case that, as Fry notes, many of the individuals who left Scotland in the nineteenth century returned or simply assimilated into the host culture, and many individuals simply did not keep a connection with the Homeland. This could certainly explain the nature of the European-based contemporary Scottish diaspora.

Nonetheless, it is important that we acknowledge the contribution that Scotland has made to such societies. Wherever the Scottish diaspora went it took myriad ideas and practices, some among the best of history, such as the ideas of the Scottish Enlightenment, some among the worst, such as slavery. Yet such an impact Scotland has clearly had. Now we do not argue here, as some have (see Herman 2002), that the Scots were responsible for 'inventing' the modern world or saving Western civilisation, but this consideration of the diaspora has, as others have, to acknowledge the positive (as well as

the negative) contributions that Scots have made in numerous societies throughout the world. The connections that exist today, and
the esteem in which Scots and Scotland are held in numerous and
different countries, surely attest to this legacy. They may also fuel
the positive attachment that many individuals, even those lacking
any familial connection, have to Scottish culture and history (Hesse
2011a, 2011b), thereby creating the affinity diaspora.

Emergent Themes

We can, therefore, move to establish some themes from the varied analyses. First, there exists among the diaspora a mythic and
romantic vision of Scotland. Such a vision may once have been
heavily influenced by earlier Hollywood visions such as '*Brigadoon,
Whisky Galore*, and *Local Hero*' (Edensor 1997: 138) but they
have been somewhat displaced by the more modern, and less fanciful, gritty explorations of Scottishness such as *Braveheart* and *Rob
Roy*, although *Brave* may well represent a return to earlier themes.
Today the expressions of Scotland and Scottishness that inform the
majority of the diaspora (and the wider world outside Scotland)
are created in London or America (see Crawford, Chapter 12). It is
the vision that is *Braveheart/Brigadoon/Brave* that is the principal
idea of Scotland and the Scots out in the wider world. Furthermore,
while these ideas of bravery, masculinity, independence and action
inform the screen, they are not the sole carrier of such a vision.
The mass market 'Kilt and Petticoat' romances, so aptly described
by Hague (see Chapter 11), fill bookshelves and e-Readers across
the English-language world. Crawford argues that Scotland needs
to ensure it can 'hold a mirror' up in order that it can be seen but
perception seems to be in the eye of the beholder, and the vision of
Scotland outside Scotland may continue to be more powerful than
the vision of Scotland from Scotland.

In addition, both Fry and Cowan, discussing the importance of
history, culture and ancestry as they do, provide similar and yet
clearly varying themes about the nature and the understanding of
the diaspora. As Fry indicates, the diaspora have a strong sense of
worship of the ancestors, while for Cowan it is the worship of culture, with some reinventing themselves as Scots. Both illustrate the
worship aspect of the diaspora, and both illustrate the components
of that worship. It is not only familial roots or known ancestry that
counts but the cultural background of Scotland and Scots that calls to

the contemporary diaspora. This is a culture that may well have never stretched across the whole of Scotland and certainly may not exist (if it ever did) in the form that the diaspora perceive it.

Yet this lack of existence or seeming misperception should not, does not, invalidate the nature of the diaspora vision, let alone the diaspora Scottishness itself. Just as the various historical associations identified by Sullivan took numerous varied forms, so do Scotland and Scottishness today. Even within Scotland, the Homeland, there is no one single perception of what Scotland is or what it should be. Despite the SNP-led Scottish Government presenting Scotland as a modern, forward-looking country, and Scottishness as a civic, inclusive-based form of belonging, this particular homeland elite perception has been subject to challenge (Leith and Soule 2012; Mycock 2012; Soule, Leith and Steven 2013). As Sullivan notes, it is important that the homeland and the Scots who inhabit Scotland respect the identity of the diaspora as much as the diaspora respect them. It will be this mutual respect that will help perpetuate and preserve the strength and size of the Scottish diaspora.

This need for a mutual recognition and co-operation between the homeland and the diaspora is echoed in several contributions, not least those of Danson and Mather, and Leith. The vitality of the diaspora, along with the potential vitality of modern Scotland operating in conjunction with that diaspora, is clearly a goal of the current (and likely any politically different) Scottish Government. They seek opportunities for Scotland, economic, cultural and, no doubt, political. It is important that Scotland understands the goodwill with which it is held. Danson and Mather argue that, just as Scotland once informed the world, today the diaspora can help inform Scotland. If a mutually rewarding relationship can be established, and Danson and Mather believe it can, then the opportunities are there, as long as the relationship is one where both sides gain something.

Yet at this juncture the need for mutual understanding and mutual awareness becomes even more important. It is clear that the diaspora has very limited understanding of the changing political and constitutional situation in Scotland and of the overall political scene itself. Even among the European diaspora, mostly first generation rather than ancestral, modern political activity and connections are almost non-existent. This is, perhaps, unsurprising, given the general inability of homeland-born members of the diaspora to engage in political activity in that homeland. While a voter may vote in UK Westminster elections for up to fifteen years after leaving the UK (in the constituency in which he/she was registered prior to leaving) members of the Scottish diaspora have no say in Scottish parliament elections, as discussed by both Mycock and Leith. Furthermore, while thirty-eight countries around the world allow diaspora members to participate in their national referendums, the UK, and thus Scotland, is not one of them.

This situation has not been widely challenged, as Mycock discusses in Chapter 7. As he illustrates, attempts to change the situation have met with limited support, and more a sense of general acceptance of the status quo. Yet, as he and Leith also point out, the current situation is that while the largest lived diaspora is unable to participate in the forthcoming referendum (namely, Scots-born individuals living in England, Wales and Northern Ireland, despite being in the same polity), Europeans, members of the reverse diaspora in Scotland, will be able to do so. Therefore, while members of the ancestral diaspora have no political involvement or input (and there are no known arguments that they should be able to do so) the same is also true for a significant number of Scots-born individuals who, while not living in Scotland, have not left the same state. In the near future though, they may well find that the state has left them.

How this particular issue may be resolved, or even if it should be resolved, is not one we seek to grapple with here. Rather, we simply wish to illustrate that there is a distinct absence of political activity within the Scottish diaspora and this, as Sim has pointed out (2011a), is yet another difference between the Scottish diaspora and others. Many diasporas have sought a connection with their homeland and an influence on political matters and affairs. Yet, even after fifteen years of devolution, even the near Scottish diaspora remains seemingly ignorant of potential outcomes, or unable to organise and voice their opinion to Scotland.

WHITHER THE DIASPORA?

There can be little doubt that since devolution, the creation of a Scottish Government and the increased activity of that government on the world stage, Scotland and the diaspora have come to know each other better. While Tartan Day (and now Week) was an invention of the diaspora, Homecoming 2009, and the more limited Homecoming 2014, were very much home-grown, and a call from home for the diaspora to come and see what the homeland is all about. Many did in 2009, and many will in 2014. The act of coming home has a symbolic impact that only those who have been members of the diaspora can truly appreciate. To come back, to come 'home', creates a strength of feeling and connects with a sense of identity like few actions do. The modern Scottish diaspora may have differing ideas of what Scotland is and what being Scottish is all about but they know where it is. More links have been forged with the diaspora since the start of this new century than were perhaps forged during the last decades of the old one. It is unlikely that the chain will stop growing now.

Notes

Chapter 3

1. The original is in the American Philosophical Society, Philadelphia, PA.
2. *The Celebrated Letter of Joseph Hume, Esq MP to William Lyon Mackenzie, Mayor of Toronto,* (Toronto 1834: 5).

Chapter 4

1. *List of Members of the Highland Society of Scotland, Instituted in 1784* [Manuscript]. APS.1.77.55. National Library of Scotland, Edinburgh; *Rules and Regulations of the Aberdeen Highland Society* [Private papers], Royal Celtic Society of Edinburgh; *Objects and Regulations of the Celtic Society, Instituted at Edinburgh, 1820* [Manuscript], APS.4.87.42(2), National Library of Scotland, Edinburgh.
2. *History Synopsis, 1777–1983, Comunn na Gaidhlig an Lunnainn (The Gaelic Society of London)* [Manuscript]. HP2.84.1240, National Library of Scotland, Edinburgh; *Highland Society of London, and Branch Societies, with a List of Members, Corrected to May 1881* [Manuscript]. ABS.1.76.282, National Library of Scotland, Edinburgh.
3. *Geelong Comunn na Feinne Society Source Book, 1854–1858* [Cuttings]. 994.529163 COM. Geelong Heritage Centre, Geelong.
4. *Rules of the St Andrew's Society of the City of Charleston, South Carolina: founded in the year one thousand seven hundred and twenty-nine* (1892) [online]. Charleston: Walker, Evans & Cogswell. Available from: http://books.google.com/ [accessed 4 April 2009].

5. *St Andrew's Society of the State of New York Constitution, City of New York on the 13th day of November, 1794* [online]. Available from: http://www.st.andrewsny.org.standrews/content/our-purpose-and-guiding-principles [accessed 4 April 2009].

6. *About the St Andrew's Society of Washington, DC* [online]. Available from: http://www.saintandrewsociety.org/about.htm [accessed 4 April 2009].

7. *Constitution of the St Andrew's Benevolent Society of Hamilton, Ontario, 1876* [Microform film]. F CIHM 13140. Toronto Central Reference Library, Toronto.

8. *Rules, Regulations, By-Laws, Precedents and Statistics of the St Andrew's Society of Aberdeen, as at 30 November 1854* [Manuscript]. L Aa M15 StA2. University of Aberdeen Library, Aberdeen; *The Glasgow St Andrew's Society, its Origin and Constitution, History and Present Position, and List of Members, November 1890* [Manuscript]. 367/J000072400. Mitchell Library, Glasgow.

9. *Geelong Comunn na Feinne Society Source Book, 1854–1858* [Cuttings]. 994.529163 COM. Geelong Heritage Centre, Geelong.

10. *Treasurer's Report, 1867, St Andrew's Society of Toronto Minute Book, 1836–1870* [Minute book]. Box 145384–1, Series 1324, File 1. City of Toronto Archives, Toronto.

11. *St Andrew's Society of Toronto Minute Book, 1871–1898* [Minute book]. Box 423625–1, Series 1324, File 2. City of Toronto Archives, Toronto.

12. *St Andrew's Society of Toronto Minute Book, 1836–1870* [Minute book]. Box 145384–1, Series 1324, File 1. City of Toronto Archives, Toronto.

13. *St Andrew's Society of Toronto Minute Book, 1899–1929* [Minute book]. Box 145394–2, Series 1324, File 3. City of Toronto Archives, Toronto.

14. *Caledonian Society of Otago Director's Minute Book, January 1868–December 1874* [Minute book]. MS–1045/001. Hocken Collections, Uare Toaka o Hakena, University of Otago, Dunedin.

15. *Membership List, 1882, Caledonian Society of Otago Director's Minute Book, 1875–1885* [Manuscript]. MS–1045/002. Hocken Collections, Uare Taoka o Hakena, University of Otago, Dunedin.

16. http://www.standrews-society.ca/ [accessed 24 November 2009].

17. http://www.scotsofaus.org.au/scottishcaledonian-societies/royalcaledonian/ [accessed 28 April 2009].

18. http://www.geocities.com/athens/acropolis/1850/caledonians.html [accessed 6 June 2007].

19. Personal communication, 8 June 2009.

CHAPTER 7

1. These figures are based on the 2001 census, with 753,286 Scots living in England, 22,533 in Wales and 14,965 in Northern Ireland.

CHAPTER 9

1. Although the younger generation of educated Gaelic singers in Scotland has shown a renewed interest in more archaic styles and content.

2. It is possible that some elements of Gaelic pyrrhic dances survive in modern Highland Dance, but there are two notes of caution. First, 'Highland Dance' was too radically altered in the nineteenth century for us to separate the inherited from the invented. Second, antiquarian interest in pyrrhic dances was already so keen in the sixteenth century that 'tradition' was being invented and altered around Europe to satisfy demand. See McGowan 2008: 122–6.

CHAPTER 10

1. https://familysearch.org/.

2. There are several related sites in different countries. See, for example, http://www.ancestry.co.uk/ and http://www.findmypast.co.uk/.

3. http://www.rootsweb.ancestry.com/. This site includes, among other resources, message boards and email lists organised by place and surname. There is also an independent British-based *Rootschat* site at http://www.rootschat.com.

4. http://www.scotlandspeople.gov.uk.

5. http://talkingscot.com/forum/.

6. http://boards.rootsweb.com/localities.britisles.scotland.ans.general/mb.ashx.

7. http://www.visitscotland.com.

8. http://www.undiscoveredscotland.co.uk/edinburgh/southleithchurch/index.html.

9. http://dna-project.clan-donald-usa.org.

10. http://www.elliotclan.com/.

CHAPTER 11

1. As a comparison, and an indication of a publishing phenomenon, 2012 was the year of E. L. James' 'Fifty Shades' erotic trilogy. Her titles occupied 14.7 per cent of the trade paperback bestsellers and sold 35,000,000 copies in the US alone (Maryles 2013). James is published by Random House.

2. *Outlander* was published in the UK with an alternative title: *Cross Stitch*.

Bibliography

Adamson, F. (2008), *Constructing the diaspora: diaspora identity politics and transnational social movements*, Paper delivered at 49th Annual Meeting of the International Studies Association, San Francisco, March 2008, accessed at http://www.serbianunity.com/serbianunitycongress/pdf/world_of_serbs/Diasp_Identity_Politics_isa08_proceeding_251176.pdf.

Aikins, K. (2011), *Categories of Diasporas*, http://www.diaspora-matters.com/categories-of-diasporas/2011/. Accessed 26 January 2013.

Aikins, K. and White, N. (2011), *The Diaspora Strategies Toolkit*, http://www.diasporamatters.com/download-the-diaspora-toolkit/2011/. Accessed 26 January 2013.

Alba, R. (2005), 'Bright vs blurred boundaries: second-generation assimilation and exclusion in France, Germany and the United States', *Ethnic and Racial Studies*, 28(1): 20–49.

Ali, M. A. (1975), 'The Passing of Empire: the Mughal case', *Modern Asian Studies*, IX: 389–96.

Allen, Jody (2013) Interview, 12 February.

Ancien, D., Boyle, M. and Kitchin, R. (2009), *The Scottish Diaspora and Diaspora Strategy: Insights and Lessons from Ireland*, Scottish Government Social Research, http://www.scotland.gov.uk/Resource/Doc/273844/0081838.pdf.

Anderson, B. (1991), *Imagined Communities: Reflections on the Origins and Spread of Nationalism* (2nd edn), London: Verso.

Andrews, H. F. (1981), 'Nineteenth-century St Petersburg: Workpoints for an exploration of image and place', in D. D. C. Pocock (ed.), *Humanistic Geography and Literature*, Totawa, NJ: Barnes and Noble Books, pp. 173–89.

Andriani, L. (2009), 'Harlequin Hits 60', *Publishers Weekly*, 256(11): 13–14.

Ang, I. (1991), *Desperately seeking the audience*, London: Routledge.

Anwar, M. (1979), *The myth of return: Pakistanis in Britain*, London: Heinemann.

Archibald, D. (1987), 'The Courland Adventure 1639–1690', in *Tobago, melancholy isle*, St Anns: Trinidad, Chap. iv.

Armitage, D. (2005), 'The Scottish Diaspora', in J. Wormald (ed.), *Scotland: A History*, Oxford: Oxford University Press, pp. 272–303.

Arnkil, R., Järvensivu, A., Koski, P. and Piirainen, T. (2010), *Exploring Quadruple Helix. Outlining user-oriented innovation models*, Final Report on Quadruple Helix Research for the CLIQ project, Työraportteja 85/2010 Working Papers, University of Tampere.

Ascherson, N. (2002), *Stone Voices: The Search for Scotland*, London: Granta Books.

Bailyn, B. (1986), *Voyagers to the West*, New York: Alfred A. Knopf.

Bailyn, B. (ed.) (2005), *Atlantic history, concept and contours*, Cambridge, MA: Harvard University Press.

Bairner, A. (1994), 'Football and the idea of Scotland', in G. Jarvie and G. Walker (eds), *Scottish Sport in the Making of the Nation: Ninety Minute Patriots?*, Leicester: Leicester University Press, pp. 9–26.

Bairner, A. (1996), 'Sportive nationalism and nationalist politics: a comparative analysis of Scotland, the Republic of Ireland, and Sweden', *Journal of Sport and Social Issues*, 20(3):314–34.

Bairner, A. (2001), *Sport, Nationalism and Globalization: European and North American Perspectives*, Albany, NY: State University of New York Press.

Bairner, A. (2004), 'Örgryte's Scots: Swedish Football and the Scottish Connection', *Soccer History*, 8: 26–30.

Bannister, S. (ed.) (1859), *The Writings of William Paterson, founder of the Bank of England*, New York.

Barna, B. (2010), 'Internal Diaspora – Assimilation – Formation of the Internal Diaspora', *European and Regional Studies*, 1(1): 59–82.

BBC (2012a), 'Corby "should have independence vote"', 29 October. Available online at: http://www.bbc.co.uk/news/uk-england-northamptonshire–20122435.

BBC (2012b), 'SNP dismisses expat voting call', 18 January. Available online at: http://www.bbc.co.uk/news/uk-scotland-scotland-politics–16607480.

BBC (2013), 'Corby Highland Gathering hit as council grant cut to £500', 2 July. Available online at: http://www.bbc.co.uk/news/uk-england-northamptonshire–23132908.

BBC Annual Report (2012), *Public Purposes 2011/12*. Available online at http://www.bbc.co.uk/annualreport/2012/trust/performance/publicpurposes/.

BBC Scotland (2011), *Management Review 2010/11*. Available online at http://downloads.bbc.co.uk/scotland/aboutus/management_review_2010_2011.pdf.

BBC Scotland (2012), *Management Review 2011/12*. Available online at http://downloads.bbc.co.uk/annualreport/pdf/bbc_nr_mr_scotland_2011_12.pdf.

BBC Trust (2011), *Delivering Quality First*. Available online at http://downloads.bbc.co.uk/aboutthebbc/reports/pdf/dqf_detailedproposals.pdf.

Baird, S., Foster, J. and Leonard, R. (2007), 'Scottish capital: still in control in the 21st century?', *Scottish Affairs*, 58(Winter): 1–35.

Barrie, J. M. (1932 [1888]), *Auld Licht Idylls*, New York: Scribner.

Basu, P. (2005), 'Macpherson country: genealogical Identities, spatial histories and the Scottish diasporic clanscape', *Cultural Geographies*, 12(2): 123–50.

Basu, P. (2007), *Highland homecomings: genealogy and heritage tourism in the Scottish diaspora*, Abingdon: Routledge.

Baxter, A. (1991), *In search of your British and Irish roots: a complete guide to tracing your English, Welsh, Scottish and Irish ancestors*, Baltimore: Genealogical Publishing Co. Inc.

Bergum, S. (2012), 'Proximity and distributed innovations. Innovations "in the shadow of the clusters"', in M. Danson and P. de Souza (eds), *Regional Development in Northern Europe: Peripherality, Marginality and Border Issues*, Abingdon: Routledge, pp. 134–47.

Bicket, D. (1999), 'Fictional Scotland: a realm of the imagination in film, drama and literature', *Journal of Communication Inquiry*, 23(1): 3–19.

Billig, M. (1995), *Banal Nationalism*, London: Sage.

Black, J. (2012), 'The Mughals Strike Twice', *History Today*, LXII: 22–6.

Black, R. (2010), 'Gaelic Orthography: The Drunk Man's Broad Road', in M. Watson and M. Macleod (eds), *The Edinburgh Companion to the Gaelic Language*, Edinburgh: Edinburgh University Press, pp. 229–61.

Blain, J. and Wallis, R. J. (2007), *Sacred sites, contested rites/rights*, Brighton: Sussex Academic Press.

Bond, R. and Rosie, M. (2010), 'National identities and attitudes to constitutional change in post-devolution UK: a four territories comparison', *Regional and Federal Studies*, 20(1): 83–105.

Bottero, W. (2010), 'Intersubjectivity and Bourdieusian approaches to "identity"', *Cultural Sociology*, 4(1): 3–22.

Boxer, C. R. (1965), *The Dutch Seaborne Empire*, New York: Alfred A. Knopf.

Boyle, M. and Motherwell, S. (2005), *Attracting and Retaining Talent: Lessons for Scottish Policy Makers from the Experiences of Scottish Expatriates in Dublin*, Scottish Economic Policy Network. Available online at: http://www.scotecon.net/publications/Boyle%20Full.pdf.

Bradbury, M. (ed.) (1996), *The Atlas of Literature*, London: De Agostini.

Braddell, R. StJ., Brooke, G. E. and Makepeace, W. (1991), *One Hundred Years of Singapore*, Oxford: Oxford University Press.

Bradley, J. M. (1998), *Sport, Culture, Politics and Scottish Society: Irish Immigrants and the Gaelic Athletic Association and Culture*, Edinburgh: John Donald.

Brah, A. (1996), *Cartographies of diaspora: contesting identities*, London: Routledge.

Brinkerhoff, J. (2009), 'Creating an enabling environment for diasporas' participation in homeland development', *International Migration* 50(1): 75–95.

Brisbin, T. (1998), *A Love Through Time*, New York: Berkley/Jove.

Brisbin, T. (2002), *Once Forbidden*, New York: Berkley/Jove.

Brisbin, T. (2012), *The Highlander's Stolen Touch*, Don Mills, Canada: Harlequin.

Brisbin, T. (2013), Interview, 20 February.

Broadie, A. (1990), *The tradition of Scottish philosophy*, Edinburgh: Polygon.

Brock, J. (1999), *The mobile Scot: a study of emigration and migration 1861–1911*, Edinburgh: John Donald.

Brockway, C. (1999), *McClairen's Isle: The Passionate One*, New York: Dell.

Brockway, C. (2000a), *McClairen's Isle: The Ravishing One*, New York: Dell.

Brockway, C. (2000b), *McClairen's Isle: The Reckless One*, New York: Dell.

Brøgger, A. W. (1929), *Ancient Emigrants: A History of the Norse Settlements of Scotland*, Oxford: Clarendon.

Brooking, T. (1985), "'Tam McCanny and Kitty Clydeside" – The Scots in New Zealand', in R. A. Cage (ed.), *The Scots Abroad: Labour, Capital, Enterprise, 1750–1914*, Sydney: Croom Helm.

Brown, P. L. (ed.) (1941–71), *Clyde Company Papers*, 7 vols, London.

Brown, R. and Danson, M. (2008), 'Fresh talent or cheap labour? Accession State migrant labour in the Scottish Economy', *Scottish Affairs*, 64: 37–52.

Brown, R. and Mason, C. (2012), 'The evolution of enterprise policy in Scotland', in R. Blackburn and M. Schaper (eds), *Government, SMEs and Entrepreneurship Development: Policy, Practice and Challenges*, Farnham: Gower, pp. 17–30.

Brubaker, R. (2005), 'The "diaspora" diaspora', *Ethnic and Racial Studies*, 28(1): 1–19.

Bruce, D. A. (1998), *The Mark of the Scots: Their Astonishing Contributions to History, Science, Democracy, Literature*, New York: Citadel Press/Kensington.

Brückner, M. and Hsu, H. L. (eds) (2007), *American Literary Geographies: Spatial Practice and Cultural Production, 1500–1900*, Newark: University of Delaware Press.

Bryce, J. (1914), *The Ancient Roman Empire and the British Empire in India*, Oxford.

Buchan, J. (1906), *A Lodge in the Wilderness*, Edinburgh and London: Blackwood.

Bulmer, M. and Solomos, J. (2009), 'Introduction: Diasporas, Cultures and Identities', *Ethnic and Racial Studies*, 32(8): 1301–3.

Bumsted, J. M. (1981), 'Scottish emigration to the Maritimes, a new look at an old theme', *Acadiensis*, X: 65–85.

Burnett, J. (2007), "'Hail brither Scots O' Coaly Tyne": networking and identity among Scottish migrants in the north east of England, ca.1860–2000', *Immigrants & Minorities*, 25(1): 1–21.

Butler, K. D. (2001), 'Defining diaspora, refining a discourse', *Diaspora*, 10(2): 189–219.

Calder, J. (2006), *Scots in the USA*, Edinburgh: Luath Press.

Cameron, G. and Danson, M. (2000), 'The European partnership model and the changing role of regional development agencies: a regional development and organisation perspective', in M. Danson, H. Halkier and G. Cameron (eds), *Governance, Institutional Change and Development*, London: Ashgate.

Campbell, M. (2001), *The Scottish Golf Book*, Revised edition, Edinburgh: Lomond Books.

Campbell, J. L. (1936), 'Scottish Gaelic in Canada', *American Speech*, 11(2): 128–36.

Campbell, J. L. (1999), *Songs Remembered in Exile*, 2nd edn, Edinburgh: Birlinn.

Campey, L. H. (2005), *The Scottish Pioneers of Upper Canada 1784–1855*, Toronto: Natural Heritage Books.

Canny, N. (ed.) (1998), *The Oxford History of the British Empire Volume 1: The Origins of Empire British Overseas Enterprise to the Close of the Seventeenth Century*, Oxford: Oxford University Press.

Carr, J. and Cavanagh L. (2009), *Scotland's Diaspora and Overseas-Born Population*, Edinburgh: Scottish Government. Available online at: http://www.scotland.gov.uk/Resource/Doc/285746/0087034.pdf.

Carrell, S. (2012), 'Scotland rallies behind *Brave* animation on hopes it will buoy tourism', *The Guardian*. Available online at: http://www.guardian.co.uk/uk/2012/jun/03/scotland-brave-tourism-animation-disney.

Carswell, A. (1937), *The Port of Leith*, Leith: Leith Chamber of Commerce.

Caughie, J. (1982), 'Scottish television: what would it look like?', in C. McArthur (ed.), *Scotch Reels: Scotland in cinema and television*, London: British Film Institute, pp. 112–22.

Cawood, I. (2012), *The Liberal Unionist Party, a history*, London: I. B. Tauris.

CEC (2010), *Europe 2020: A Strategy for Smart, Sustainable and Inclusive Growth*, Brussels. Available online at: http://eur-lex.europa.eu/LexUriServ/LexUriServ.do?uri=COM:2010:2020:FIN:EN:PDF.

CEC (2011), *Research and Innovation Strategies for Smart Specialisation*, Brussels. Available online at: http://ec.europa.eu/regional_policy/sources/docgener/informat/2014/smart_specialisation_en.pdf.

CEC (2012), *Industrial innovation. Innovation Union Scoreboard*. Available online at: http://ec.europa.eu/enterprise/policies/innovation/facts-figures-analysis/innovation-scoreboard/index_en.htm.

Cecchini, P. (1988), *The European Challenge 1992: The Benefits of a Single European Market*, Aldershot: Wildwood House.

Césaire, A. (1955), *Discours sur le Colonialisme*, Paris.

Cheape, H. (2009), 'Traditional Origins of the Piping Dynasties', in J. Dickson (ed.), *The Highland Bagpipe: Music, History, Tradition*, Aldershot: Ashgate, pp. 97–126.

Chisholm, A. H. (1950), *Scots Wha Hae: History of the Royal Caledonian Society of Melbourne*, Sydney: Angus & Robertson.

Clarke, A. J. (2003), *Feasts and Fasts: Holidays, Religion and Ethnicity in Nineteenth-Century Otago*, Thesis (PhD), Dunedin: University of Otago.

Cloke, K. (2008), *The Crossroads of Conflict: A Journey into the Heart of Dispute Resolution*, Calgary: Janus Publications Inc.

Cohen, R. (1996), 'Diasporas and the nation-state: from victims to challengers', *International Affairs*, 72(3): 507–20.

Cohen, R. (2008), *Global diasporas: an introduction* (2nd edn), London: Routledge.

Collectanea (1847), *Collectanea de Rebus Albanicis*, Edinburgh: Iona Club.

Conn, S. (2012), *Carn Mor de Chlachan Beaga, A Large Cairn from Small Stones: Multivocality and Memory in Cape Breton Gaelic Singing*, PhD thesis at University of Toronto.

Conner, W. (1986), 'The impact of homelands upon diasporas', in G. Sheffer, *Modern Diasporas in International Politics*, London: Croom Helm, pp. 16–46.

Cosgrove, S. (1991), *Hampden Babylon. Sex and Scandal in Scottish Football*, Edinburgh: Canongate.

Cowan, E. J. (1984), 'Myth and identity in Early Medieval Scotland', *Scottish Historical Review*, lxiii: 111–35.

Cowan, E. J. (1998), 'The Discovery of the *Gàidhealtachd* in Sixteenth Century Scotland', *Transactions of the Gaelic Society of Inverness*, lx: 259–84.

Cowan, E. J. (1999), 'The Myth of Scotch Canada', in M. Harper and M. E. Vance (eds), *Myth, Migration and the Making of Memory: Scotia and Nova Scotia c.1700–1990*, Halifax: Fernwood, pp. 49–72.

Cowan, E. J. (2008), *For Freedom Alone: The Declaration of Arbroath*, 2nd edn, Edinburgh: Birlinn.

Cowan, E. J. (2012), 'The Age of Emigration', in E. J. Cowan (ed.), *Why Scottish History Still Matters*, Edinburgh: Saltire Society, pp. 73–88.

Cox, L. (1994), 'Gaelic and the Schools in Cape Breton', *Nova Scotia Historical Review*, 14: 20–40.

Craig, C. (1982), 'Myths against history: Tartanry and Kailyard in Nineteenth Century Scottish literature', in C. McArthur (ed.), *Scotch Reels: Scotland in cinema and television*, London: British Film Institute, pp. 7–15.

Crang, M. (1998), *Cultural Geography*, Abingdon: Routledge.

Crockett, S. R. (1893), *The Stickit Minister*, New York: Caldwell.

Curtice, J., Devine, P. and Ormston, R. (2013), 'Devolution', in A. Park, C. Bryson, E. Clery, J. Curtice and M. Phillips (eds) (2013), *British Social Attitudes: the 30th Report*, London: NatCen Social Research, pp. 139–72.

Curtice, J. and Ormston, R. (2011), 'On the road to divergence? Trends in public opinion in Scotland and England', in A. Park, E. Clery, J. Curtice, M. Phillips and D. Utting (eds), *British Social Attitudes: the 28th Report*, London: Sage, pp. 21–36.

Curtice, J. and Steven, M. (2011), *The 2011 Scottish Parliament election In-depth*, Electoral Reform Society. Available online at: http://www.electoral-reform.org.uk/publications/.

Daily Record (2012), 'Scots expats will NOT get to vote in independence referendum say SNP', 18 January. Available online at: http://www.dailyrecord.co.uk/news/politics/scots-expats-will-not-get-to-vote-in-independence–1114214.

Danson, M. (2012), Presentation to 'Growth versus the Scottish Government's "Golden Rules" and Economic Strategy', Economy, Energy and Tourism Committee and Scottish Trades Union Congress Seminar, 13–20, Scottish Parliament. Available online at: http://www.scottish.parliament.uk/S4_EconomyEnergyandTourismCommittee/General%20Documents/Proceedings_v2.pdf.

Danson, M., Helinska-Hughes, E., Hughes, M. and Whittam, G. (2005), 'National and local agency support for Scottish SME internationalisation activity: lessons for small transition economies', *International Journal of Entrepreneurship and Small Business* 2(4): 312–30.

Danson, M. and de Souza, P. (eds) (2012), *Regional Development in Northern Europe: Peripherality, Marginality and Border Issues*, Abingdon: Routledge.

Danson, M. and Lloyd, G. (2012), 'Beyond devolution: roads to coherent autonomies?', *Environment & Planning C*, 30(1): 78–94.

Danson, M. and Whittam, G. (2001), 'Power and the spirit of clustering', *European Planning Studies*, 9(8): 949–63.

Darby, P. (2009), *Gaelic Games, Nationalism and the Irish Diaspora in the United States*, Dublin: University College Dublin Press.

Darby, P. and Hassan, D. (eds) (2008a), *Emigrant Players. Sport and the Irish Diaspora*, London: Routledge.

Darby, P. and Hassan, D. (2008b), 'Introduction: Locating Sport in the Study of the Irish Diaspora', in P. Darby and D. Hassan (eds)

(2008a), *Emigrant Players. Sport and the Irish Diaspo*ra, London: Routledge, pp. 1–14.

Dargis, M. (2012), 'Who Needs a Prince when Fun's Afoot', *New York Times*. Available online at: http://movies.nytimes.com/2012/06/22/movies/brave-pixars-new-animated-film.html?pagewanted=all&_r=1&.

Day, M. (2002), 'Scots sweep romance readers off their feet', *The Enquirer* (Cincinnati), 13 August. Available online at: http://www.enquirer.com/editions/2002/08/13/tem_scots_sweep_romance.html.

Defence (1699), *A Defence of the Scots Settlement at Darien*, Edinburgh.

Delaney, B. (2010), 'Willie Anderson', in The Editors of Salem Press (eds), *Great Athletes. Golf and Tennis*, Pasedena, CA: Salem Press, pp. 3–5.

Dembling, J. (1997), *Joe Jimmy Alex Visits the Mod and Escapes Unscathed: The Nova Scotia Gaelic Revivals*, Master of Arts thesis at Saint Mary's University, Halifax.

Dembling, J. (2005), 'You Play It As You Would Sing It: Cape Breton, Scottishness, and the Means of Cultural Production', in C. Ray (ed.), *Transatlantic Scots*, Tuscaloosa: University of Alabama Press, pp. 180–97.

Dembling, J. (2006), 'Gaelic in Canada: new evidence from an old census', in W. McLeod, J. Fraser and A. Gunderloch (eds), *Cànan & Cultar/Language & Culture: Rannsachadh na Gàidhlig 3*, Edinburgh: Dunedin Academic Press, pp. 203–14.

Deming, E. (2000), *The New Economics for Industry, Government and Education*, 2nd edn, Cambridge, MA: MIT Press.

Dennett, A. and Stillwell, J. (2011), 'A new area classification for understanding internal migration in Britain', *Population Trends*, 145: 1–26.

Denver, D. (2007), *Elections and Voters in Britain*, Basingstoke: Palgrave Macmillan.

Devine, T. (1975), *The Tobacco Lords*, Edinburgh: Edinburgh University Press.

Devine, T. (ed.) (1992), *Scottish Emigration and Scottish Society*, Edinburgh: John Donald.

Devine, T. (1994), *Clanship to Crofters' War: The Social Transformation of the Scottish Highlands*, Manchester: Manchester University Press.

Devine, T. (1999), *The Scottish Nation 1700–2000*, London: Penguin.

Devine, T. (2011), *To the Ends of the Earth: Scotland's Global Diaspora, 1750–2010*, London: Allen Lane.

Devine T. and Hesse, D. (eds) (2011), *Scotland and Poland: Historical Encounters, 1500–2010*, Edinburgh: John Donald.

Devine, T. and Logue, P. (2002), *Being Scottish*, Edinburgh: Polygon.

Dezell, M. (2002), *Irish America: coming into clover*, New York: Anchor.

Dixon, T. (1905), *The Clansman*, New York: Doubleday Page.

Dobson, D. (2005), 'Seventeenth-Century Scottish Communities in the Americas', in A. Grosjean and S. Murdoch (eds), *Scottish Communities Abroad in the Early Modern Period*, Leiden: Brill, pp. 105–30.

Dollarhide, W. (2001), *The Census Book, a genealogist's guide to federal census facts, schedules and indexes*, North Salt Lake, UT.

Donaldson, W. (2000), *The Highland Pipe and Scottish Society, 1750–1950*, East Linton: Tuckwell Press.

Duke, V. and Crolley, L. (1996), *Football, Nationality, and the State*, Harlow: Longman.

Dunlay, K. (1992), 'The Playing of Traditional Scottish Dance Music: Old and New World Styles and Practices', in C. Byrne, M. Harry and P. Ó Siadhail (eds), *Celtic Languages and Celtic Peoples: Proceedings of the Second North American Congress of Celtic Studies*, Halifax: Saint Mary's University, pp. 173–91.

Dunn, C. (1991 [1953]), *Highland Settler: A Portrait of the Scottish Gael in Cape Breton and Eastern Nova Scotia*, Wreck Cove, Nova Scotia: Breton Books.

Dyer, J. (2002), '"We all speak the same round here": Dialect levelling in a Scottish-English community', *Journal of Sociolinguistics*, 6(1): 99–116.

Edensor, T. (1997), 'Reading *Braveheart*: representing and contesting Scottish identity', *Scottish Affairs*, 21, 135–58.

Eirich, F. and McLaren, J.-G. (2008), 'Engaging the Scottish Diaspora – Internal Document', The Scottish Government's Europe, External Affairs and Culture Analytical Unit.

EKOS (2010), *Homecoming Scotland 2009 Economic Impact*, Report for Homecoming Scotland, Glasgow.

Elliott, L. and Atkinson, D. (2012), *Going South: Why Britain will have a Third World Economy by 2014*, Basingstoke: Palgrave Macmillan.

Encouragements For such as shall have intention to bee Under-takers in the new plantation of Cape Briton, now New Galloway in

America, by Mee Lochinvar, Edinburgh 1625 in D. Laing (ed.). *Royal Letters and Charters etc Relating to Nova Scotia.*

English, S. (2005), 'Devil in a Kilt may be ravishing the US, but the reality leaves Scots women cold', *The Times*, 2 April.

Entwistle, E. R. (1981), *History of the Gaelic Society of New Zealand, 1881–1981*, Dunedin: Gaelic Society of New Zealand.

Ernst & Young (2012), *Staying Ahead of the Game. Ernst & Young's 2012 Attractiveness Survey United Kingdom*. Available online at: http://www.ey.com/Publication/vwLUAssets/2012_UK_Attractiveness_Survey/$FILE/EY_2012_UK_Attractiveness_Survey%20.pdf.

Esman, M. (2009), *Diasporas in the contemporary world*, Cambridge: Polity.

ESPON (2010), *New Evidence on Smart, Sustainable and Inclusive Territories. Polycentric Europe: smart, connected places*, First ESPON 2013 Synthesis Report. Available online at: http://www.espon.eu/export/sites/default/Documents/Publications/Synthesis-Report/FirstOctober10/fullversion.pdf.

EventScotland (2008), *Scotland – The Perfect Stage: A strategy for the events industry in Scotland 2009–2020*, Edinburgh: EventScotland.

Fairbank, J. and Teng, S. (1979), *China's Response to the West*, Cambridge, MA: Harvard University Press.

Fairney, J. (2010), 'The Branches of the Highland Society of London', in K. Nilsen (ed.), *Rannsachadh na Gàidhlig 5/Fifth Scottish Gaelic Research Conference*, Sydney, Nova Scotia: Cape Breton University Press, pp. 67–77.

Faist, T. (2000), 'Transnationalization in international migration: Implications for the study of citizenship and culture', *Ethnic and Racial Studies*, 23(2): 189–222.

Faist, T. (2008), 'Migrants as transnational development agents: An inquiry into the newest round of the migration-development nexus', *Population, Space and Place*, 14(1): 21–42.

Farole, T., Rodríguez?Pose, A. and Storper, M. (2011), 'Cohesion policy in the European Union: growth, geography, institutions', *Journal of Common Market Studies*, 49(5): 1089–1111.

Ferguson, B. (2008), 'Whisky, haggis and shortbread take a back seat as Tartan Week becomes Scotland Week', *The Scotsman*, 8 March.

Fielding, A. (1992), 'Migration and social mobility: South-east England as an escalator region', *Regional Studies*, 26(1): 1–15.

Finch, T., Latorre, M. and Andrew, H. (2010), *Global Brit: Making the Most of the British Diaspora*, London: Institute for Public Policy Research.

Finlayson, I. (1987), *The Scots: a portrait of the Scottish soul at home and abroad,* New York: Atheneum.

Fitzgerald, P. (2005), 'Scottish Migration to Ireland in the Seventeenth Century', in A. Grosjean and S. Murdoch (eds), *Scottish Communities Abroad in the Early Modern Period,* Leiden: Brill, pp. 27–52.

Flesch, J. (2004), *From Australia with Love: A history of modern Australian popular romance novels,* Fremantle: Curtin University Books.

Flett, J. and Flett, T. (1972), 'The History of Scottish Reel as a Dance-Form: I', *Scottish Studies* 16: 91–120.

Flett, J. and Flett, T. (1996), *Traditional Step-Dancing in Scotland,* Edinburgh: Scottish Cultural Press.

Flinn, M. et al. (1977), *Scottish Population History,* Cambridge: Cambridge University Press.

Forsyth, R. (1990), *The Only Game. The Scots and World Football,* Edinburgh: Mainstream.

Forsyth, R. (1992), 'Sport', in M. Linklater and R. Denniston (eds), *Anatomy of Scotland,* Edinburgh: Chambers, pp. 334–53.

Foucault, M. and Miskowiec, J. (transl.) (1986), 'Of other spaces', *Diacritics* 16(1): 22–7.

Frängsmyr, T. (1976), *Ostindiska Kompaniet,* Stockholm.

Frankl, V. (2006), *Man's Search for Meaning,* Boston: Beacon Press.

Frantz, S. S. G. and Selinger, E. M. (eds) (2012), *New approaches to popular romance fiction: critical essays,* Jefferson, NC: McFarland.

Fraser, A. (ed.) (1900), *Fraser's Scottish Annual: A Literary and Historical Repository and Register of Events Interesting to the Scots at Home and Abroad, Canadian Edition, Volume 1,* Toronto: publisher unknown.

Fraser, J. E. (2009), *From Caledonia to Pictland: Scotland to 795, New History of Scotland vol. 1,* Edinburgh: Edinburgh University Press.

Frontline (2007), Evaluation of Globalscot: Report for Scottish Enterprise National. Available online at: http://www.evaluationsonline. org.uk/evaluations/Browse.do?ui=browse&action=show&id=74 &taxonomy=ITA. Accessed 19 March 2013.

Fry, M. (1992), *The Dundas Despotism,* Edinburgh: Edinburgh University Press.

Fry, M. (2001), *The Scottish Empire,* Edinburgh: Birlinn.

Gabaldon, D. (2005 [1991]), *Outlander,* New York: Dell.

Gale (2013), *Business Insights: Essentials and Company Intelligence Database.*

Gans, H. (1979), 'Symbolic ethnicity: the future of ethnic groups and cultures in America', *Ethnic and Racial Studies,* 2(1): 1–20.

Gans, H. J. (1999), *Making Sense of America: Sociological Analyses and Essays,* Lanham: Rowman & Littlefield Publishers Inc.

Gardner, E. S. (ed.) (1947), *The First Two Hundred Years of the St Andrew's Society of Philadelphia,* Philadelphia: St Andrew's Society of Philadelphia.

Garwood, J. (1991 [1989]), *The Bride,* New York: Pocket/Simon and Schuster.

Garwood, J. (1992), *The Secret,* New York: Pocket/Simon and Schuster.

Garwood, J. (1996), *The Wedding,* New York: Pocket/Simon and Schuster.

General Register Office for Scotland (2003), Scotland's Census 2001. Available online at: http://www.gro-scotland.gov.uk/census/census-shm/index.html.

Gibson, J. (1998), *Traditional Gaelic Bagpiping: 1745–1945,* Edinburgh: Edinburgh University Press.

Gifford, B. (2012a), *Return of the Border Warrior,* Don Mills, Canada: Harlequin.

Gifford, B. (2012b), *Captive of the Border Lord,* Don Mills, Canada: Harlequin.

Gifford, B. (2013a), Interview, 25 January.

Gifford, B. (2013b), *Taken by the Border Rebel,* Don Mills, Canada: Harlequin.

Gifford, B. (2013c), *Tempted By The Border Captain.* Available online at: www.harlequin.com. Accessed 24 February–22 March.

Giulianotti, R. (2005), 'Towards a critical anthropology of voice: the politics and poets of popular culture, Scotland and football', *Critique of Anthropology,* 25(4): 339–59.

Giulianotti, R. and Robertson, R. (2006), 'Glocalization, globalization and migration: the case of Scottish football supporters in North America', *International Sociology,* 21(2): 171–98.

Giulianotti, R. and Robertson, R. (2007), 'Forms of glocalization: globalization and the migration strategies of Scottish football fans in North America', *Sociology,* 41(1): 133–52.

Gladstone, W. E. (1971), *Midlothian Speeches 1879,* Leicester.

Glazer N. and Moynihan, D. P. (1963), *Beyond the melting pot: the Negroes, Puerto Ricans, Jews, Italians and Irish of New York City*, Cambridge, MA: MIT Press.

Graham, G. (2006), *The Cape Breton Fiddle*, Sydney: Cape Breton University Press.

Greig, J. Y. T. (ed.) (1969), *The Letters of David Hume*, Oxford: Oxford University Press.

Grenier, K. H. (2005), *Tourism and identity in Scotland, 1770–1914; creating Caledonia*, Aldershot: Ashgate.

Gründer, H. and Johanek, P. (2006), *Kolonialstädte, europäische Enklaven oder Schmelztiegel der Kulturen*, Münster.

Guthrie, D. (1946), 'Leiden and Edinburgh: a medical partnership', *British Medical Bulletin*, 4(3): 218.

Habermann, I. and Kuhn, N. (2011), 'Sustainable fictions – geographical, literary and cultural intersections in J. R. R. Tolkien's *The Lord of the Rings*', *Cartographic Journal*, 48(4): 263–73.

Hagen, R. (2003), 'At the Edge of Civilisation: John Cunningham Lensmann of Finnmark, 1619–51', in S. Murdoch and A. Mackillop (eds), *Military Governors and Imperial Frontiers c. 1600–1800: A Study of Scotland and Empires*, Leiden: Brill, pp. 29–51.

Hague, E. (1999–2000), 'Scotland on Film: Attitudes and opinions about *Braveheart*', *Etudes Ecossaises*, 6: 75–89.

Hague, E. (2002a), 'The Scottish diaspora: Tartan Day and the appropriation of Scottish identities in the United States', in D. C. Harvey, R. Jones, N. McInroy and C. Milligan (eds), *Celtic Geographies: Old culture, new times*, London and New York: Routledge, pp. 139–56.

Hague, E. (2002b), 'National Tartan Day: Rewriting history in the United States', *Scottish Affairs*, 38: 94–124.

Hague, E. (2006), 'Representations of race and romance: The portrayal of people of Scottish descent in North America by British newspapers, 1997–1999', *Scottish Affairs*, 57: 39–69.

Hague, E. and Stenhouse, D. '"A Very Interesting Place" – Representing Scotland in US Romance Novels', in B. Schoene (ed.), *The Edinburgh Companion to Contemporary Scottish Literature*, Edinburgh: Edinburgh University Press, pp. 354–61.

Haley, A. (1976), *Roots: the saga of an American family*, Garden City, NY: Doubleday.

Hall, A. J. (2003), *The American Empire and the Fourth World*, Montreal and Kingston: McGill-Queen's University Press.

Hall, S. (1975), 'Encoding and decoding in the television discourse', *Education and Culture*, 6, Strasbourg: Council of Europe.

Hall, S. (1990), 'Cultural identity and diaspora', in J. Rutherford (ed.), *Identity: Community, Culture, Difference*, London: Lawrence and Wishart, pp. 222–37.

Handlin, O. (1973), *The Uprooted: The Epic Story of the Great Migrations that Made the American People*, Boston: Little, Brown.

Harland, J. (2009), 'Island heritage and identity in the Antipodes: Orkney and Shetland Societies in New Zealand', in T. Bueltmann, A. Hinson and G. Morton (eds), *Scottish Associational Culture in the Diaspora*, Guelph: Centre for Scottish Studies.

Harper, M. (2003), *Adventurers and exiles: the great Scottish exodus*, London: Profile.

Harper, M. (2013), '"Come to Corby": A Scottish Steel Town in the Heart of England', *Immigrants and Minorities*, 31(1): 27–47.

Hassan, G. (2012), 'Ignorant, and proud of it: the independence debate outside of Scotland', *Open Democracy*, 3 July. Available online at: http://www.opendemocracy.net/ourkingdom/gerry-hassan/ignorant-and-proud-of-it-independence-debate-outside-of-scotland.

Heffer, S. (2013), 'Why the Scots MUST vote for independence! It'll save the rest of us a fortune', *Daily Mail*, 18 September. Available online at: http://www.dailymail.co.uk/debate/article–2424713/Scots-MUST-vote-independence-Itll-save-rest-fortune-says-SIMON-HEFFER.html#ixzz2l1H392NH.

Hart, F. R. (1930), *The Disaster of Darien: The Story of the Scots Settlement and the Causes of its Failure 1699–1701*, London: Constable.

Harvie, C. (1994), *Scotland and Nationalis: Scottish Society and Politics 1707–1994* (2nd edn), London: Routledge.

Heather, P. (2009), *Empires and Barbarians: Migration, Development and the Birth of Europe*, London: Macmillan.

Henley, V. (1998), *A Year and a Day*, New York: Dell/Random House.

Hepburn, D. and Douglas, J. (1923), *The Chronicles of the Caledonian Society of London*, Leith: David Davidson.

Herdman, J. (2008), *The Cape Breton Fiddling Narrative: Innovation, Preservation, Dancing*, Unpublished Master's Thesis, University of British Columbia.

Hesse, D. (2011a), 'Scots for a day: the Highland Games of mainland Europe', *History Scotland*, 11(3): 24–30.

Hesse, D. (2011b), 'Roots and hearts: Homecoming Scotland 2009 and the Scots of Europe', *Scottish Affairs*, 77: 90–109.

Hewitson, J. (1993), *Tam Blake & Co.: The Story of the Scots in America*, Edinburgh: Canongate.

Higounet, C. (1976), *Les Allemands en Europe centrale et orientale au Moyen Age*, Paris.

Hinderaker, E. and Horn, R. (2010), 'Territorial crossings, histories and historiographies of the early Americas', *William and Mary Quarterly*, 67: 395–432.

Hinton, L. (2001), *How to Keep Your Language Alive: A Commonsense Approach to One-On-One Language Learning*, Berkeley, CA: Heyday.

HM Government (2013), *Scotland Analysis: Devolution and the Implications of Scottish Independence*. Available online at: https://www.gov.uk/government/uploads/system/uploads/attachment_data/file/79417/Scotland_analysis_Devolution_and_the_implications_of_Scottish_Independan ... __1_.pdf.

Hobsbawm, E. (1983), 'Introduction: inventing tradition', in E. Hobsbawm and T. Ranger (eds), *The Invention of Tradition*, Cambridge: Cambridge University Press, pp. 1–14.

Hock, D. (2005), *One from Many*, San Francisco: Berrett Koehler Publishers, Inc.

Houston, D., Findlay, A., Harrison, R. and Mason, C. (2008), 'Will attracting the "creative class" boost economic growth in old industrial regions? a case-study of Scotland', *Geografiska Annaler: Series B, Human Geography*, 90(2): 133–49.

Hunter, J. (1994), *A Dance Called America. The Scottish Highlands, the United States and Canada*, Edinburgh: Mainstream.

Hunter, J. (2005), *Scottish Exodus: Travels Among a Worldwide Clan*, Edinburgh: Mainstream.

Hutchinson, R. (1996), *Empire Games. The British Invention of Twentieth-Century Sport*, Edinburgh: Mainstream.

Hutchison, I. G. C. (1986), *Political History of Scotland 1832–1924*, Edinburgh: John Donald.

Hutchison, R. (2005), *A Waxing Moon: The Modern Gaelic Revival*, Edinburgh: Mainstream Publishing.

Hyslop, J. (2006), 'The world voyage of James Keir Hardie: Indian nationalism, Zulu insurgency and the British labour diaspora 1907–1908', *Journal of Global History*, 1: 343–62.

Ichijo, A. (2004), *Scottish nationalism and the idea of Europe: concepts of Europe and the nation*, London: Routledge.

Insh, G. P. (1922), *Scottish Colonial Schemes 1620–1686*, Glasgow: Maclehose.

Institute of Public Policy Research (2013), *England and its two unions: The anatomy of a nation and its discontents*, London: IPPR.

James, E. (2008), 'Some like it Scots', *Barnes & Noble Review*, 4 August. Available online at: http://bnreview.barnesandnoble. com/t5/Reading-Romance/Some-Like-It-Scots/ba-p/555. Accessed 24 February 2013.

Jarvie, G. (1991), *Highland Games: The Making of the Myth*, Edinburgh: Edinburgh University Press.

Jarvie, G. (2000), 'Highland Games', in G. Jarvie and J. Burnett (eds), *Sport, Scotland and the Scots*, East Linton: Tuckwell, pp. 128–42.

Jarvie, G. (2005), 'The North American Émigré, Highland Games, and Social Capital in International Communities', in C. Ray (ed.), *Transatlantic Scots*, Tuscaloosa: The University of Alabama Press, pp. 198–214.

Jarvie, G. and Walker, G. (1994), 'Ninety minute patriots? Scottish sport in the making of the nation', in G. Jarvie and G. Walker (eds), *Scottish Sport in the Making of the Nation: Ninety Minute Patriots?*, Leicester: Leicester University Press, pp. 9–26.

Jenkins, R. (2008), *Social identity* (3rd edn), London: Routledge.

Johnson, S. (2013a), 'Thousands of Scottish servicemen denied special deal in independence referendum', *Daily Telegraph*, 18 March. Available online at: http://www.telegraph.co.uk/news/ uknews/scotland/9937920/Thousands-of-Scottish-servicemen-de-nied-special-deal-in-independence-referendum.html.

Johnson, S. (2013b), 'Alistair Darling appeals to Scots in England to save UK', *Daily Telegraph*, 6 June. Available online at: http:// www.telegraph.co.uk/news/uknews/scotland/10102099/Alistair-Darling-appeals-to-Scots-in-England-to-save-UK.html.

Johnson, T. and Broms, A. (2000), *Profit Beyond Measure: Extraordinary Results through Attention to Work and People*, New York: Free Press.

Kalra, V. S., Kaur, R. and Hutnyk, J. (2005), *Diaspora and Hybridity*, London: Sage.

Karras, A. (1992), *Sojourners in the Sun, Scottish migrants in Jamaica and the Chesapeake*, Ithaca, NY: Cornell University Press.

Kay, J. (2004), *The Truth About Markets. Why Some Nations are Rich But Most Remain Poor*, London: Penguin.

Keating, M. (2001), *Nations Against the State: The New Politics of Nationalism in Quebec, Catalonia and Scotland* (2nd edn), Basingstoke: Palgrave Macmillan.

Kellas, J. G. (1998), *The Politics of Nationalism and Ethnicity* (2nd edn), Basingstoke: Macmillan.

Kelly, S. (2011), *Scott-land: the man who invented a nation*, Edinburgh: Polygon.

Kelman, J. (1994), *How Late It Was, How Late*, London: Secker and Warburg, London.

Kennedy, M. (2002), *Gaelic Nova Scotia: An Economic, Cultural, and Social Impact Study*, Halifax: Nova Scotia Museum.

King, S. (1995), *The Raven's Wish*, New York: Topaz.

King, S. (1998), *Laird of the Wind*, New York: Topaz.

King, S. F. (2008), *Lady Macbeth*, New York: Crown.

King, S. F. (2010), *Queen Hereafter*, New York: Crown.

King, S. F. (2013), Interview, 30 January.

Kowalski, W. (2005), 'The Placement of Urbanised Scots in the Polish Crown during the Sixteenth and Seventeenth Centuries', in A. Grosjean and S. Murdoch (eds), *Scottish Communities Abroad in the Early Modern Period*, Leiden: Brill, pp. 53–104.

Kneale, J. (2003), 'Secondary Worlds: Reading novels as geographical research', in A. Blunt, P. Gruffudd, J. May, M. Ogborn and D. Pinder (eds), *Cultural Geography in Practice*, London: Arnold, pp. 39–51.

Krentz, J. A. (ed.) (1992), *Dangerous Men and Adventurous Women: Romance writers on the appeal of the romance*, Philadelphia: University of Pennsylvania Press.

Kuznetsov, Y. (2011), *Diaspora Networks and the International Migration of Skills: How Countries Can Draw on Their Talent Abroad*, Washington, DC: World Bank Institute.

Laing, D. (ed.) (1867), *An Encouragement to Colonies by Sir William Alexander Knight*, London 1624 in *Royal Letters, Charters and Tracts Relating to the Colonization of New Scotland and the Institution of Knight Baronets of Nova Scotia 1621–1638*, Edinburgh: Bannatyne Club.

Lamb, W. (2011), 'Is there a future for regional dialects in Scottish Gaelic?', unpublished talk at Forum for Research on the Languages of Scotland (FRLSU) Colloquium.

Landsman, N. (ed.) (2001), *Nation and Province in the First British Empire: Scotland and the Americas, 1600–1800*, Cranbury Press.

Langford, P. (2005), 'South Britons' reception of North Britons, 1707–1820', in T. C. Smout (ed.), *Anglo-Scots Relations from 1603 to 1900*, Oxford: Oxford University Press, pp. 143–70.

Larsen, K. (1907), *De Dansk-Ostindiske Koloniers Historie*, Copenhagen.

Law, A. (2001), 'Near and far: banal national identity and the press in Scotland', *Media, Culture and Society*, 23(3): 299–317.

Leith, M. S. (2006), *Nationalism and national identity in Scottish politics*. PhD thesis, University of Glasgow.

Leith, M. S. (2008), Scottish National Party Representations of Scottishness and Scotland, *Politics*, 28(2): 83–92.

Leith, M. S. (2012), 'The View from Above: Scottish National Identity as an Elite Concept', *National Identities*, 14(1): 40–51.

Leith, M. S. and Sim, D. (2012), 'Second generation identities: the Scottish diaspora in England', *Sociological Research Online*, 17(3): 11. Available online at: http://www.socresonline.org.uk/17/3/11.html.

Leith, M. S. and Soule, D. P. J. (2012), *Political Discourse and National identity in Scotland*, Edinburgh: Edinburgh University Press.

Lester, A. (2012), 'Empire on the Eastern Sea, the influence of Asian and western imperialism on national identity formation in Japan and China', *Emergence*, 4: 1–6.

Leveson Inquiry (2012), Witness Statements. Available online at: http://www.levesoninquiry.org.uk/wp-content/uploads/2012/04/Witness-Statement-of-Keith-Rupert-Murdoch2.pdf.

Linklater, M. (1992), 'The media', in M. Linklater and R. Denniston (eds), *Anatomy of Scotland*, Edinburgh: Chambers, pp. 126–44.

Lobdell, H. (2013), Review of *The Chieftain* by Margaret Mallory. Available online at: http://freshfiction.com/review.php?id=36168. Accessed 24 February 2013.

Lofty, C. (2012), *Starlight*, New York: Pocket Books.

Lucassen, J., Lucassen, L. and Manning, P. (2011), 'Migration History: Multidisciplinary Approaches', in J. Lucassen, L. Lucassen and P. Manning (eds), *Migration History in World History*, Leiden: Brill.

Lundvall, B.-A. and Lorenz, E. (2012), 'On the role of social investment in the globalising learning economy – A European perspective', in N. Morel, B. Palier and J. Palme (eds), *Towards a Social Investment Welfare State? Ideas, Policies, Challenges*, Bristol: Policy Press.

Luxemburg, R. (1913), *Die Akkumulation des Kapitals, ein Beitrag zur ökonomischen Erklärung des Imperialismus*, Berlin.

Lynch, M. (1992), *Scotland: a new history*, London: Pimlico.

Lyons, T. and Mandaville, P. (2010), 'Diasporas and Politics', in K. Knott and S. McLoughlin (eds), *Diasporas: Concepts, Intersections, Identities*, London: Zed Books.

MacAlister, K. (2003), *Men in Kilts*, New York: Penguin.

MacAskill, K. and McLeish, H. (2007), *Wherever the Saltire Flies*, Edinburgh: Luath Press.

MacDonald, A. (1995), *The Relationship between Pibroch and Gaelic Song: its Implications on the Performance Style of the Pibroch Ùrlar*, Unpublished Master's dissertation at the University of Edinburgh.

Macdonald, C. M. M. (2012), 'Imagining the Scottish Diaspora: Emigration and Transnational Literature in the Late Modern Period', *Britain and the World*, 5(1): 12–42.

Macdonald, H. (2013), 'Murray: I will declare my hand on Independence', *The Herald*, 9 July. Available online at: http://www.heraldscotland.com/politics/referendum-news/murray-i-will-declare-my-hand-on-independence.21560118.

Macdonell, A. J. (The Younger of Greenfield) (1884), *An Account of the Highland Society of Canada, a Branch of the Highland Society of London*, Montreal: Armour and Ramsay.

MacGregor, G. (1980), *Scotland. An Intimate Portrait*, Boston: Houghton Mifflin.

MacGregor, J. (1828), *Historical and Descriptive Sketches of the Maritime Colonies of British America*, London: Longman, Rees, Orme, Brown and Green.

Macinnes, A. I. (2007), *Union and Empire: The Making of the United Kingdom in 1707*, Cambridge: Cambridge University Press.

MacInnes, J. (2006), *Dùthchas nan Gàidheal: Selected Essays of John MacInnes*, ed. Michael Newton, Edinburgh: Birlinn.

Macintyre, M. E. (2011), 'Ex-premier seeks to defuse fallout at Gaelic College', *Halifax Chronicle Herald*, 14 December. Available online at: http://thechronicleherald.ca/novascotia/42558-ex-premier-seeks-defuse-fallout-gaelic-college.

MacKay, A. [Sue-Ellen Welfonder] (2012), *Haunted Warrior*, New York: Signet/Penguin.

Mackay, A. [Sue-Ellen Welfonder] (2008), *Tall, Dark and Kilted*, New York: Signet/Penguin.

MacKay, D. (1969), *Geographical Mobility and the Brain Drain: A Case Study of Aberdeen University Graduates, 1860–1960*, London: George Allen and Unwin Ltd.

MacKay, D. (ed.) (2011), *Scotland's Economic Future*, Edinburgh: Reform Scotland. Available online at: http://reformscotland.com/public/publications/scotlandseconomicfuture.pdf.

MacKenzie, Anabel (n.d.), 'Anabel MacKenzie's Guide to Scottish Romance and Historical Fiction'. Available online at: http://www.scottishromance.com/. Accessed 11 January 2013.

Mackinder, H. (1907), *Britain and the British Seas*, London: Heinemann.

MacKinnon, R. (2009), *Discovering Cape Breton Folklore*, Sydney, Nova Scotia: Cape Breton University Press.

MacLellan, L. (2000), *Brìgh an Òrain/A Story in Every Song*, ed. John Shaw, Montreal and Kingston: McGill-Queen's University Press.

MacMillan, D. S. (1967), *Scotland and Australia, 1788–1850: Emigration, Commerce and Investment*, Oxford: Clarendon Press.

MacRae, M. and Wight, M. (2011), *The Role of Home Organizations in Home Countries: Globalscot and Scottish Enterprise*, World Bank. Available online at: http://info.worldbank.org/etools/docs/library/152387/mairimacrae.pdf.

Maguire, J. A. (1999), *Global Sport*, Cambridge: Polity Press.

Maley, W. (2005), 'Introduction', in W. Maley (ed.), *100 Best Scottish Books of All Time*, Edinburgh: The List, pp. 2–4.

Mallory, M. (2011a), *The Guardian*, New York and Boston: Forever Books.

Mallory, M. (2011b), *The Sinner*, New York and Boston: Forever Books.

Mallory, M. (2012), *The Warrior*, New York and Boston: Forever Books.

Mallory, M. (2013a), Interview, 19 February.

Mallory, M. (2013b), *The Chieftain*, New York and Boston: Forever Books.

Mallory, W. E. and Simpson-Housley, P. (eds.) (1987), *Geography and Literature: A meeting of the disciplines*, Syracuse: Syracuse University Press.

Maryles, D. (2013), 'A look at a year of bestsellers lists', *Publishers Weekly*, 260(2): 22, 25.

Massie, A. (1984), *A Portrait of Scottish Rugby*, Edinburgh: Polygon Books.

McArthur, A. and Long, H. Kingsley (1984 [1935]), *No Mean City*, London: Corgi.

McArthur, C. (1982), *Scotch Reels*, London: British Film Institute.

McArthur, C. (2003), *Brigadoon, Braveheart and the Scots: Distortions of Scotland in Hollywood Cinema*, London: I. B. Tauris.

McCarra, K. (1984), *Scottish Football. A Pictorial History From 1867 To The Present Day*, Glasgow and Edinburgh: Third Eye Centre and Polygon Books.

McCarthy, A. (2005), 'National identities and twentieth-century Scottish migrants in England', in W. L. Miller (ed.), *Anglo-Scottish Relations from 1900 to Devolution and Beyond*, Oxford: Oxford University Press, pp. 171–82.

McCarthy, A. (2006) (ed.), *A Global Clan: Scottish Migrant Networks and Identities since the Eighteenth Century*, London: Tauris Academic Studies.

McCarthy, A. (2007a), *Personal Narratives of Irish and Scottish Migration 1921–65*, Manchester: Manchester University Press.

McCarthy, A. (2007b), 'The Scots' Society of St Andrew, Hull, 1910–2001: immigrant, ethnic and transnational association', *Immigrants and Minorities*, 25(3): 209–33.

McCarthy, J. and Hague, E. (2004), 'Race, nation and nature, the cultural politics of Celtic identification in the American West', *Annals of the Association of American Geographers*, 94(2): 387–408.

McCrone, D. (1989), 'Representing Scotland: Culture and nationalism', in D. McCrone, S. Kendrick and P. Straw (ed.), *The Making of Scotland: Nation, culture and social change*, Edinburgh: Edinburgh University Press, pp. 161–74.

McCrone, D. (2001 [1992]), *Understanding Scotland: The sociology of a stateless nation* (2nd edn), London: Routledge.

McCrone, D. (2013), 'Getting Scotland: Re-Reading Eric Hobsbawm', *Scottish Affairs*, 83: 1–9.

McCrone, D., Morris, A. and Kiely, R. (1995), *Scotland – The Brand: The making of Scottish heritage*, Edinburgh: Edinburgh University Press.

McCulloch, J. H. (1954), *North Range: A Record of Hard Living and Adventure on the Colourful Northern Rim of the British Empire*, London: Chambers.

McDaniel, I. (2013), *Adam Ferguson in the Scottish Enlightenment*, Cambridge, MA: Harvard University Press.

McGarvey, N. and Cairney, P. (2013), *Scottish Politics: An Introduction* (2nd edn), London: Palgrave Macmillan.

McGilvary, G. (2008), *East India Patronage and the British State, the Scottish elite and politics in the eighteenth century*, London: I. B. Tauris.

McGoldrick, M. (1995), *The Thistle and the Rose*, New York: Topaz.

McGowan, M. (2008), *Dance in the Renaissance: European Fashion, French Obsession*, New Haven: Yale University Press.

McKean, C., Harris, B. and Whatley, C. A. (2009), 'Introduction', in C. McKean, B. Harris and C. A. Whatley (eds), *Dundee:*

renaissance to enlightenment, Dundee: Dundee University Press, pp. xxi–xxxi.

McKinstry, L. (2005), *Rosebery, statesman in turmoil*, London: John Murray.

McVeigh, K. (2005), 'Kilted heroes' novel role as US women's heart-throbs', *The Scotsman*, 29 March.

McWhiney, G. (1988), *Cracker Culture, Celtic ways in the Old South*, Tuscaloosa: University of Alabama Press.

Maddox, D. (2013), 'UK passport loss indication', *The Scotsman*, 11 June. Available online at: http://www.scotsman.com/news/uk/scottish-independence-uk-passport-loss-indication–1-2961819.

Martin, M. (2010), 'Regional economic resilience, hysteresis and recessionary shocks', *Journal of Economic Geography*, 12(1): 1–32.

Matthew, H. C. G. (1995), *Gladstone 1875–1898*, Oxford: Oxford University Press.

Maxwell, S. (2012), *Arguing for Independence: Evidence, Risk and the Wicked Issues*, Edinburgh: Luath Press.

Melin, M. (2012), *Exploring the Percussive Routes and Shared Commonalities in Cape Breton Step Dancing*, Unpublished PhD thesis, University of Limerick.

Miller, A. (2013), 'Let us Scottish "expats" vote on independence', *The Guardian*, 2 July. Available online at: http://www.theguardian.com/commentisfree/2013/jul/02/scots-scotland-vote-on-independence.

Miller, D. (2000), *Citizenship and national identity*, Cambridge: Polity Press.

Miller, W. (2005), 'Introduction', in W. Miller (ed.), *Anglo-Scottish relations: from 1900 to devolution*, Oxford: Oxford University Press, pp. 1–16.

Mitchell, J. (1995), 'Lobbying Brussels: the case of Scotland Europa', *European Urban and Regional Studies*, 2(4): 287–98.

Mitchell, J. (1996), *Strategies for Self-Government: The Campaigns for a Scottish Parliament*, Edinburgh: Polygon.

Moorhouse, H. F. (1987), 'Scotland against England: football and popular culture', *International Journal of the History of Sport*, 4(2): 189–202.

Moreno, L. (1988), 'Scotland and Catalonia: the path to home rule', in D. McCrone and A. Brown, (eds), *Scottish Government Yearbook 1988*, Edinburgh: Edinburgh University Press, pp. 166–81.

Moulaert, F. and Sekia, F. (2003), 'Territorial innovation models: a critical survey', *Regional Studies*, 37(3): 289–302.

Murdoch, S. (2003), 'Scotsmen on the Danish–Norwegian Frontiers c. 1580–1680', in S. Murdoch and A. MacKillop (eds), *Military Governors and Imperial Frontiers c. 1600–1800: A Study of Scotland and Empires*, Leiden: Brill, pp. 1–28.

Murdoch, S. (2007), 'The French connection: Bordeaux's "Scottish" networks in context, c.1670–1720', in G. Leydier (ed.), *Scotland and Europe, Scotland in Europe*, Newcastle: Cambridge Scholars, pp. 26–55.

Mycock, A. (2012), 'SNP, identity and citizenship: re-imagining state and nation', *National Identities*, 14(1): 53–69.

Nagel, J. (1994), 'Constructing ethnicity: creating and recreating ethnic identity and culture', *Social Problems*, 41: 1001–26.

Nairn, T. (1981), *The Break-Up of Britain: Crisis and Neo-Nationalism*, 2nd (expanded) edn, London: Verso.

Napier, P. (1995), *Barbarian Eye: Lord Napier in China, the prelude to Hong Kong*, London: Brassey.

Newton, M. (2003), '"Becoming Cold-Hearted Like the Gentiles Around Them": Scottish Gaelic in the United States 1872–1912', *eKeltoi*, 2: 63–131.

Newton, M. (2005), '"This Could Have Been Mine": Scottish Gaelic Learners in modern North America', *eKeltoi*, 1: 1–37.

Newton, M. (2009), *Warriors of the Word: The World of the Scottish Highlanders*, Edinburgh: Birlinn.

Newton, M. (2010), 'Paying for the Plaid: Scottish Gaelic Identity Politics in Nineteenth-century North America', in I. Brown (ed.), *From Tartan to Tartanry: Scottish Culture, History and Myth*, Edinburgh: Edinburgh University Press, pp. 63–81.

Newton, M. (2011), 'Scotland's Two Solitudes Abroad: Scottish Gaelic Immigrant Identity and Culture in North America', in J. A. Campbell, E. Ewan and H. Parker (eds), *The Shaping of Scottish Identities: Sex, Nation, and the Worlds Beyond*, Guelph: Guelph Series in Scottish Scottish Studies, pp. 215–33.

Newton, M. (2012), 'The Hidden History of Highland Dance'. Available online at: http://www.academia.edu/1788050/The_Hidden_History_of_Highland_Dance. Accessed February 2013.

Newton, M. (forthcoming), '"*Dannsair air ùrlar-déile thu*": Gaelic evidence about dance from the mid–17th to late–18th century Highlands'.

Nilsen, K. (2000), 'Living Celtic Speech: Celtic Sound Archives in North America', in R. F. E. Sutcliffe and G. Ó Néill (eds), *The Information Age, Celtic Languages and the New Millennium: 6th*

Annual Conference of the North American Association for Celtic Language Teachers, Limerick, Ireland: North American Association for Celtic Language Teachers, pp. 89–94.

Nilsen, K. (2002), 'Some Notes on pre-*Mac-Talla* Gaelic Publishing in Nova Scotia', in C. Ó Baoill and N. McGuire (eds), *Rannsachadh na Gàidhlig 2000*, Aberdeen, Scotland: An Clò Gàidhealach, pp. 127–40.

Northamptonshire Telegraph (2012), 'Campaign against Scottish independence comes to Corby', 13 November. Available online at: http://www.northantstelegraph.co.uk/news/top-stories/campaign-against-scottish-independence-comes-to-corby–1–4471789.

Novak, M. (1971), *The rise of the unmeltable ethnics: politics and culture in the seventies*, New York: Macmillan.

O'Connor, S. B. (2008), *The St Andrew's Society of Toronto: Scottish Associational Culture in the Nineteenth and Early Twentieth Centuries*, Thesis (MA), University of Guelph.

Osterhammel, J. (2004), *Colonialism, a theoretical overview*, Göttingen.

Otago Daily Times (1881), 25 March.

Otago Daily Times (2006), 'Gaelic Numbers Dwindle, but Spirit Remains', 3 March.

Otago Witness (1883), 'Donald Dinnie', 24 November.

Park, A., Clery, E., Curtice, J., Philips, M. And Utting, D (eds) (2012), *British Social Attitudes: the 20th Report*, London: NatCen Social Research. Available online at: www.bsa–29.natcen.ac.uk.

Parr, J., Hewings, G., Sohn, J. and Nazara, S. (2002), 'Agglomeration and trade: some additional perspectives', *Regional Studies*, 36: 675–84.

Paterson, L., Bechhofer, F. and McCrone, D. (2004), *Living in Scotland: Social and Economic Change since 1980*, Edinburgh: Edinburgh University Press.

Perks, K. and Hughes, M. (2008), 'Entrepreneurial decision-making in internationalization: Propositions from mid-size firms', *International Business Review*, 17(3): 310–30.

Petersoo, P. (2007), 'What does "we" mean? National deixis in the media', *Journal of Language and Politics*, 6(3): 419–38.

Petrie, D. (2000), *Screening Scotland*, London: British Film Institute.

Petrie, D. (2009), 'Screening Scotland: a reassessment', in Murray, J. et al. (eds), *Scottish Cinema Now*, Newcastle: Cambridge Scholars Publishing, pp. 153–70.

Philo, G. (2007), 'Can discourse analysis successfully explain the content of media and journalistic practice?', *Journalism Studies*, 8(2): 175–96.

Pires-Hester, L. (1999), 'The emergence of bilateral diaspora ethnicity among Cape Verdean-Americans', in I. Okpewho, C. Davies and A. Mazrui (eds), *The African diaspora: African origins and New World identities*, Bloomington, IN: Indiana University Press, pp. 485–503.

Piskorski, J. M. (1999), 'The Historiography of the so-called "East Colonisation" and the Current State of Research', in B. Nagy and M. Sebôk (eds), *The Man of Many Devices: Festschrift in honour of Janos Bak*, Budapest, pp. 654–67.

Pittock, M. (1998), *Jacobitism*, Basingstoke: Macmillan.

Pocock, D. D. C. (1981), 'Introduction: Imaginative literature and the Geographer', in D. D. C. Pocock (ed.), *Humanistic Geography and Literature*, Totawa, NJ: Barnes and Noble Books, pp. 9–19.

Porter, M. (2000), 'Location, competition, and economic development: local clusters in a global economy', *Economic Development Quarterly*, 14(1): 15–34.

Prentis, M. (2008), *The Scots in Australia*, Sydney: University of New South Wales Press.

Price, A. and Levinger, B. (2011), 'The flotilla effect: Europe's small economies through the eye of the storm', mimeo, Center for International Development, Harvard.

Radhakrishnan, R. (2003), 'Ethnicity in an age of diaspora', in J. Braziel and A. Mannur (eds), *Theorizing diaspora: a reader*, Oxford: Blackwell, pp. 119–31.

Radway, J. (1984), *Reading the Romance: Women, Patriarchy, and Popular Literature*, Chapel Hill: University of North Carolina Press.

Ramblings from this Chick (2013), 'Forever's Scottish Seduction Tour'. Available online at: http://ramblingsfromthischick.blogspot.com/2013/02/forevers-scottish-seduction-tour.html. Accessed 24 February.

Ranney, K. (2013), 'About Me'. Available online at: http://karenranney.com/author/. Accessed 3 March.

Ray, C. (2001), *Highland heritage: Scottish-Americans in the American South*, Chapel Hill, NC: University of North Carolina Press.

Ray, C. (ed.) (2005), *Transatlantic Scots*, Tuscaloosa: University of Alabama Press.

Reading Between the Wines (2013), 'Character Love Letters'. Available online at: http://readingbetweenthewinesbookclub. blogspot.com/2013/02/character-love-letters-seduction-of. html?zx=53f5aef2a6e343ba. Accessed 1 March.

Redmond, G. (1971), *The Caledonian Games in Nineteenth-Century America*, Rutherford: Fairleigh Dickinson University Press.

Regis, P. (2003), *A Natural History of the Romance Novel*, Philadelphia: University of Pennsylvania Press.

Richards, E. (1999), *Patrick Sellar and the Highland Clearances: Homicide, Eviction and the Price of Progress*, Edinburgh: Polygon.

Richards, E. (2000), *The Highland Clearances: People, Landlords and Rural Turmoil*, Edinburgh: Birlinn.

Riddington, G. (2010), *The Economic Evaluation of Homecoming Scotland 2009*, A Review for the Economy, Energy and Tourism Committee of the Scottish Parliament, EET/S3/10/23/2.

Roberts, D. (1999), 'Your clan or ours?', *Oxford American,* September–October: 24–30.

Robinson, M. (1995), 'Cherishing the Irish diaspora', Address to the Houses of the Oireachtas, 2 February. Available online at: http://www.oireachtas.ie/viewdoc.asp?fn=/documents/addresses/ 2Feb1995.htm. Accessed January 2013.

Romance Reader (2006), 'Authors of Scottish Historical Romance'. Available online at: http://romancereaderatheart.com/scotland/ AuthorsACl.htm. Accessed 4 March 2013.

Romance Reader (2008), 'Great Romance Novels in Scottish Settings'. Available online at: http://romancereaderatheart.com/ scotland/great_reads.htm. Accessed 4 March 2013.

Romance Times Book Reviews (2013), 'Choose Margaret Mallory's Hottest Highlander'. Available online at: http://www.rtbookre- views.com/rt-daily-blog/choose-margaret-mallorys-hottest-high- lander-giveaway. Accessed 1 March.

Romance Writers of America (2013a), 'Romance Industry Statistics'. Available online at: http://www.rwa.org/p/cm/ld/fid=580. Accessed 11 January.

Romance Writers of America (2013b), 'Romance Reader Statistics'. Available online at: http://www.rwa.org/p/cm/ld/fid=582. Accessed 11 January.

Rosie, M., Petersoo, P., MacInnes, J., Condor, S. and Kennedy, J. (2004), 'Nation speaking unto nation? Newspapers and national identity in the devolved UK', *Sociological Review*, 42(4): 437–58.

Rosie, M., Petersoo, P., MacInnes, J., Condor, S. and Kennedy, J. (2006), 'Mediating which nation? Citizenship and national identities in the British press', *Social Semiotics*, 16(2): 327–44.

Ross, A. (1995), 'Out of Kilter', *Artforum International*, 34 (October) 18: 114.

Rutherford, A. (2009), *Engaging with the Scottish Diaspora: Rationale, Benefits and Challenges*, Edinburgh: Scottish Government.

Safran, W. (1991), 'Diasporas in modern societies: myths of homeland and return', *Diaspora* 1(1): 83–99.

Salmond, A. (2012a), 'Hugo Young Annual Lecture', *The Guardian*, 25 January. Available online at: http://www.theguardian.com/politics/2012/jan/25/alex-salmond-hugo-young-lecture.

Salmond, A. (2012b), 'Scottish Independence good for England', Liverpool, February 13. Available online at: http://www.snp.org/blog/post/2012/feb/scottish-independence-good-england.

Salmond, A. (2013), 'Annual Conference Address', Perth, 19 October. Available online at: http://www.snp.org/blog/post/2013/oct/alex-salmond-address-conference–2013.

Samanta, I. (2012), *Modelling the Relationships in B2B under E-Marketing Practices: Moving from the Traditional Business Environment to Innovative E-Commerce. The Case of Greek Firms*, unpublished PhD thesis, Paisley: UWS.

Scarles, C. (2004), 'Mediating landscapes: the processes and practices of image construction in tourist brochures of Scotland', *Tourist Studies*, 4(1): 43–67.

Schechner, R. (1993), *The future of ritual: writings of culture and performance*, London and New York: Routledge.

Schlesinger, A. M. Jr. (1991), *The disuniting of America*, Knoxville, TN: Whittle.

Schoene, B. (ed.) (2007), *The Edinburgh Companion to Contemporary Scottish Literature*, Edinburgh: Edinburgh University Press.

Scott, J. and Hughes, M. (1980), *Anatomy of Scottish Capital*, London: Croom Helm.

Scottish Affairs Committee (2013), *Sixth Report: The Referendum on Separation for Scotland: The proposed section 30 Order. Can a player also be the referee?*, HMSO: London.

Scottish Executive (2001), *Scotland: A Global Connections Strategy*. Available online at: http://www.scotland.gov.uk/Resource/Doc/158429/0042932.pdf.

Scottish Government (2010), *Diaspora Engagement Plan – Reaching out to Scotland's International Family*, Edinburgh: Scottish Government.

Scottish Government (2011a), *Government Economic Strategy*. Available online at: http://www.scotland.gov.uk/Publications/2011/09/13091128/0.

Scottish Government (2011b), *Scottish Digital Network Panel Final Report*. Available online at: http://www.scotland.gov.uk/Publications/2011/01/19140602/5.

Scottish Government (2013), *Scotland's Future: From the Referendum to Independence and a Written Constitution*, Edinburgh: Scottish Government.

Scottish National Party (2002), *The Scottish Constitution*. Available online at: http://www.constitutionalcommission.org/production/byre/images/assets/file/Resources%20Folder/SNP_2002_text.pdf.

Scullion, A. (2004), 'Byrne and the Bogie Man', *Atlantic Studies*, 1(2): 210–27.

Seidel, K. G. (1992), 'Judge Me by the Joy I Bring', in J. A. Krentz (ed.), *Dangerous Men and Adventurous Women: Romance Writers on the Appeal of the Romance*, Philadelphia: University of Pennsylvania Press, pp. 159–79.

Selinger, E. M. (2007), 'Rereading the romance', *Contemporary Literature*, 48(2): 307–24.

Serruys, M. W. (2005), 'Oostende en de Generale Indische Compagnie, de opbloie en neergang van een koloniale handelshaven 1713–1740', *Tijdschrift voor Zeegeschiedenis*, 24: 23–49.

Shain, Y. and Barth, A. (2003), 'Diasporas and international relations theory', *International Organizations*, 57: 449–79.

Shaw, G. (1992–3), 'Language, Music and Local Aesthetics, Views from Gaeldom and Beyond', *Scottish Language*, 11/12: 37–61.

Shaw, G. (2003), 'Gaelic Cultural Maintenance and the Contribution of Ethnography', *Scotia*, 27: 34–48.

Shaw, G. (2007) (ed.), *Na Beanntaichean Gorma agus Sgeulachdan Eile à Ceap Breatainn/The Blue Mountains and Other Gaelic Stories from Cape Breton*, Montreal and Kingston: McGill-Queen's University Press.

Shaw, J. (1988), 'Observations on the Cape Breton Gàidhealtachd and its relevance to present-day Celtic Studies', in G. MacLennan (ed.), *Proceedings of the First North American Congress of Celtic Studies*, Ottawa: University of Ottawa, pp. 75–87.

Shears, B. (2008), *Dance to the Piper: The Highland Bagpipe in Nova Scotia*, Sydney: Cape Breton University Press.

Sheffer, G. (1986), 'A new field of study: Modern diasporas in international politics', in G. Sheffer (ed.), *Modern Diasporas in International Politics*, London: Croom Helm, pp. 1–15.

Sheffer, G. (2003), *Diaspora Politics: At Home Abroad*, Cambridge: Cambridge University Press.

Shuval, J. (2000), 'Diaspora migration: definitional ambiguities and a theoretical paradigm', *International Migration*, 38(5): 41–57.

Sillars, J. (2009), 'Admitting the Kailyard', in J. Murray et al. (eds), *Scottish Cinema Now*, Newcastle: Cambridge Scholars Publishing, pp. 122–38.

Sim, D. (2011a), 'The Scottish community and Scottish organisations on Merseyside: development and decline of a diaspora', *Scottish Journal of Historical Studies*, 31(1): 99–118.

Sim, D. (2011b), *American Scots: The Scottish Diaspora and the USA*, Edinburgh: Dunedin Academic Press.

Sim, D. (2012), 'Scottish devolution and the Scottish diaspora', *National Identities*, 14(1): 99–114.

Sim, D. and Leith, M. (2013), 'Diaspora tourists and the Scottish Homecoming 2009', *Journal of Heritage Tourism*, 8(4): 259–74.

Sim, D. and McIntosh, I. (2007), 'Connecting with the Scottish diaspora', *Scottish Affairs*, 58: 78–95.

Sked, P. (2005), *Culross: a short history of the Royal Burgh*, Edinburgh: National Trust for Scotland.

Skilling, D. (2012), 'In uncertain seas: positioning small countries to succeed in a changing world', Discussion Paper, Singapore: Landfall Strategy Group.

Sloat, A. (2000), 'Scotland and Europe: links between Edinburgh, London and Brussels', *Scottish Affairs*, 31: 92–110.

Small, B. (1978a), *The Kadin*, New York: Avon Books.

Small, B. (1978b), *Love Wild and Fair*, New York: Avon Books.

Smith, A. (1976 edn), *An Inquiry into the Nature and Causes of the Wealth of Nations*, Oxford: Oxford University Press.

Smith, J. A. (1965), *John Buchan, a biography*, London: Hart-Davis.

Smout, T. C. (1961), 'The Early Scottish Sugar Houses 1660–1720', *Economic History Review*, 14: 240–53.

Smout, T. C. (1985), *A history of the Scottish people 1560–1830*, London: Fontana.

Smout, C. (1995), 'The culture of migration: Scots as Europeans 1500–1800', *History Workshop Journal*, 40(1): 108–17.

Smout, T. C., Landsman, N. C. and Devine, T. M. (1994), 'Scottish Emigration in the Seventeenth and Eighteenth Centuries', in

N. Canny (ed.), *Europeans on the Move: Studies on European Migration, 1500–1800*, Oxford: Clarendon, pp. 76–112.

Sparling, H. (2005), *Song Genres, Cultural Capital and Social Distinctions in Gaelic Cape Breton*, Unpublished PhD thesis, York University.

Sparling, H. (2011), 'Cape Breton Island: Living in the Past?', in G. Baldacchino (ed.), *Island Songs: A Global Repertoire*, Lanham and Toronto: Scarecrow Press, pp. 49–63.

Sriskandarajah, D. and Drew, C. (2006), *Brits abroad: mapping the scale and nature of British emigration*, London: Institute for Public Policy Research.

Stenhouse, D. (2005), 'America is turned on by Kilt Ripping Yarns', *The Sunday Times*, 27 March.

Stenhouse, D. (2009), 'Not Made in Scotland: Images of the Nation from Furth of the Forth', in J. Murray et al. (eds), *Scottish Cinema Now*, Newcastle: Cambridge Scholars Publishing, pp.171–87.

Stephenson, A. (1997), 'Diana Gabaldon: her novels flout convention', *Publishers Weekly*, 244(1): 50–1.

Stevenson, R. L. (1896), *Weir of Hermiston: An Unfinished Romance*, London.

Stock, F. (2010), 'Home and memory', in K. Knott and S. McLoughlin (eds), *Diasporas: concepts, intersections, identities*, London: Zed, pp. 24–8.

Stone, R. C. J. (1982), *Young Logan Campbell*, Auckland: Auckland University Press.

Sturgeon, N. (2013). 'A welfare system for Scotland', 8 January. Available online at: http://www.snp.org/blog/post/2013/jan/sturgeon-welfare-system-scotland.

Sullivan, K. (2010), *Scots by Association: Scottish Diasporic Identities and Ethnic Associationism in the Nineteenth-Early Twentieth Centuries and the Present Day*, Thesis (PhD), Dunedin: University of Otago.

Taylor, M. (2002), 'Administrators', in R. Cox, D. Russell and W. Vamplew (eds), *Encyclopedia of British Football*, London: Frank Cass, pp. 2–6.

Teo, H.-M. (2012a), '"Bertrice teaches you about history and you don't even mind!" History and Revisionist Historiography in Bertrice Small's *The Kadin*', in S. S. G. Frantz and E. M. Selinger (eds), *New Approaches to Popular Romance Fiction: Critical Essays*, Jefferson, NC: McFarland, pp. 21–32.

Teo, H.-M. (2012b), *Desert Passions: Orientalism and Romance Novels*, Austin, University of Texas Press.

Terry, C. S. (1909), *A Catalogue of the Publications of Scottish Historical and Kindred Clubs and Societies, 1780–1909*, Glasgow: James MacLehose & Sons.

The Argus (1859), 'The Caledonian Gathering', 10 October.

The Cyclopedia of Victoria (Illustrated) in Three Volumes: An Historical and Commercial Review, Volume II (1903), Melbourne: The Cyclopedia Company Publishers [book]. SLTF 994.502 C99. State Library of Victoria, Melbourne.

The Scotsman (2013), 'Scottish independence: 47% support union – poll', 7 November. Available online at: http://www.scotsman.com/news/politics/top-stories/scottish-independence–47-support-union-poll–1–3177800.

Tignor, R. (1998), 'Preface', in J. Osterhammel, *Colonialism: a theoretical overview*, Princeton: Markus Wiener Publishers.

Timothy, D. (2011), *Cultural heritage and tourism: an introduction*, Bristol: Channel View.

TNS (System 3) (2007), *USA Strategy Research Report*, Edinburgh: Scottish Government Social Research.

Torrance, D. (2006), *The Scottish Secretaries*, Edinburgh: Birlinn.

Trench, A. (2008), 'Scotland and Wales: the evolution of devolution', in R. Hazell (ed.), *Constitutional Futures Revisited: Britain's Constitution to 2020*, London: Palgrave Macmillan.

Trevor-Roper, H. (1983), 'The Invention of Tradition: The Highland Tradition of Scotland', in E. Hobsbawm and T. Ranger (ed.), *The Invention of Tradition*, Cambridge: Cambridge University Press, pp. 15–41.

Twain, M. (1996 [1883]), *Life on the Mississippi*, New York: Oxford University Press.

Tyler, K. (2009), 'Whiteness studies and laypeople's engagements with race and genetics', *New Genetics and Society*, 28(1): 37–50.

Ullah, P. (1990), 'Rhetoric and ideology in social identification: the case of second generation Irish youths', *Discourse and Society*, 1(2): 167–88.

UNESCO (n.d.), 'Cultural Landscape'. Available online at: http://whc.unesco.org/en/culturallandscape/.

Ury, W. (2000), *The Third Side: Why We Fight and How We Can Stop*, New York: Penguin Books.

Vance, M. (2005), 'Powerful pathos: the triumph of Scottishness in Nova Scotia', in C. Ray (ed.), *Transatlantic Scots*, Tuscaloosa: University of Alabama Press, pp. 156–79.

van der Heyden, U. (2001), *Der Rote Adler an Afrikas Küste, die brandenburgisch-preussische Kolonie Grossfriedrichsburg in Westafrika*, Berlin.

The Vinland Sagas: The Norse Discovery of America (1965), trans. Magnus Magnusson and Hermann Pálsson, Harmondsworth: Penguin.

VisitScotland (2011), *The Winning Years: VisitScotland Corporate Plan 2012/2015*, Edinburgh: VisitScotland.

VisitScotland (2012), 'VisitScotland and Disney announce marketing campaign for upcoming Disney Pixar film "Brave"'. Available online at: http://www.visitscotland.org/media_centre/visitscotland_disney_partners.aspx.

Vivanco, L. (2011), *For Love and Money: The Literary Art of the Harlequin Mills & Boon Romance*, Penrith: Humanities-Ebooks.†

Vivanco, L. (2010), 'Braving the Scottish Romance'. Available online at: http://teachmetonight.blogspot.com/2010/12/braving-scottish-romance.html. Accessed 11 January 2013.

Walter, B., Morgan, S., Hickman, M. J. and Bradley, J. M. (2002), 'Family stories, public silence: Irish identity construction amongst the second-generation Irish in England', *Scottish Geographical Journal*, 118(3): 201–17.

Waters, M. C. (1990), *Ethnic Options: Choosing Identities in America*, Berkeley, CA: University of California Press.

Watson, M. (2005), 'Scotland's English Clan', *History Today*, 55(6). Available online at: http://www.historytoday.com/murray-watson/scotlands-english-clan.

Watson, S. (2010), 'Tomhais air dualchainntean Gàidhlig ann an Ceap Breatainn', in K. Nilsen (ed.), *Rannsachadh na Gàidhlig 5/Fifth Scottish Gaelic Research Conference*, Sydney, Nova Scotia: Cape Breton University Press, pp. 31–41.

Watt, D. (2007), *The Price of Scotland: Darien, Union and the Wealth of Nations*, Edinburgh: Luath.

Welfonder, S.-E. (2001), *Devil in a Kilt*, New York: Warner.

Welfonder, S.-E. (2011a), *Sins of a Highland Devil*, New York: Forever/Hachette.

Welfonder, S.-E. (2011b), *Temptation of a Highland Scoundrel*, New York: Forever/Hachette.

Welfonder, S.-E. (2013), 'Sue-Ellen Welfonder: Where Scotland's Past Lives On: Biography', Available online at: http://welfonder.com/biography/. Accessed 11 January.

Werbner, P. (2010), 'Complex Diasporas', in K. Knott and S. McLoughlin (eds), *Diasporas: Concepts, Intersections, Identities*, London: Zed Books.

Whigham, S. (2011), *'Anyone But England'? Exploring Anti-English sentiment as part of Scottish National Identity in Sport*. Unpublished MSc thesis. Loughborough University, UK.

Whigham, S. (in press), "'Anyone but England'? Exploring anti-English sentiment as part of Scottish national identity in sport', *International Review for the Sociology of Sport*. Published online before print, 28 August 2012, doi: 10.1177/1012690212454359.

Whyte, C. (ed.) (1995), *Gendering the Nation: Studies in modern Scottish literature*, Edinburgh: Edinburgh University Press.

Widdowson, H. G. (2007), *Discourse Analysis*, Oxford: Oxford University Press.

Williams, K. (2003), *Understanding Media Theory*, London: Hodder Arnold.

Williamson, A. H. (1996), 'Scots, Indians and Empire: The Scottish Politics of Civilization 1519–1609', *Past & Present*, 150: 46–83.

Willis, B. (2008), *Bagpipes, Bowlers and Cabers: History of the Maryborough Highland Society*, Maryborough: Maryborough Highland Society.

Wilson, A. (1995), *Irish America and the Ulster conflict 1968–1995*, Belfast: Blackstaff Press.

Withers, C. W. J. (1984), '"The Image of the Land": Scotland's Geography through her languages and literature', *Scottish Geographical Magazine*, 100(2): 81–95.

Withers, C. W. J. (1985), 'Kirk, club and cultural change: Gaelic chapels, Highland Societies and the urban Gaelic subculture in eighteenth-century Scotland', *Social History*, 10(1): 171–92.

Wodak, R., de Cilla, R., Reisigl, M. and Liebhart, K. (2009), *The discursive construction of national identity* (2nd edn), Edinburgh: Edinburgh University Press.

Woodward, G. S. (1963), *The Cherokees*, Norman: University of Oklahoma Press.

Word Wenches (2013), 'A Professor Studies Scottish Romance'. Available online at: http://wordwenches.typepad.com/word_wenches/2013/03/susan-here-the-word-wenches-are-

pleased-to-welcome-dr-euan-hague-associate-professor-of-geogra-
phy-at-depaul-university-to.html#comments. Accessed 15 April.

World Economic Forum (2012), *The Global Competitiveness Report
2011–2012*. Available online at: http://www.weforum.org/reports/
global-competitiveness-report–2011–2012.

Worthington, D. (2012), *British and Irish Experiences and Impres-
sions of Central Europe, c. 1560–1688*, Farnham: Ashgate.

Zarnowski, F. (1998), 'The amazing Donald Dinnie: the nineteenth
century's greatest athlete', *Iron Game History*, 5(1): 3–11.

Index

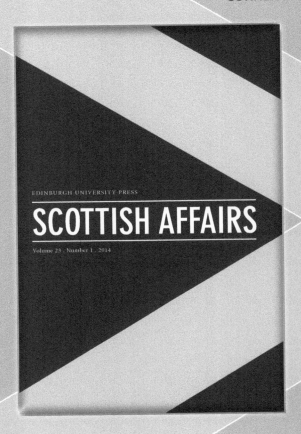